Life

STUDENT'S BOOK AND WORKBOOK | ADVANCED

PAUL DUMMETT

JOHN HUGHES

HELEN STEPHENSON

Australia • Brazil • Mexico • Singapore • United Kingdom • United States

Contents Split Edition A

Unit	Grammar	Vocabulary	Real life (functions)	Pronunciation
1 Lessons for life pages 9–20	time phrases the continuous aspect	personality and identity wordbuilding: binomial pairs word focus: *life*	getting to know people	linking in word pairs merged words in everyday phrases
VIDEO: Arctic wisdom page 18 ▶ REVIEW page 20					
2 More than a job pages 21–32	perfect forms passive forms	wordbuilding: phrasal verb *get* idioms: safety word focus: *foot/feet* personal qualities	presenting yourself	word stress
VIDEO: Climbing Yosemite page 30 ▶ REVIEW page 32					
3 Design for life pages 33–44	qualifiers intensifying adverbs	describing towns adverb + adjective collocations word focus: *ground*	expressing opinions	*quite, fairly* and *pretty* stress in intensifying adverbs linking vowel sounds (intrusion)
VIDEO: A story of solutions page 42 ▶ REVIEW page 44					
4 Innovation pages 45–56	future probability past modals	wordbuilding: *-able* phrasal verb *come* word focus: *give*	making a short pitch speaking skill: making key points	weak forms in past modals word stress
VIDEO: This man risked it all page 54 ▶ REVIEW page 56					
5 The magic of travel pages 57–68	emphatic structures avoiding repetition	repeated word pairs wordbuilding: synonyms word focus: *matter*	telling an anecdote speaking skill: linking events	*do, does* and *did* stress in short responses long sounds
VIDEO: On the road: Andrew McCarthy page 66 ▶ REVIEW page 68					
6 Body matters pages 69–80	phrasal verbs verb patterns	wordbuilding: compound words injuries idioms: health word focus: *face*	discussing proposals speaking skill: proposing and conceding a point	stress in two-syllable verbs toning down negative statements
VIDEO: The art of parkour page 78 ▶ REVIEW page 80					

COMMUNICATION ACTIVITIES page 81 ▶ GRAMMAR SUMMARY page 83 ▶ AUDIOSCRIPTS page 96

Listening	Reading	Critical thinking	Speaking	Writing
two speakers talk about important lessons in life a talk by a sociologist about understanding what makes people who they are	an article about the lessons we learn from the past an article about the language of Shakespeare	purpose	your favourite saying situations in your life call my bluff	taking notes writing skill: using abbreviations
a talk about the livelihood of Kazakh nomads an interview with a firefighter	an article about the Moken people of Myanmar an article about rock climbing in Yosemite	analysing language	more than a job safety features your comfort zone	a covering letter or email writing skill: fixed expressions
a description of a photograph an interview with an architect about small homes	an article about two towns with individual characters an article about the architect Zaha Hadid	summarizing	your home town a bit of luxury how spaces affect you	an opinion essay writing skill: discourse markers
a news report about bionic body parts an interview about the inspiration for inventions	an article about the future of bendable technology an article about a social entrepreneur	finding counter arguments	future solutions how people managed in the past a social business	a proposal writing skill: making recommendations
an extract from a talk by a travel writer a radio interview about holidays to unknown places	a travel blog about different approaches to travelling an article about travel in graphic novels	evaluating sources	how you travel a mystery tour knowing places	a review writing skill: using descriptive words
a conversation between two friends about health and exercise an interview with an ultrarunner about sports injuries	an article about different exercise regimes an article about beauty	author influence	exercise trends describing an injury does beauty sell?	a formal report writing skill: avoiding repetition

Contents Split Edition B

Unit	Grammar	Vocabulary	Real life (functions)	Pronunciation
7 Digital media	passive reporting verbs nominalization	wordbuilding: verb prefix *out* idioms: business buzz words word focus: *break*	making a podcast speaking skill: hedging language	new words
VIDEO: Talking dictionaries ▶ REVIEW			
8 The music in us	the adverb *just* purpose and result	themes of songs idioms: music word focus: *hit*	your favourite music speaking skill: responding to questions	expressions with *just* intonation to express uncertainty
VIDEO: A biopic ▶ REVIEW			
9 Window on the past	linking words present and perfect participles	wordbuilding: verb + preposition crime and punishment word focus: *board*	checking, confirming and clarifying	silent letters
VIDEO: Collecting the past ▶ REVIEW			
10 Social living	adverbs and adverbial phrases negative adverbials and inversion	being a good member of society having fun word focus: *free*	making conversation speaking skill: showing interest	sentence stress intonation and elision
VIDEO: Initiation with ants ▶ REVIEW			
11 Reason and emotion	unreal past forms conditionals and inversion	feelings wordbuilding: heteronyms word focus: *beyond*	recognizing feelings	heteronyms adjectives ending in *-ed*
VIDEO: Madeline the robot tamer ▶ REVIEW			
12 Mother nature	approximation and vague language *would*	wordbuilding: adverb + adjective collocations idioms: adjective collocations word focus: *move*	a debate speaking skill: interrupting	intonation in interruptions
VIDEO: Three years and 6,000 miles on a horse ▶ REVIEW			

Listening	Reading	Critical thinking	Speaking	Writing
a talk by a journalist about digital technology an interview about social media marketing	a study of global facts about selfies an article about a day at a hackers' conference	identifying personal opinion	the impact of digital media brands attitudes to security	a news report writing skill: cautious language
an interview with a busker a talk by a neuroscientist about music therapy	an interview with a musician about cultural influences a review of a documentary about Bob Marley	identifying key points	themes of songs how to relax a charity concert	a description writing skill: parallel structures
a talk about the significance of historical objects a story about an unusual crime	an article about what personal letters reveal about our past a story about hidden treasure	unanswered questions	an important past event a case of fraud historical irony	describing a past event writing skill: sequencing events
an extract from a radio programme about ethnic communities a podcast about the importance of play	an article about ant society an article about the Hadza of Tanzania	reading between the lines	being a good member of society social games feeling free	a discursive essay writing skill: referring to evidence
a short talk by a photographer about photographing people a lecture about irrational thinking	an article about understanding emotions an article about artificial intelligence in the future	analysing structure	modern life mind games technology and occupations	an email message writing skill: avoiding misunderstandings
three people describe the landscape where they live an extract from a radio interview about the Japanese poet Basho	an article about the importance of geo-literacy an article about how wildlife are moving into our cities	different perspectives	natural and man-made features events in nature the animal and human worlds	a letter to a newspaper writing skill: persuasive language

Life around the world – in 12 videos

Unit 11 Madeline the robot tamer

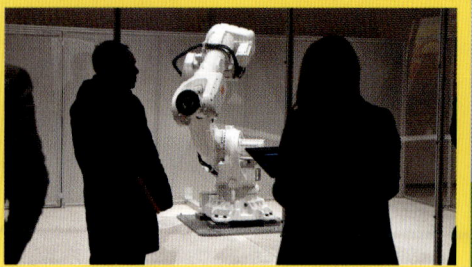

Discover how one project is bringing humans and robots closer together.

Unit 1 Arctic wisdom

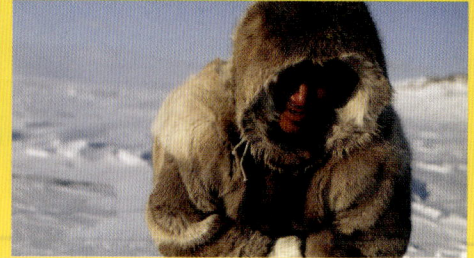

Learn how generations pass on their accumulated wisdom in Iqaluit, Canada.

Canada

USA

Unit 2 Climbing Yosemite

Find out how Jimmy Chin made a career out of mountaineer photography.

France

Spain

Jamaica

Unit 3 A story of solutions

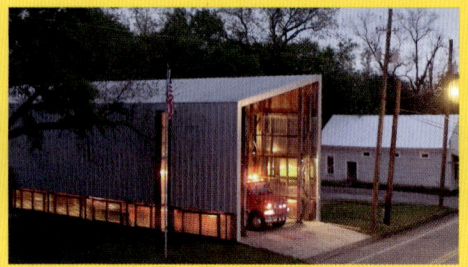

Find out about how an architecture company made an impact on a small town in the USA.

Unit 5 On the road: Andrew McCarthy

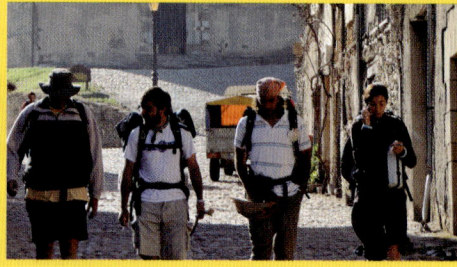

Learn how a travel experience changed the life of travel writer Andrew McCarthy.

Brazil

Unit 8 A biopic

Learn about the inspiration behind the making of the biopic Marley.

Unit 10 Initiation with ants

Find out about an unusual ceremony in the Amazonian jungle in Brazil.

Life videos, Split Editions A and B

Unit 6 The art of parkour

Learn about the history of free running.

Unit 7 Talking dictionaries

Learn about a project which is helping to preserve dying languages.

Unit 12 Three years and 6,000 miles on a horse

Find out about the impact of an unusual journey on horseback.

Russia

Mongolia

Palestine

China

Unit 9 Collecting the past

Find out how China's cultural heritage is being preserved by shopping.

Uganda

Unit 4 This man risked it all

Learn how Sanga Moses took a risk to set up a social enterprise in Uganda.

7

Split Editions A and B

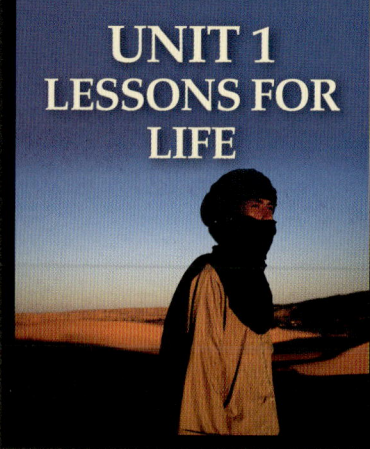
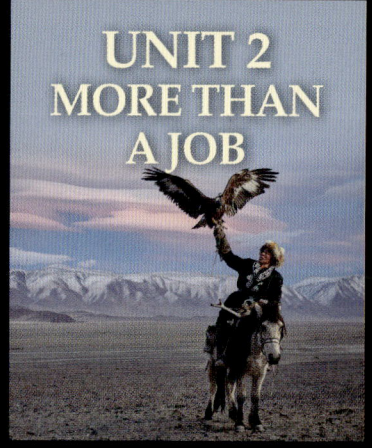
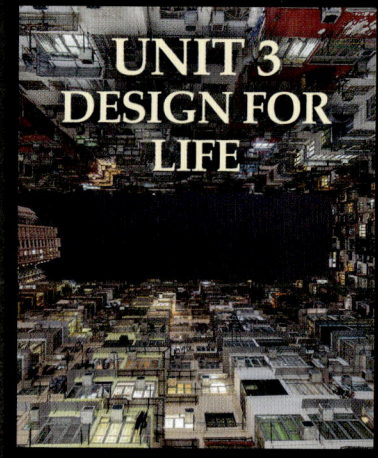

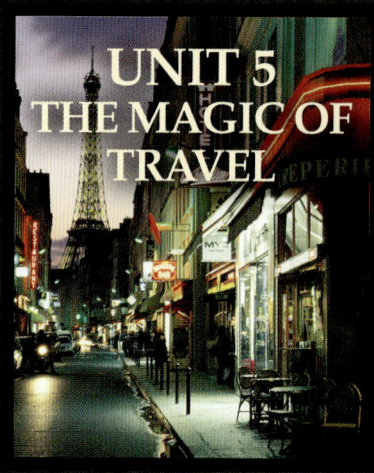

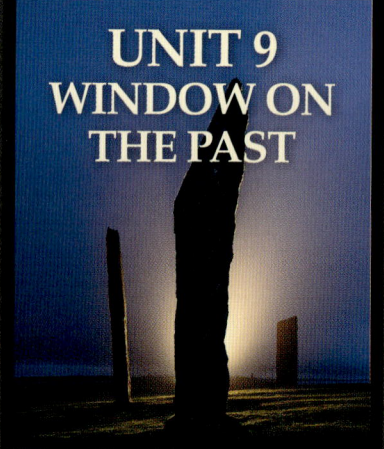

Unit 1 Lessons for life

A Tuareg tribesman at twilight, Libya

FEATURES

10 Learning from the past

The lessons we learn from the past

12 What makes us who we are?

Understanding what makes people who they are

14 Immortal words

The language of Shakespeare

18 Arctic wisdom

A video about how Inuit elders pass on their knowledge

1 Work in pairs. Look at the photo and these Tuareg proverbs. What do the proverbs tell you about the Tuareg attitude to life?

"Better to walk without knowing where than to sit doing nothing."

"In life, it is always possible to reach agreement in the end."

"Acquiring things you do not need will kill you."

2 ▶1 Listen to two people talking about important lessons they have learned in life. Answer the questions.

1 What advice does each speaker now try to follow?
2 What experience led them to learn this lesson?
3 Which lesson do you think a Tuareg person would agree with? Why?

3 ▶1 Complete the phrases the speakers use to describe the life lessons they have learned. Then listen again and check.

1 The most _____ lesson I've learned was …
2 That's become a sort of _____ principle for me …
3 A good rule of _____ is …
4 But it's a lot easier _____ than done …
5 I always make a _____ of not getting …

4 Think of an occasion when you learned an important lesson or found a good way of doing something (e.g. about people, friends, family, money, work, health, risk, fun). Describe what happened. What did you do? What have you learned from it?

my life ▶ YOUR FAVOURITE SAYING ▶ SITUATIONS IN YOUR LIFE ▶ CALL MY BLUFF ▶ GETTING TO KNOW PEOPLE ▶ TAKING NOTES

9

reading **lessons in life** • grammar **time phrases** • speaking **your favourite saying**

1a Learning from the past

Reading

1 Work in pairs. Read the quotation. Do you think this is good advice? Is it easy to follow? Discuss with your partner.

" Learn from the mistakes of others. You can't live long enough to make them all yourself. "

Eleanor Roosevelt, Diplomat

2 Read the article. Match the person (1–2) with the type of lesson they taught (a–c). There is one extra type of lesson.

1 Confucius
2 Nelson Mandela

a a lesson that is difficult to follow
b a lesson that has been misinterpreted
c a lesson that has been forgotten

3 Read the article again. According to the article, are the sentences true (T) or false (F)?

1 Sometimes people don't want to follow the lessons of the past.
2 A lot of Chinese people feel that their society is not interested in the past.
3 China's rapid development has begun to slow down.
4 Mandela was not opposed to violence in principle.
5 Nelson Mandela wanted the two sides in South Africa to forget what had happened in the past.
6 The writer suggests that most people are too selfish.

4 Find words or expressions in the article with these meanings.

1 show the right direction (para 1)
2 period of significant growth (para 2)
3 do something as a result of information or advice (para 3)
4 work hard towards a goal (para 4)
5 copy someone's behaviour (para 4)

LEARNING FROM THE PAST

▶ 2

Why do we never seem to learn from the past? The mistakes or correct actions of others should point the way for us in the future. But either we forget these lessons or we fail to follow them or, in some cases, we deliberately choose to ignore them. Of all the lessons that we have to learn, perhaps the most difficult is how not to be selfish or think only of ourselves.

In China, the government is trying to remind people of the lessons given by Confucius, the ancient philosopher. Because of China's economic boom in recent years, the government has become worried that people are becoming more selfish and individualistic. Many Chinese have been saying for some time that the traditional values in society of harmony, respect and hard work have been lost. Accordingly, a few years ago the government focused attention again on the teachings of Confucius.

Prior to the 1990s, Confucianism had not been fashionable, but in a country which is currently developing at a dizzying speed, his teachings offer a sense of stability and order. Nowadays, people often talk about Confucius' idea of a 'harmonious society', even if they do not always act on it.

Sometimes it is difficult to learn lessons because the standards of the 'teacher' are so high. This is certainly the case with Nelson Mandela, who tried to spread the message of reconciliation to two sides in South Africa who hated and distrusted each other deeply. Mandela had always been committed to peace, and while he was living in prison, he decided that the only way to unite his divided country was if the two sides could talk about what had happened in the past and begin to rebuild some measure of trust. All those who strive for peace know that in the long term they will have to begin a dialogue with their enemy. Yet few are able to follow the example set by Mandela, because it requires such a high degree of unselfishness. It seems that heeding this warning – not to be selfish – is perhaps the hardest lesson of all for people to learn.

'Consideration for others is the basis of a good life, a good society.'
Confucius

'If you want to make peace with your enemy, you have to work with your enemy.'
Nelson Mandela

dizzying (adj) /ˈdɪziɪŋ/ very fast and confusing
reconciliation (n) /ˌrek(ə)nsɪlɪˈeɪʃ(ə)n/ making peace and re-establishing relations

Grammar time phrases

> **TIME PHRASES**
>
> Certain time phrases are commonly (but not always) used with certain tenses.
>
> **Present simple:** *often, never, every week, generally*
> **Present continuous:** *now, at the moment, this week*
> **Past simple:** *two days ago, last week, at the time, when*
> **Past continuous:** *at the time*
> **Present perfect simple:** *just, recently, so far, over the last two years, how long, for, since (2010), already, yet, ever, never*
> **Present perfect continuous:** *how long, for, just, recently, since*
> **Past perfect simple and continuous:** *already, before that, up to then*
> **will, going to and present continuous for future:** *next week, in three days / in three days' time, soon, on Friday*
>
> For further information and practice, see page 84.

5 Look at the grammar box and the time phrases (1–8) below. Then follow the steps (a–b).

1 in recent years 5 currently
2 for some time 6 nowadays
3 a few years ago 7 while
4 prior to the 1990s 8 in the long term

a Find the verbs that are used in the article with each of the time phrases and identify the tenses.
b Match the time phrases (1–8) with the tense in the grammar box.

6 Complete the sentences with these time phrases.

at the moment	at the time	before that
ever	fifty years ago	for years
in the coming years	nowadays	often
over the last 25 years		

a ¹_____ military service was compulsory in the UK. But ²_____ young people don't have to go into the army. I think this will change ³_____ because there is a feeling that young people need more discipline.

b ⁴_____, people have definitely become more greedy. I've been saying ⁵_____ that it is not right for anyone to earn a hundred times the average salary.

c I'm having an interesting debate with my father ⁶_____. He says that young people don't ⁷_____ show respect to their elders anymore. But I don't think you can just demand respect; you have to earn it.

d When I was forty, I decided to stop working so hard. ⁸_____, I was working sixty hours a week. It was the best decision that I have ⁹_____ made. ¹⁰_____, I had had no time to enjoy life.

7 Complete the conversations with the correct form of the verbs. Use the time phrases to help you decide which form to use.

1 A: How long _____ (you / learn) Japanese? You speak it really well.
  B: Thanks! I _____ (start) having lessons two years ago. But I _____ (learn) a few words on a trip to Japan before that.

2 C: _____ (you / try) out the new gym yet? I _____ (go) last night. It's great.
  D: No. Every week I _____ (tell) myself I'm going to go, but I never _____ (seem) to make it. I'm sure I _____ (get) there in the end, though.

3 E: What _____ (you / work) on currently?
  F: Well, for the last two weeks I _____ (do) some work at the university computing department.
  E: Oh, that explains it. I _____ (see) you outside the university building the other day.

8 Complete the sentences by writing facts about yourself. Write one sentence which is not true. Then work in pairs. Compare sentences with your partner and try to guess the false sentence.

1 My work? Currently, I …
  Currently, I'm looking for a new job.
2 I like seeing new places. A few years ago, I …
3 In my free time, I usually …
4 I have never … , but I've always wanted to.
5 I didn't … last weekend, because I had already …
6 I met my best friend when I … . I … at the time.
7 I … for several years.
8 I don't have the time or money at the moment, but sooner or later I …

9 Complete the advice about life using these words. Then compare answers with your partner. Which piece of advice do you like most? Why?

| ever | for | in | never | now | while |

1 Life is what happens _____ you are making other plans.
2 Value your friends. If you ignore them _____ a long time, they will start to ignore you.
3 When you're feeling stressed, ask yourself this question: _____ five years, will the problem still seem so important?
4 No one has _____ become poor by giving.
5 Get out more. A whole world of amazing experiences is waiting for you right _____.
6 You should _____ take yourself too seriously.

Speaking my life

10 Work in groups. Each write down two of your favourite (or least favourite!) sayings about life. Then discuss your choices.

my life ▶ YOUR FAVOURITE SAYING ▶ SITUATIONS IN YOUR LIFE ▶ CALL MY BLUFF ▶ GETTING TO KNOW PEOPLE
▶ TAKING NOTES

vocabulary and listening personality and identity • wordbuilding binomial pairs •
pronunciation linking in word pairs • grammar the continuous aspect • speaking situations in your life

1b What makes us who we are?

A Paris painter next to his self-portrait

Vocabulary and listening
personality and identity

1 Work in pairs. Look at the photo and caption. Discuss the questions.

1 Why is the painter putting his hands up?
2 What impression of the painter do you get from his self-portrait?

2 Look at the expressions to describe people. Answer the questions.

> a control freak   a dreamer
> a driven person   a family person
> a free spirit   a joker
> the life and soul of the party
> an outgoing type

1 What do you think each expression means?
2 Which expressions do you think are positive, negative or neutral?
3 Give an example of someone you know who fits each description.

3 Look at these factors which can give people information about you. Which do you think are the most significant? Number them in order (1–8) of importance.

a your friends   e your life experiences
b your work   f your interests/hobbies
c your age   g your background
d your character   h your beliefs and values

4 ▶3 Listen to a sociologist describing how we define ourselves. Tick (✓) the factors in Exercise 3 that he mentions. Which is the most important, according to him?

5 ▶3 Listen to the talk again. Choose the correct option to complete the sentences.

1 The speaker thinks the question 'What do you do?' can sound *aggressive / judgmental* as a conversation starter.
2 Sally has been defined by her background because she didn't grow up in *the city / a normal family*.
3 Sarah has dedicated her life to helping people who *are ill / live in poor countries*.
4 The most important thing for John about his work is the *challenge / security*.
5 Jack hasn't been in a relationship since he was *34 / 25*.
6 Anne wants school children to eat *better / more vegetarian* food.

Wordbuilding binomial pairs

> **WORDBUILDING binomial pairs**
>
> Certain pairs of words in English are irreversible, i.e. they always appear in the same order.
> *rock and roll* (never *roll and rock*), *law and order*
>
> For further practice, see Workbook pages 107 and 111.

6 Look at the wordbuilding box. Choose the correct form of these irreversible word pairs (a–b).

a He picks up *pieces and bits / bits and pieces* of work *as and when / when and as* he can.
b It seems that what defines people *first and foremost / foremost and first* is experience.

7 Complete the word pairs using these words. Discuss what you think each phrase means.

| fro | games | large | pains | quiet | sound |
| sweet | then | wide | | | |

1 I need **peace and** _____ to concentrate.
2 They all came back from their canoeing trip **safe and** _____. No one was injured, but most of them had a few **aches and** _____.
3 Try not to give a long talk. **By and** _____, it's better to keep it **short and** _____.
4 People come from **far and** _____ to see Stonehenge. There are busloads of tourists coming **to and** _____ all day.
5 You think my job is all **fun and** _____, but actually **now and** _____ we do some serious work too!

8 Pronunciation linking in word pairs

▶ 4 Listen to the word pairs in Exercise 7. Notice a) how the words are linked and b) the pronunciation of *and* in the word pairs. Then practise reading the sentences.

Grammar the continuous aspect

> **THE CONTINUOUS ASPECT**
>
> **Present continuous**
> 1 *… you feel as if people **are always judging** you …*
> 2 *It's now **becoming** a national movement.*
>
> **Present perfect continuous**
> 3 *He **has been saying** that since he was 35.*
>
> **Past continuous**
> 4 *When his children were born, he **was working** as a carpet salesman.*
>
> **Past perfect continuous**
> 5 *At one point, he **had been intending** to leave the company …*
>
> **Future continuous**
> 6 *In a few years, he **won't be moving** about anymore.*
>
> For further information and practice, see page 84.

9 Look at the grammar box. Which verb form in bold describes something which:

a is a current trend?
b we expect to be happening (now or) in the future?
c started in the past and is still continuing?
d is the background to another more important event in the past?
e was in progress up to a point in the past?
f happens regularly and is irritating?

10 Work in pairs. What is the difference in meaning, if any, between these verb forms?

1 What *do you do / are you doing*?
2 My husband *is always phoning / always phones* me at work.
3 *I've been reading / I've read* the book you gave me.
4 When I left school, I *was working / worked* at a restaurant at weekends.
5 This time next week, *I'll be sitting / I'll sit* on a beach in the Bahamas.
6 He *had been working / had worked* as a nurse before he became a paramedic.
7 She *was living / had been living / lived* in Germany before she moved to this country.
8 California is eight hours behind us. Anne-Marie *will be going / usually goes* to bed now.

11 Complete the sentences using the appropriate continuous form of the verbs.

1 Marlon's a fantastic football player, isn't he? I _____ (watch) him playing the other day. I expect in a few years he _____ (play) professionally. Apparently, some clubs _____ (already / watch) him.
2 Katja is such a great friend. Last week I _____ (feel) really fed up about work and she gave me some chocolates that she _____ (save) for a special occasion.
3 Marta _____ (get) very eccentric. She keeps budgerigars and recently she's started letting them out of their cages; so they _____ (fly) all over the house. I _____ (sit) in her kitchen the other day and one flew down and landed on the table.

Speaking my life

12 Think of examples of the following things. Then work in pairs and take turns to tell each other your ideas and ask follow-up questions.

- a habit of other people that irritates you
- two things that you imagine people you know will be doing right now
- a situation that you hope is temporary
- something you haven't finished but keep meaning to
- something you had been intending to do but then changed your mind

1c Immortal words

Reading

1 Work in pairs. Discuss the questions.

1 Who are the most famous writers in your country's history? What did they write?
2 What Shakespeare plays or characters can you name? What do you know about them?

2 Read the article. According to the author, why are Shakespeare's plays still so popular today?

3 Read the article again and answer the questions.

1 What adjective describes what England was like in Shakespeare's time? (para 1)
2 What new element did Shakespeare bring to play writing, according to Bloom?
3 Why does Hamlet find it difficult to make a decision?
4 In *Romeo and Juliet*, what is the nurse's attitude to relationships?
5 Which adverb means that Shakespeare was good at expressing ideas in just a few words? (para 4)
6 What verb tells you that Shakespeare created new words and expressions? (para 4)

4 Look at the expressions in italics in paragraph 4. Use them to replace the words in bold below.

1 I need a new jacket. This one **is past its best.**
2 I'm 24. I have money and a university degree. **I can do anything I want to.**
3 He said that one of the shops in town would have the right battery, but it turned out to be **a search for something that couldn't be found.**
4 What the critics say is **not significant**. What matters is whether the public like the film.
5 Everyone says it's **an obvious result** that Johanna will win, but I'm not so certain.
6 There's no point telling her he's no good. **You can't see the faults in the person you love.**
7 The teacher got us to play a game to **help people relax at the start.**
8 After six different jobs, I'm with my first company again. I've **arrived back at the starting point.**

Critical thinking purpose

5 Which option(s) (a–d) describes the author's main purpose for writing this article? Underline the sentences in the article that tell you this.

a to review Harold Bloom's book
b to explain why Shakespeare is popular today
c to examine if Shakespeare's reputation is justified
d to examine Shakespeare's contribution to modern-day English

6 Did the author state her purpose at any point? In which of these writing types do you think it is important for an author to begin by stating the reason for writing?

- a description
- a job application
- a business report
- a personal letter

7 Do you think the author achieved her purpose? Why? / Why not?

Word focus life

8 Look at the article again. Find words or expressions with the word *life* that mean:

1 realistic (para 2)
2 for all one's life (para 2)
3 with a 'big' personality (para 3)

9 Work in pairs. Look at the expressions with *life* in bold. Discuss what they mean.

1 I sold my old Citroen 2CV car last year for £300. Now I've just read that they've become really valuable! That's **the story of my life.**
2 Work stress is just **a fact of life** these days – you have to learn to deal with it.
3 There were people at the conference from **all walks of life** – writers, students, business people.
4 My son was worried about going to university, but now he's **having the time of his life**.
5 Thanks for driving me to the station – it was a real **life-saver**. I'd have missed my train.

10 Work in groups. Each think of a personal example for two of the expressions in Exercises 8 and 9.

Not doing well in exams has been the story of my life!

Speaking my life

11 Work in two groups of three. Play the game *Call my bluff* using words coined by Shakespeare.

Group A: Turn to page 81.

Group B: Turn to page 82.

- For each word, rewrite the true definition in your own words, then write two false definitions. Write example sentences for each definition.
- Group A reads the three definitions of the first word. Group B must guess which is the true definition.
- Group B then reads the definitions of their first word for Group A to guess the true one.
- Then repeat this procedure with the other words.

12 Think of an aspect of your life. Choose a word related to this, and find the English word. Then play *Call my bluff* with that word.

Unit 1 Lessons for life

▶ 5

The sixteenth-century dramatist Ben Jonson generously called his rival, Shakespeare, a writer 'not of an age, but for all time'. And so it has proved to be, because Shakespeare's plays are still the most translated and most performed of any playwright's in the world. But if you ask people the reason for Shakespeare's continued popularity, you get different answers. Some say he was a great storyteller, others that the magic lies in the beauty of his poetry. Some say it is simply because he left us a huge volume of work, which was written during a vibrant time in English history, particularly in the theatre.

A more interesting answer that I came across recently is one put forward by the critic Harold Bloom in his book *Shakespeare: The Invention of the Human*. Bloom argues that Shakespeare gave us something that the world had not seen in literature before – characters with personalities, and particularly weaknesses, that we could relate to. These lifelike characters and the observations that Shakespeare made about the human condition are really what Jonson was referring to when he talked about Shakespeare's universal appeal. For Bloom, a lifelong fan of the poet, English speakers have Shakespeare to thank for much of their current language, cultural references and their understanding of human psychology.

While some might disagree with Bloom's assertion about the invention of 'personality' in literature – many earlier storytellers like Homer and Petrarch could claim this – there is no doubt that Shakespeare's characters resonate with people very strongly. We sympathize with poor Hamlet because we all know that frustrating situation where our hearts tell us one thing must be true and our heads another. We laugh at the larger-than-life nurse in *Romeo and Juliet* because of the amusing way she offers advice to Juliet about relationships, putting practical considerations before romance; she is a person that we too have met. The name Lady Macbeth has become synonymous with cold, over-ambitious women; while the character of Iago still serves as a warning about the dangers of jealousy and how it leads to the manipulation of others.

Of course the language plays a big part too. The observations about people and life are made more memorable by the way in which they are phrased, both succinctly and poetically. Shakespeare has been dead for 400 years, but certain words and sayings of his still exist in the English language today. Whether you are 'fashionable' or 'faint-hearted', thank Shakespeare, who probably coined the terms. Iago promises to 'wear his heart on his sleeve', a phrase still commonly used for people who do not try to hide their true feelings. In fact, it is amazing just how great Shakespeare's influence on everyday modern language has been. Take, for example, these commonly used phrases: *a foregone conclusion, come full circle, has seen better days, break the ice, neither here nor there, the world is my oyster, a wild goose chase, love is blind.*

Bloom's title *The Invention of the Human* may seem a bit strong. 'The enduring humanity of Shakespeare', on the other hand, would not be an exaggeration.

---

enduring (adj) /ɪnˈdjʊərɪŋ/ lasting a long time
faint-hearted (adj) /ˌfeɪnt ˈhɑː(r)tɪd/ lacking courage to act
resonate with (v) /ˈrezəneɪt/ create a feeling that something is familiar or relevant

Immortal words

my life ▶ YOUR FAVOURITE SAYING ▶ SITUATIONS IN YOUR LIFE ▶ CALL MY BLUFF ▶ GETTING TO KNOW PEOPLE
▶ TAKING NOTES

real life getting to know people • **pronunciation** merged words in everyday phrases

1d How did you get into that?

Real life getting to know people

1 Work in pairs. Discuss the questions.
  1. What kind of subjects do you generally like to talk about – sport, entertainment, the news, family and friends, work, something else?
  2. What do you find are good conversation topics for getting to know other people?

2 Write three tips for a blog about 'getting to know people'. Then share your ideas with the class.

3 ▶6 Look at the conversation openers for getting to know people. Then listen to six short conversations. Tick (✓) the conversation opener they use in each conversation.

> ▶ **GETTING TO KNOW PEOPLE**
>
> Hi, I don't think we've met. I'm …
> Hi. Is it your first day at college too?
> Hey, I like your jacket.
> Whereabouts are you from?
> So, what do you do?
> What did you think of the show?
> This is a long queue, isn't it?
> Have you seen that film everyone's talking about?
> I'm supposed to have given up sweet things, but I can't stop eating this cake.

4 ▶6 Listen to the conversations again. Make notes on the follow-up questions that each person starting the conversation asked. Then compare answers with your partner.

5 Pronunciation merged words in everyday phrases

a ▶7 Listen to these questions and notice how the underlined words merge together when said quickly.
  1. I <u>don't think</u> we've met.
  2. Is it <u>your first day</u> too?
  3. <u>What do you</u> do?
  4. What did you <u>think of the</u> show?
  5. <u>What kind of films</u> do you like?

b ▶8 Listen to these questions and write in the missing words.
  1. _____ eat here?
  2. _____ living in New York?
  3. _____ apartment have you got?
  4. _____ the new building?
  5. _____ coffee or something?

6 Work in pairs. Act out two of the conversations for getting to know people you heard in Exercise 3. Use the same conversation openers and follow-up questions. Answer as naturally as possible.

7 Work with a new partner. Act out two more conversations. Follow these steps.
  - Choose two of the conversation openers in the box that you did not hear in Exercise 3.
  - Think of follow-up questions you might ask.
  - Act out the conversations.

16 my life ▶ YOUR FAVOURITE SAYING ▶ SITUATIONS IN YOUR LIFE ▶ CALL MY BLUFF ▶ GETTING TO KNOW PEOPLE ▶ TAKING NOTES

writing taking notes • writing skill using abbreviations
Unit 1 Lessons for life

1e Your first day

Writing taking notes

1 Do you write notes sometimes on things you read or listen to? In what situations do you write notes? What do the notes consist of? What do you do with them?

2 ▶9 Look at the notes taken by a student at a university orientation day. Then listen to an extract from the talk and complete the information where the student put ??? in points 1 and 2.

```
Talk by Principal to new students      ???
1 Course reg 10 a.m. – 3 p.m. Mon in main uni hall –
  compulsory.
2 Overseas students. i.e. all except UK and ???,
  must take docs to Admissions office – incl.
  education certificates, student visas + bank
  account details – by end of next week.
3 Uni has 'buddy' system (a 2nd year student)
  to help OS sts know where things are and what
  to do.
4 Most courses approx. 9–12 contact hrs p.w.; plan
  study time carefully. Lots of places to work,
  e.g. faculty library, main library, IT centre.
5 If worried about study or sthg else, see student
  counsellor. NB each group has native speaker
  counsellor.
6 Extra academic writing skills tuition available for
  1st year sts – details in student booklet (times,
  level, etc.).
```

3 Work in pairs. What other information did the speaker give that isn't in notes 1 and 2? Discuss with your partner.

4 ▶9 Listen again and check your answers. Why do you think this information wasn't included?

5 Writing skill using abbreviations

a Work in pairs. How many different abbreviations can you find in the notes? Try to guess what each one means.

b Compare your answers in Exercise 5a with another pair. Did you guess the same meanings? Which abbreviations have the following meanings?

Shortened words
a including
b roughly
c please note
d and so on

Latin abbreviations
e for example
f that is to say

c We use abbreviations in semi-formal writing and when writing in note form, but not in more formal contexts. In which of the following could abbreviations be used?

1 an academic essay
2 your notes on a book you have read
3 a letter of complaint
4 an internal email to a close colleague

d Look at this email message and rewrite it in note form. Exchange notes with your partner, cover the original email and try to reconstruct it from the notes.

> Please note that the meeting with Ellis & Company will be tomorrow, Tuesday 12th May at 3 o'clock. Please can you let me know approximately how many people from your department will be attending and if you need further information. Thanks.

6 ▶10 Listen to a talk from a university tutor about reading for your university course and take notes. Remember to include only the relevant points and to use abbreviations where necessary.

7 Exchange notes with your partner. Use these questions to check your notes.

• Do the notes include the same relevant points?
• Have they left out unnecessary information?
• Do they use abbreviations correctly?

my life ▶ YOUR FAVOURITE SAYING ▶ SITUATIONS IN YOUR LIFE ▶ CALL MY BLUFF ▶ GETTING TO KNOW PEOPLE
▶ TAKING NOTES

17

1f Arctic wisdom

An Inuit man ice fishing, Nunavut Territory, Canada

Unit 1 Lessons for life

Before you watch

1 Look at the photo and the map of where the Inuit people live. Discuss with your partner what you think this place is like. Talk about:

- Population (many/few, old/young, etc.)
- Weather
- Communications (transport, internet, speaking/writing, etc.)
- Way of life (traditional/modern/changing, stressful/relaxed, etc.)

2 Key vocabulary

a Read the sentences. The words in bold are used in the video. Guess the meaning of the words.

1 They have asked the government to **fund** the building of a new community centre.
2 The **elders** of the tribe meet once a week to discuss any problems in the community.
3 He has low **self-esteem** because as a child he was always criticized for not being clever enough.
4 Thank you for all your comments on my essay. They have been **invaluable**.
5 A **disproportionate** number of the university's students are from wealthy backgrounds.

b Match the words in bold in Exercise 2a with these definitions.

a extremely useful
b too large or small in comparison to something else
c older members of a group
d finance, provide the money for
e how good you feel about yourself

While you watch

3 ▶ 1.1 Watch the video and check your ideas from Exercise 1. What is your overall impression of the place?

4 ▶ 1.1 Watch the first part of the video (0.00 to 2.24) again which features an interview with the Mayor of Iqaluit. Answer the questions.

1 What has happened to the elders in a short time?
2 What is important about the elders?
3 What phrase is still relevant and is often used in Iqaluit?
4 How did these people's parents live?
5 How were traditions passed down between generations?

5 ▶ 1.1 Watch the second part of the video (2.25 to 3.39) and complete the summary.

In the past, elders were [1] _____ for the others in the community. Each one was an [2] _____ on a particular area, helping the community to [3] _____: on the weather, on the environment, on different kinds of [4] _____. Inuits were happy with the [5] _____. The woman's mother told her daughter that she would see many [6] _____, but she said, 'Never [7] _____ who you are.'

6 Watch the third part of the video (3.40 to the end) and answer the questions.

1 What has happened to the Iqaluit population in recent times? Why?
2 Name two things the woman mentions when talking about the key to a happy life.
3 Why does she have a communication problem with the younger generation?
4 What is significant about the number 23?
5 What was the main characteristic of the culture of the Iqaluit in the past?
6 What does the narrator say is the key to these people's future?

After you watch

7 Vocabulary in context

a ▶ 1.2 Watch the clips from the video. Complete the collocations. Then discuss your answers.

b Complete the sentences in your own words. Then compare your sentences with a partner.

1 I always seek advice when …
2 The last time I experienced a communication barrier was when …
3 The key to living a happy life is …

8 Work in pairs. Discuss the questions.

1 Is the advice and wisdom of elders highly respected in your society?
2 Is this as it should be? Why? / Why not?

9 Think of a story that one of your grandparents (or an older person in your community) told you and retell the story to your partner. Do the stories have a lesson that is still relevant today? Why? / Why not?

---

infant mortality (n) /ˈɪnfənt mɔː(r)ˈtæləti/ the number of children that die before they are two years old
nomadic (adj) /nəʊˈmædɪk/ with no fixed home, wandering from place to place

19

UNIT 1 REVIEW AND MEMORY BOOSTER

Grammar

1 Read the article. What is a 'griot'? What lesson did the writer take away from his visit to Timbuktu?

2 Choose the correct options to complete the article.

Some years ago I ¹ *visited / have visited* Timbuktu in Mali. Generally, people ² *are thinking / think* of Timbuktu as a desert town somewhere at the end of the world. But once upon a time, Timbuktu ³ *was / has been* a thriving city and key trading post, a place in Africa with a long and rich history. In the marketplace you get a sense of this: women in brightly coloured clothes selling produce of all kinds. But my attention was drawn to a very old man who ⁴ *had sat / was sitting* in a corner. For a while, people ⁵ *had gathered / had been gathering* around him, so I joined them. He was a griot, or traditional storyteller.
Griots ⁶ *have been singing / sang* about kings and magicians, wars and journeys for generations. This is how Malians ⁷ *learned / have learned* about their history. He poured me a glass of tea and then I ⁸ *listened / was listening* to him tell the story of King Mansa and the golden age of Timbuktu, a story he ⁹ *told / had told* countless times before. At the end, the griot quoted old Mali saying: 'To succeed you need three things – a brazier, time and friends.' The brazier is to heat water for tea. Time and friends are what you need to share stories. It's advice that ¹⁰ *will stay / will be staying* with me in future years.

3 ▶▶ MB Find six time phrases in the article. Which tenses are used with each time phrase? Then choose four of the phrases and make your own sentences with them.

I CAN
use the correct tense with specific time phrases
use the continuous aspect to describe actions in progress

Vocabulary

4 Complete the expressions.

1 a lifel_____ painting
2 people from all w_____ of life
3 to have the t_____ of your life
4 a lifel_____ passion
5 it's the s_____ of my life
6 just a f_____ of life

5 ▶▶ MB Work in pairs. Which of these phrases best describes these people: your best friend, your mother, your sister or brother? Give reasons.

| a control freak   a dreamer   a driven person |
| a family person   a free spirit   a joker |
| the life and soul of the party |
| an outgoing person |

6 ▶▶ MB Correct the underlined words to complete these phrases about life lessons. Then give an example from your own experience that illustrates each phrase.

1 Trying to remain positive is a lot easier <u>spoken</u> than done.
2 A good rule of <u>finger</u> is: if you want something done properly, do it yourself.
3 It's a good idea to put a little money aside <u>then</u> and when you can.
4 My <u>leading</u> principle in life is: by and <u>whole</u>, it's better to ignore what others say about you.

I CAN
describe different types of personality
use idioms and expressions about life

Real life

7 Work in pairs. Complete the conversation starters.

1 Hi, I don't think we _____. I'm _____.
2 Hi. Is it your first _____ too?
3 Hey, I like _____.
4 So, whereabouts _____?
5 So, _____ you do?
6 What did you think _____?
7 This is a long queue, _____?
8 Have you seen that film everyone _____?

8 ▶▶ MB Choose four of the conversation starters from Exercise 7. Act out four short conversations, using follow-up questions and answers.

I CAN
start a conversation with someone I don't know
ask follow-up questions to get to know someone better

Unit 2 More than a job

A golden eagle with a Kazakh hunter, Mongolia

FEATURES

22 Living off the sea
The last nomads of the sea

24 Smokejumpers
A firefighter who risks her life to save others

26 Daring, defiant and free
Rock climbing unaided

30 Climbing Yosemite
A video about the mountaineering photographer Jimmy Chin

1 ▶ 11 Work in pairs. Look at the photo and caption. What do you think this man is doing? Then listen to an anthropologist talking about these people and check your ideas.

2 ▶ 11 Listen to the speaker again and answer the questions.

1 What is the livelihood of the nomads in western Mongolia?
2 How are many Kazakhs making a living these days?
3 What is their more traditional way of life?
4 What task requires great patience?
5 What does the hunter share with his eagle?
6 What sort of activity do people think eagle hunting is these days?

3 Look at the phrases in bold. Discuss the difference in meaning between the phrases in each pair.

1 it's **my occupation** and it's **my vocation**
2 **a trade** and **a profession**
3 it's **a living** and it's **my livelihood**
4 **a job** and **a task**
5 **work** and **a job** *(grammatical difference)*

4 Work in groups. Can you think of (at least) two examples of each of the following things?

a people who depend on animals for their livelihood
b a traditional occupation which is now dying out
c a task that requires great patience

my life ▶ MORE THAN A JOB ▶ SAFETY FEATURES ▶ YOUR COMFORT ZONE ▶ PRESENTING YOURSELF
▶ A COVERING LETTER OR EMAIL

21

reading the Moken people • wordbuilding phrasal verb *get* • grammar perfect forms • speaking more than a job

2a Living off the sea

Reading

1 Work in pairs. Look at the facts about the sea and try to complete the missing numbers. Then check your answers on page 81. Did any of the numbers surprise you?

SEA FACTS

1 .... % of the Earth's surface is covered by water.
2 About .... % of the world's population live in coastal regions.
3 .... % of the world's goods are transported by sea.
4 .... % of the world's animals live in the sea.
5 The average consumption of fish per person per year is .... kg.
6 Fish is the main source of protein for .... people.
7 The average time someone can hold their breath underwater is ....

2 Read the article about the Moken people. Answer the questions.

1 Are there more or fewer people living off the sea now than in the past?
2 How do the Moken 'live off' the sea?
3 What special qualities do the Moken possess?
4 What does the future hold for the Moken people?

Wordbuilding phrasal verb *get*

▶ **WORDBUILDING phrasal verb *get***

Get is one of many common verbs (e.g. *take, come, go*) which change their meaning when combined with a particle (e.g. *by, on, with, across*) to make a phrasal verb.
get by (on/with), get on with, get round to

For further practice, see Workbook pages 112 and 119.

▶ 12

Humans have been living off the land for thousands of years, developing the skills to hunt animals and harvest edible plants. But they have been living off the sea for probably just as long. However, in recent years, with the industrialization of fishing, the number of people who depend on the sea for their livelihood has declined. Yet in one corner of the world, true 'sea people' can still be found.

The Moken people, who migrated from China 4,000 years ago, live among the islands dotted across the Andaman Sea off the coast of Myanmar. Their homes are small hand-built boats called 'kabang' on which they live, eat and sleep for eight months of the year. The Moken came to public attention in 2004, when many of them escaped the tsunami that devastated coastal settlements around the Indian Ocean. Because of their intimate knowledge of the sea, they had felt the tsunami coming long before others realized the danger.

The Moken use nets and spears to forage for food and get by on what they take from the sea and beaches each day – fish and molluscs to eat; shells and oysters to trade with Malay and Chinese merchants. To get these things, they have to dive underwater for up to six minutes at a time. Their extraordinary ability to do this has fascinated scientists. Anna Gislen of the University of Lund was particularly interested in how the Moken could see so well underwater. She discovered that Moken children, once they had entered the water, were able to quickly change both the size of their pupils and the shape of their eye lens so that their underwater vision was at least twice as good as European children of a similar age.

Although their way of life poses no threat to others, the Moken have been constantly pressured by the authorities to settle on the land. Ten years ago, 2,500 Moken still led a traditional seafaring life. Now that number stands at 1,000. In another ten years, this unique way of life and the Mokens' extraordinary skills will probably have disappeared from the sea completely.

3 Look at the wordbuilding box on page 22. Find the phrasal verb with *get* (line 20) in the article. Does it mean 'manage or survive' or 'eat or feed'?

4 Look at these other phrasal verbs with *get*. Try to guess what they mean.

1 Sorry I haven't **got round to** fixing the tap yet.
2 I know you were disappointed not to win, but you've just got to **get over** it and move on.
3 I won't be free by 5.30. I have a meeting at 5 p.m. and I can't **get out of** it.
4 He just invents facts and no one contradicts him. I don't know how he **gets away with** it.
5 Thanks for sending me the details. I'll **get back to** you if I have any questions.

Grammar perfect forms

> **PERFECT FORMS**
>
> **Present perfect simple**
> 1 *The number of people who depend on the sea for their livelihood* **has declined***.*
> 2 *The Moken* **have been** *constantly* **pressured** *by the authorities to settle on the land.*
>
> **Present perfect continuous**
> 3 *They* **have been living** *off the sea for just as long.*
>
> **Past perfect simple**
> 4 *They* **had felt** *the tsunami coming long before others realized the danger.*
>
> **Future perfect simple**
> 5 *In another ten years, these unique people* **will** *probably* **have disappeared** *from the sea completely.*
>
> For further information and practice, see page 86.

5 Look at the grammar box. Which sentence(s) in the grammar box describe(s) an event or action:

1 that started in the past and is not finished?
2 that will be completed at a point in the future?
3 that is completed but might be repeated or continued and has a (strong) present connection?
4 completed before the main event in the past?

6 Work in pairs. Discuss the differences in meaning between the pairs of sentences.

1 a I've really enjoyed travelling around Laos.
  b I really enjoyed travelling around Laos.
2 a I've only met John once.
  b I only met John once.
3 a The meeting started when we arrived.
  b The meeting had started when we arrived.
4 a The votes will all be counted on the Thursday after the election.
  b The votes will all have been counted by the Thursday after the election.
5 a No one has taught him how to hold his breath underwater.
  b No one had taught him how to hold his breath underwater.

7 Choose the correct options to complete the text.

Before 2004, few people in the West ¹ *heard / had heard* of the Moken people. But since then, their way of life and their situation ² *have attracted / had attracted* a lot of interest. People are amazed, for example, that Moken children ³ *learn / had learned* to swim before they can walk, and that they ⁴ *became / have become* experts at reading the ways of the sea. This knowledge, which their ancestors ⁵ *acquired / have acquired* and then ⁶ *passed / have passed* down to them, is now in danger of being lost as more and more Moken ⁷ *are forced / had been forced* to settle on the land.

Sadly, this is not the first time that people ⁸ *try / have tried* to interfere in the Moken's way of life and it probably ⁹ *won't be / won't have been* the last. The Moken ¹⁰ *just want / have just wanted* to be left alone. The ones I met ¹¹ *were / have been* proud of their simple way of life. But I suspect in ten or twenty years' time their situation ¹² *will change / will have changed*.

8 ▶ **13** Complete the description. Use the correct perfect or non-perfect form of the verbs in brackets. Then listen and check.

My grandfather was a forestry commissioner, which meant he ¹ _____ (be) responsible for managing forests. I think he ² _____ (intend) originally to be a biologist, but then he ³ _____ (get) a job looking after forests in Wales. He ⁴ _____ (retire) now, but he's still fascinated by trees and plants. I guess his job was a way of life for him because it ⁵ _____ (occupy) all his time and he ⁶ _____ (spend) so much of his life living in or around forests. Over the years, I ⁷ _____ (often / think) about working outdoors too, but I don't think I ⁸ _____ (follow) in his footsteps.

Speaking my life

9 Work in groups. Look at these jobs and decide which are a way of life (i.e. much more than a job) for the people who do them. Give reasons.

Have they chosen to work in an unusual environment? Is this a job that previous generations in their family had done?

banker   coal miner   graphic designer
IT consultant   farmer   firefighter
fisherman/woman   lorry driver
physiotherapist   teacher

10 Think of another job (from the past, present or future) that is a way of life. Describe the job and your reasons for adding this job to the list. Is your job or studies a way of life for you?

listening **smokejumpers** • idioms **safety** • grammar **passive forms** • speaking **safety features**

2b Smokejumpers

Listening

1 Work in pairs. Look at these verbs. Which verbs collocate with *fire* and which collocate with *a fire*? Try to put each collocation in a sentence.

be on	catch	contain	fight	light
put out	set ... to	set on	start	

be on fire: We could see smoke in the distance but we couldn't see what was on fire.

2 Look at the photos and answer the questions.
   1 What kind of fire is shown in the photo on page 25? How does this kind of fire start? How can they be stopped?
   2 What qualities are needed to be a firefighter? Is it a job you could do?

3 ▶ 14 Listen to an interview with smokejumper, Kerry Franklin. Are the sentences true (T) or false (F)?
   1 Smokejumpers are sent into places that are difficult to reach.
   2 Their job is to evaluate a fire, not to fight it.
   3 Being a woman in this profession isn't easy.

4 ▶ 14 Listen to the interview again and answer the questions.
   1 What are the consequences if a smokejumper is a) too heavy? b) too light?
   2 What is Kerry's view of her own personal safety?
   3 When are smokejumpers sent to fight a fire?
   4 How do they usually try to contain a bad fire?
   5 How do you become a smokejumper?

Idioms safety

5 Look at this idiom Kerry used about safety in her job. What does it mean? Then complete the idioms about safety in the text below using these words.

" *... in this job you can't* **wrap people in cotton wool**. "

be	become	cut	do	err	follow

The first rule of safety is always to ¹_____ **things by the book**. Don't try to make up your own rules or to improvise or to ²_____ **corners**. You'll find that if you ³_____ **the correct procedure** each time, soon it will ⁴_____ **second nature to you** – you won't even think about it. If you're in any doubt about how something should be done, always try to ⁵_____ **on the side of caution**. It's **better to** ⁶_____ **safe than sorry**.

6 Think of something you regularly do or have done that involves risk. What do/did you do to keep safe? Use idioms from Exercise 5 in your description.

Grammar passive forms

▶ **PASSIVE FORMS**

Tenses
1 *Smokejumpers are firefighters with parachutes who* **are dropped** *into inaccessible areas ...*
2 *Kerry Franklin explained her career choice when she* **was interviewed** *by this programme.*
3 *That's* **been known** *to happen.*
4 *We* **get dropped** *in with tools.*

Modal verbs
5 *If ... there's a strong wind, you* **might be carried** *a long way ...*
6 *You* **can get injured** *when you hit the ground.*

Infinitives and gerunds
7 *This information has* **to be relayed** *back to base ...*
8 *First, the fire needs* **to be assessed** *...*
9 *The job involves* **being trained** *to a certain standard ...*

For further information and practice, see page 86.

24

7 Look at the grammar box on page 24. Answer the questions.

1 What tenses are the passive verb forms in bold in sentences 1–3?
2 How is the passive infinitive formed (sentences 7 and 8)? And the passive gerund (sentence 9)?
3 What verb is used (informally) in place of *are* and *be* in sentences 4 and 6?

8 Rewrite the sentences using passive forms of the underlined phrases.

1 <u>You always need to treat fire</u> with caution.
2 <u>He burned his hands badly</u> while he was trying to put a fire out.
3 I did the training course three times before <u>they accepted me</u>.
4 I was very grateful <u>to the fire service for giving me the opportunity</u>.
5 <u>People or natural causes</u>, like lightning, <u>can start forest fires</u>.
6 <u>Smokejumpers sometimes make their smokejumper suits themselves</u>.
7 <u>We haven't seen forest fires</u> in our region since 1996.
8 Above all, firefighters need to be calm. It's easy <u>for the situation to overwhelm you</u>.

9 Complete the sentences with passive forms. Use these verbs.

| arrest | catch | do | explain | force |
| pay |

1 It doesn't need _____ – it's obvious how to do it.
2 It wasn't my choice to be here. I _____ to come.
3 I _____ at the end of every month. Usually I'm broke for a week before that.
4 If you _____ speeding in your car, you risk _____ .
5 It's too late. What _____ cannot be undone.

10 Look at sentences 1–5 in the grammar box again. Find these sentences in the audioscript on page 97 (track 14). Then match each sentence with these uses (a–c) of the passive.

a The agent (person doing the action) is obvious, unknown or unimportant.
b We are following a series of actions that happen to the same subject.
c We want to give emphasis to the agent by putting it at the end of the sentence.

11 Choose the most appropriate form (active or passive) to complete the text. Sometimes both forms are possible.

> If you are thinking of a career in firefighting, there are a few facts you should know. It is a highly respected profession; in most countries ¹ *people rank it / it is ranked* in the top ten respected jobs. The money is also good. ² *We need to compensate firefighters / Firefighters need to be compensated* well for the risks ³ *they take / that are taken by them*. But it is not all adventure. Firefighters spend sixty per cent of their time waiting ⁴ *for someone to call them / to be called* into action. Moreover, eighty per cent of the events ⁵ *they attend / that are attended by them* are not even fires. Most are medical emergencies: for example, ⁶ *freeing someone / someone being freed* from a crashed car. Others are things like building inspections to make sure that ⁷ *people are following fire regulations / fire regulations are being followed*. And the hours are long, with some firefighters working shifts of up to 24 hours without ⁸ *anyone giving them / being given* a break.

Speaking my life

12 Work in pairs. List two safety and security features for the following things. Say how each feature works and what its purpose is. Use passive forms.

- my mobile phone
- a car
- my home or office block

My mobile phone is protected by a password. Some phones use fingerprint recognition so the phone can only be unlocked by the owner. I guess that's probably safer.

13 Work in groups. Look at the idea for car safety. Then think of your own 'new' safety feature for one of the items in Exercise 12. Follow the steps below.

> I think a lot of accidents **could be prevented** if people always drove with two hands on the wheel. My idea is that if people didn't have two hands on the wheel, an alarm would go off. That way, people **would be discouraged** from using their phones or eating while driving.

- Decide what a good feature would be.
- Write a short description of it and how it would work.
- Describe your feature to another group.
- In class, vote on the best idea.

my life ▶ MORE THAN A JOB ▶ SAFETY FEATURES ▶ YOUR COMFORT ZONE ▶ PRESENTING YOURSELF ▶ A COVERING LETTER OR EMAIL

reading climbing Yosemite • critical thinking analysing language • word focus *foot/feet* • speaking your comfort zone

2c Daring, defiant and free

Reading

1 Look at the photo and answer the questions.

1 How do you think the man got to this place?
2 How do you think he is going to get out of there?
3 How do you think the photo was taken?

2 Read the article and find the answers to the questions in Exercise 1.

3 Read the article again and answer the questions.

1 What are the three things you need for free-soloing?
2 How did Honnold feel after climbing for two hours and 45 minutes?
3 Why did Honnold carry on after his moment of panic on the rock face?
4 What was the effect of this climb on Honnold's reputation?
5 What is Jimmy Chin's greatest passion?
6 When he is on an assignment as a mountaineer-photographer, what does he believe is his first job?

4 Find words and expressions in the article with the following meanings.

1 an adjective meaning 'almost vertical' (para 1)
2 a noun meaning 'the top of a mountain' (para 1)
3 an adjective meaning 'oily' (para 1)
4 an adverb meaning 'perfectly' (para 2)
5 an adjective meaning 'very surprised' (para 3)
6 an adjective meaning 'very skilled and capable' (para 4)
7 a phrase meaning 'made a very strong impression on' (para 4)
8 a verb meaning 'thought about the past' (para 4)

Critical thinking analysing language

5 Find three examples of each of the following language techniques (a–d) which the author uses to make the description more dramatic.

a short sentences (nine words or fewer)
b use of the historic present (present tense to describe past events)
c words with a strong meaning (e.g. *sheer*, line 3)
d use of direct speech

6 Work in pairs. Rewrite these sentences to include the features (a–d) in Exercise 5. Then compare your more dramatic version with another pair.

Chin watched as the climber above him held onto the rock by one hand, hesitating at first to take the picture. He wondered if it would be right to take the picture in case the man then fell and hurt himself, but then he decided that he had to, because it was his job.

Word focus *foot/feet*

7 Work in pairs. Find two words or expressions in the article with the word *foot* in them and discuss what they mean.

8 Read the sentences. Look at the other expressions with *foot* or *feet* in bold. Discuss what each expression means.

1 It's all a bit new: the college, the accommodation, the people. But I'm sure I'll **find my feet** in a few weeks.
2 When she told them at the interview that money wasn't important to her, she really **shot herself in the foot**.
3 You **put your foot in it** when you asked Jim about his job – he was made redundant two weeks ago.
4 She **followed in her mother's footsteps** and became a dentist.
5 Well, I like dancing, but I'm not sure anyone else likes my dancing. I'**ve got two left feet**.
6 We're friends now, but we **got off on the wrong foot** when we first met.

9 Work in pairs. Ask each other these questions.

1 In what kind of organization/sector is it difficult to get your foot in the door?
2 When was the last time you put your foot in it?
3 When have you got off on the wrong foot?

Speaking my life

10 Work in pairs. Climbers like to live at the limits of their comfort zone. Do the quiz on page 81 to find out what your comfort zone is.

11 Look at the answers to the quiz on page 82 to find out what your comfort zone is. Discuss if you agree with the answers.

26

DARING, DEFIANT & FREE

▶ 15

It's a bright Saturday morning in September and a young man is standing on a small ledge high up on the north-west face of Half Dome, a sheer 650-metre wall of granite in the heart of Yosemite Valley in California. He's alone, far off the ground and without aids. Most climbers take two days to climb the face, using ropes and carrying up to 20 kilos of equipment and bivouacking for the night half-way up. Not Honnold. He is attempting the route free-solo, which means climbing with only a chalk bag and his rock shoes, and is trying to reach the top in less than three hours. But less than 30 metres from the summit, something potentially disastrous happens. He loses the smallest amount of confidence. 'What am I doing here?' he says to himself, staring at a greasy bump on the rock face. 'My foot will never stay on that.'

For two hours and 45 minutes, Honnold has been in the zone, flawlessly performing one precise athletic move after another, and not once has he hesitated. In free-soloing, confidence is everything. All you have is belief in your own ability. If Honnold merely believes his fingertips can't hold, he will fall to his death. Now, with mental fatigue and a glass-like slab of rock above him, he's paralysed, out of his comfort zone. He hadn't felt like this two days before when he'd raced up the same route with a rope. For a few minutes, he stands there, staring out at the sky, unable to look up or down for fear of falling. Then suddenly, he's in motion again. He steps up, planting his shoe on the smooth stone. It sticks. He moves his hand to another hold, repeats the move, and within minutes, he's at the top.

'I rallied because there was nothing else I could do,' Honnold says later, with a boyish laugh. 'I stepped up and trusted that foothold and was freed of the prison where I'd stood silently for five minutes.' Word of his three-hour free-solo of Half Dome flashed around the world. Climbers were stunned, and the blog writers were buzzing. On that warm autumn day in 2008, a shy 23-year-old from the suburbs of Sacramento had just become a climbing legend.

That is the magic of Yosemite: it creates heroes. But for the climbers, they are just doing what they love and – if they're lucky – get paid for as a bonus. One such person is Jimmy Chin, who took this photograph. He is also an accomplished mountaineer; the difference between him and Honnold is that Chin always works closely with other climbers, taking photographs as he climbs. He was actually brought up in the flat countryside of southern Minnesota, but rock climbing has been his passion since Glacier National Park first 'blew his mind' on a family vacation as a boy. Photography came later, when an outdoor clothing company bought one of the photos he had taken on an expedition. As a photographer, it isn't easy to get your foot in the door with a good client, so Chin, encouraged by their interest, bought his own camera. He hasn't looked back.

Combining a natural gift for photographic composition with his mountaineering skills, Chin has become one of the leading specialists in what has been called 'participatory photography'. He is able to carry a camera where few dare to go, at the same time remaining a reliable member of the climbing team. For Chin, that is always the priority.

bivouac (v) /ˈbɪvʊˌæk/ to make a temporary camp without a tent
chalk (n) /tʃɔːk/ soft white stone (formed from limestone)
ledge (n) /ledʒ/ a narrow horizontal surface projecting from a wall
slab (n) /slæb/ a large thick flat piece of stone

vocabulary personal qualities • pronunciation word stress • real life presenting yourself

2d Tell me a bit about yourself

Vocabulary personal qualities

1 Look at these words and expressions people use to describe themselves at interviews. Which of the words and expressions match the situations (a–d)? Sometimes there is more than one answer.

| conscientious   enthusiastic   a fast learner |
| flexible   focused   motivated |
| reliable   resourceful   well-organized |

a It was too late to post all the invitations, so I researched each person's email address and emailed them instead.
b I regularly stayed late to finish the job. Sometimes you have to do that.
c I didn't miss a single day at work all last year.
d I had to do all sorts of jobs as Head of Social Events: booking venues, dealing with entertainers, greeting new students, making food sometimes.

2 Pronunciation word stress

a ▶16 Mark where you think the stress falls on each of the words in Exercise 1. Then listen and check.

b Work in pairs. Practise saying the words with the correct stress.

Real life presenting yourself

3 Read the advice about a common interview question. What are some examples of things you probably shouldn't talk about when asked this question?

> Almost every interview will either begin with or include the question 'Can you tell me a bit about yourself?' While it's important not to give a scripted answer, it *is* important to think about how you'll answer this. The interviewer doesn't want your whole life story. What they really want to know is: your relevant background, what has brought you to this point in your career and your hopes and goals for the future.

4 Work in pairs. Make a list of five more questions that are often asked at an interview. Use these words to help you. Then compare your questions with another pair.

| goals   this job/position   strengths |
| in five years   weaknesses |

5 ▶17 Listen to Katy presenting herself to a careers advisor. Note down the questions that the careers advisor asks. What kind of work is Katy looking for and why is she suited to this?

6 ▶17 Look at the expressions for presenting yourself. Complete the expressions with a suitable preposition. Then listen to the interview again and check your answers.

▶ **PRESENTING YOURSELF**

Background
I graduated [1] _____ there last June …
I've been looking [2] _____ a job [3] _____ journalism …

Goals
My ambition is to …
The media is not an easy sector to break [4] _____ …
That's what I'm working [5] _____ .
I'd be (perfectly) happy to start [6] _____ the bottom and then work my way [7] _____ .
I wouldn't mind -ing …

Qualities
I'm good [8] _____ -ing …
Once I start something, I follow it [9] _____ .
When it comes [10] _____ -ing … , I …
I have some experience [11] _____ -ing …
I have a tendency [12] _____ …*

* for discussing weaknesses only

7 Work in pairs. Take turns to act out the roles of either a career advisor and an interviewee OR an employer and a job applicant. Follow these steps:

- decide what type of interview it is
- interviewer: make some notes on the questions you want to ask
- interviewee: make some notes on the answers you are going to give
- act out a short (e.g. five-minute) interview.
- begin the interview with the question 'Tell me a bit about yourself.'

my life ▶ MORE THAN A JOB ▶ SAFETY FEATURES ▶ YOUR COMFORT ZONE ▶ PRESENTING YOURSELF
▶ A COVERING LETTER OR EMAIL

2e A letter of application

Writing a covering letter or email

1 Read the letter of application. Find and underline the following key elements of a covering letter. Then compare answers with your partner.

1. the job applied for
2. where and when it was advertised
3. the candidate's current situation
4. why the writer is a good candidate
5. thanks for reading the letter
6. how and when the candidate can be contacted

2 Look at the statements about a covering letter. Using the letter as a model, say if the statements are true (T) or false (F). Explain your answers.

> 1. Keep it short. The letter should basically just refer the reader to your CV.
> 2. Show interest in and knowledge of the organization you are writing to.
> 3. Just mention your general suitability for the job. The letter should not respond to specific requirements the company has listed.
> 4. The letter should give a personal touch to your application.

3 Writing skill fixed expressions

The writer follows the conventions of letter writing by using certain fixed expressions. Find words and expressions in the letter with the following meanings.

a. I am looking for
b. I am sending
c. a good person to consider
d. I am free to come
e. the things you say you need
f. I am answering
g. feel free to
h. I liked the look of
i. I hope you will reply
j. my CV shows you that
k. thanks for reading this

Dear Mr Fairburn

I am writing in response to your advertisement in last Tuesday's *Guardian* newspaper for a Trainee Marketing Assistant. Please find attached my CV. The job attracted me because it emphasizes opportunities for people who are keen to learn and also because of your company's reputation for innovative and high-quality travel books. I am currently doing some freelance travel writing.

As a recent graduate from university, I am well aware that I still have much to learn and it is exactly this kind of challenging environment that I am seeking. You will see from my CV that I am someone who believes in getting results. My two proudest achievements are raising over £15,000 for a local charity and organizing a highly successful student Arts Week.

Regarding the requirements you mention, I think I am a suitable candidate as:

- I have a degree in Business Studies with a specialization in marketing
- I am flexible about where in the south-east I work
- I have good organizational skills, acquired as head of the Student Social Committee

I am available for interview at any time. Thank you for taking time to consider this application and please do not hesitate to contact me at any time by phone or in writing if you have questions about any of the above.

I look forward to hearing from you.
Yours sincerely

Philip Morrissey

Philip Morrissey

---

4 Write a covering email to a company that you would like to work for. Make sure you include the key elements mentioned in Exercise 1.

5 Exchange emails with your partner. Look at their email as if you were the employer. Use these questions to check.

- Is it well organized and does it include all the key elements?
- Is it grammatically correct and without spelling mistakes?
- Does it use appropriate fixed expressions?
- Does it specify the key skills the organization needs?
- Is it interesting and does it have a personal touch?
- Does the application seem convincing?

2f Climbing Yosemite

Jimmy Chin climbs Half Dome, Yosemite, California, USA.

Unit 2 **More than a job**

Before you watch

1 Look at the photo. Write down two words or expressions to describe what is happening. Then share your words with the class. What were the most common words?

2 Key vocabulary

a Read the sentences. The words in bold are used in the video. Guess the meaning of the words.

1 My work **as a surgeon** is very physical, but it's also very **cerebral**.
2 The acting in the film was so bad that it made me **cringe** at times.
3 We'll need to **shovel** all this sand into a big wheelbarrow and take it to the back of the house.
4 It's no good rushing an editing job. You have to be very patient and **methodical**.
5 On my first day at the company, they gave me a very simple **assignment** – to learn everyone's name in the office!

b Match the words in bold in Exercise 2a with these definitions.

a shrink back in embarrassment
b work or study task
c involving great thought and concentration
d going through something slowly and carefully (often in a certain order)
e move with a large spade

While you watch

3 ▶ 2.1 Watch the first part of the video (0.00 to 1.03). Note the adjectives Jimmy Chin used to describe his work. Did any of these adjectives surprise you? Were any of them the same ones you used in Exercise 1?

4 ▶ 2.1 Read these sentences about Jimmy Chin's career. Then watch the second part of the video (1.04 to the end). Are the sentences true (T) or false (F)?

1 Jimmy Chin's parents hoped he would follow a professional career.
2 Chin realized straightaway that climbing was something he wanted to do permanently.
3 Chin felt very at home in Yosemite.
4 Chin's real ambition was to be a photographer.
5 Being a photographer has allowed him to visit countries all over the world.

5 ▶ 2.1 Watch the second part of the video again (1.04 to the end) and complete the notes about Jimmy Chin's career. Use one word in each space.

1 In college he was part of the _____ team.
2 After college he went to the Bay area to find a job in the _____ realm.
3 Not finding a job, he decided to take a _____ off and ski full time.
4 Seven years later he was still living in the back of his _____ and doing various jobs, shovelling snow and waiting _____ .
5 He spent most of his time in Yosemite, where he found his _____ .
6 After some time in Yosemite, he decided he would like to visit the _____ ranges of the world.
7 He took a photo which a friend sold for $_____ and realized taking photos could help him continue what he was doing.
8 Yosemite is a special place for him because it helped to _____ his career.

6 Do you think Jimmy Chin made a good career choice? Why? / Why not? How do you think his career will develop?

After you watch

7 Vocabulary in context

a ▶ 2.2 Watch the clips from the video. Choose the correct meaning of the words and expressions.

b Complete the sentences in your own words. Then compare your sentences with a partner.

1 Before I go, I'll need to sort out a few odds and ends, like …
2 We left the house and headed out …
3 My parents freaked out when I said I wanted to …

8 Look at these things people do before starting out on a career. What are the benefits of each one, do you think?

- travelling
- doing military service
- doing various odd jobs (working in restaurants, shops, on building sites, etc.)
- building up a range of practical skills – driving, speaking languages, computer skills (e.g. Excel)
- doing some voluntary work in the community

31

UNIT 2 REVIEW AND MEMORY BOOSTER

Grammar

1 Complete the article. Use the correct tense and form (active or passive) of the verbs.

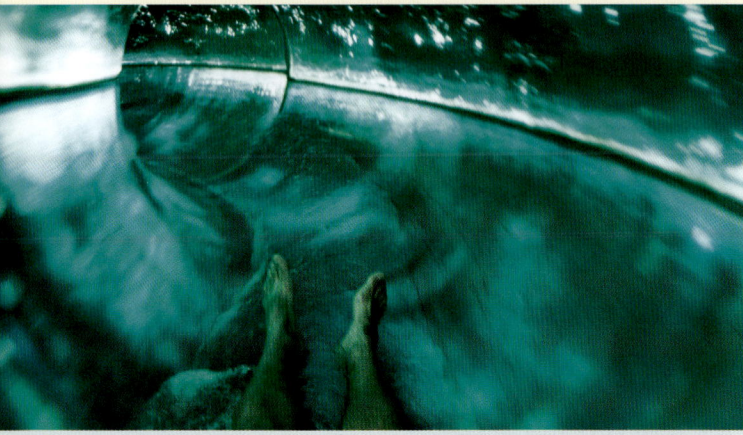

What would be your dream job? Tommy Lynch believes that he [1] _____ (find) his. Two years ago, he [2] _____ (employ) as a waiter in a restaurant, but more recently he [3] _____ (travel) around the world testing water slides at holiday resorts. That's because Tommy [4] _____ (give) the job by holiday operator First Choice of helping them to include the best water parks in their holiday brochures. So far, he [5] _____ (test) over fifty water slides and pools.
After the company [6] _____ (create) their own selection of 'Splash Resorts', they soon realized that they would need the quality of the facilities [7] _____ (check) regularly. A First Choice spokesperson said, 'We knew that to offer the best, we would have to appoint a full-time tester. Tommy [8] _____ (be) great.'
He was chosen from hundreds of applicants and [9] _____ (put) straight to work.
'I [10] _____ (have) the time of my life,' he says, 'but it's hard work. New resorts [11] _____ (add) to the list all the time. So I spend a lot of my time travelling and doing paperwork. But if customers have had a great time on holiday, then all my work [12] _____ (be) worthwhile!'

2 **MB** Work in pairs. Find five passive forms in the article. Discuss the reason the passive has been used in each case. (Refer to the reasons (a–c) in Exercise 10 on page 25, if necessary.)

3 Answer the questions.
  1 Who created Tommy's job and why?
  2 What does the job involve?

I CAN	
use perfect forms to look back at actions at an earlier time	
use a variety of passive forms	

Vocabulary

4 **MB** Choose the correct option to complete the questions about work. Then discuss the questions with your partner.
  1 What do you consider a reasonable monthly salary to get *along / by* on?
  2 In their careers, have any of your family followed in their parents' *footsteps / shoes*?
  3 What are the advantages and disadvantages of being in the teaching *trade / profession*?
  4 In a new work environment, how long does it take you to *find / set* your feet?
  5 Is getting *on / forward* in life and moving up the career ladder important to you?
  6 Would you rather do a challenging job or stay on the safe *road / side* and do something easy?

5 **MB** What are these people talking about, do you think? Discuss with your partner.
  1 'You need to get over it and move on.'
  2 'Sorry, I haven't got round to it, but I will.'
  3 'I'd like to get out of it, but I can't.'

I CAN	
talk about jobs and careers	
use phrasal verbs with *get*	

Real life

6 Match the questions (1–4) with the beginnings (a–g) of the answers someone might give.
  1 So can you tell me a bit about your background?
  2 Where do you hope to be in five years' time?
  3 What are your strengths?
  4 And your weaknesses?

  a My ambition is to …
  b I graduated from …
  c I have a tendency to …
  d When it comes to … , I …
  e I'm working towards …
  f I'm conscientious …
  g I've recently been …

7 **MB** Look at these adjectives. Can you think of a job for which each quality is especially important? Give reasons.

| conscientious | enthusiastic | flexible |
| motivated | reliable | resourceful |

8 **MB** Work in pairs. Ask and answer the questions (1–4) in Exercise 6.

I CAN	
present myself at an interview	

Unit 3 Design for life

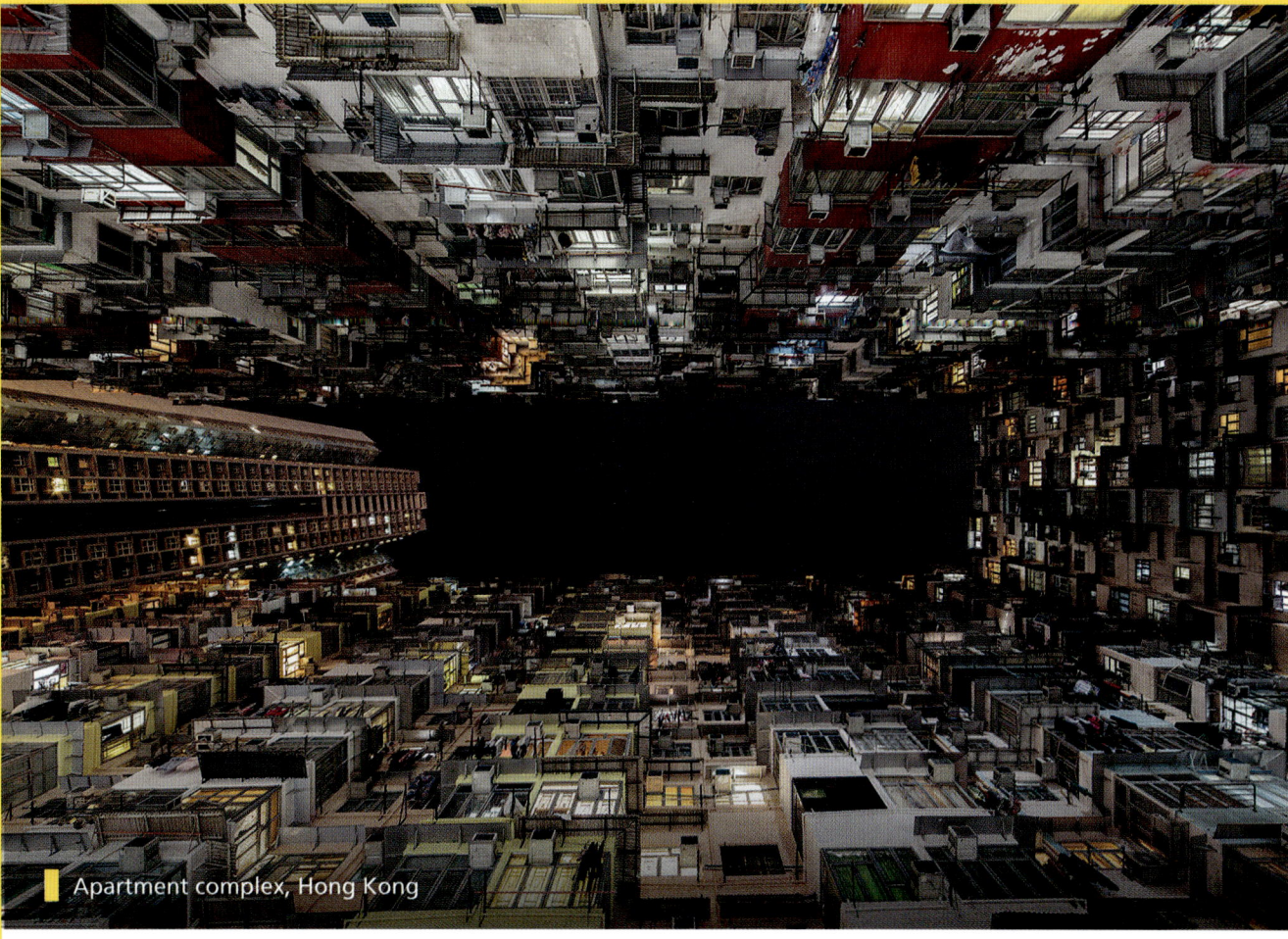

Apartment complex, Hong Kong

FEATURES

34 Towns with character
Two towns with individual characters

36 Compact living
A focus on small homes

38 The paper architect
The life and work of architect Zaha Hadid

42 A story of solutions
A video about the human impact of architecture

1 Look at the photo and caption. Discuss the questions.
   1 What do you think it's like to live in this place?
   2 How would you describe these buildings and what features can you see on them?

2 ▶ 18 Listen to someone discussing the photo. Compare your ideas from Exercise 1.

3 ▶ 18 Listen again. What adjectives does the speaker use to describe these things?
   1 apartments   3 buildings
   2 climate   4 the city

4 Look at these adjectives. Make adjective + noun collocations with these nouns: *apartment, building, street, area*. Which adjective can collocate with all four nouns?

> brick   built-up   deprived   first-floor   four-storey
> high-rise   imposing   main   narrow   one-way
> pedestrianized   residential   run-down   spacious   studio
> tree-lined   two-bedroom

5 Think of an area or neighbourhood you know. Describe this place and the buildings in it, saying what you like or dislike about it.

my life   ▶ YOUR HOME TOWN   ▶ A BIT OF LUXURY   ▶ HOW SPACES AFFECT YOU   ▶ EXPRESSING OPINIONS
▶ AN OPINION ESSAY

33

vocabulary describing towns • reading the character of towns • grammar qualifiers •
pronunciation *quite, fairly* and *pretty* • speaking and writing your home town

3a Towns with character

Vocabulary describing towns

1 Work in pairs. Look at these different types of town and answer the questions.

| boom town   ghost town   historic town |
| holiday town/resort   industrial town   market town |
| port (town)   regional capital   shanty town |
| spa town   university town |

1 What are the characteristics of each type of town?
2 Can you give an example of three of these types of town from your own experience?

2 Look at these adjectives which describe towns. Make pairs of opposites or near opposites.

| lively   modern and characterless   quaint   scruffy |
| self-contained   sleepy   sprawling   well-kept |

Reading

3 Look at the photos of two towns with a special identity. Read the descriptions of each town that residents have written. Then match the statements (1–6) with the towns (Granada or Billund).

1 It is not a town that pretends to be something it isn't.
2 It is known for its period buildings.
3 It is very busy with visitors from outside.
4 Its residents seem happy and comfortable.
5 It has a relaxed feel to it.
6 Its economy has grown in recent decades.

▶ 19

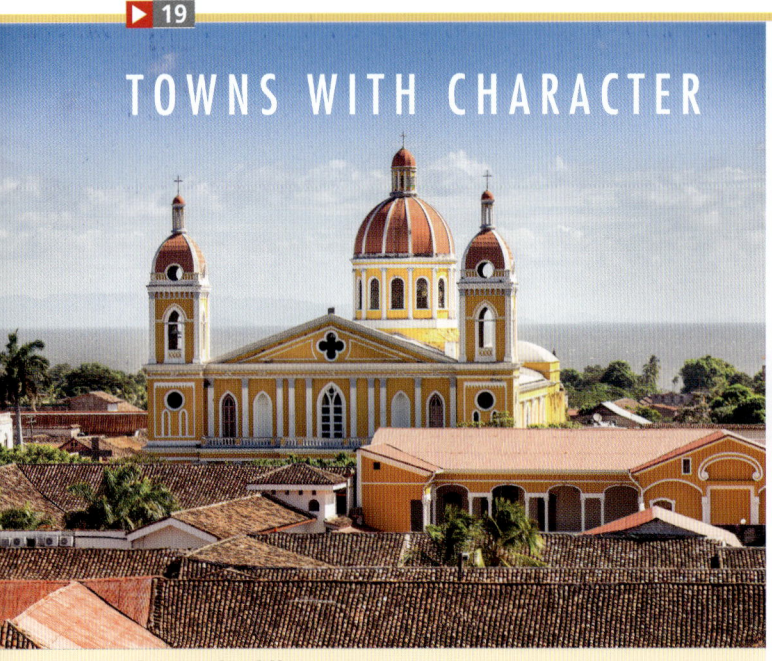

TOWNS WITH CHARACTER

Granada, Nicaragua

It might be cheating slightly to call Granada a town: it's officially a city, but not a big sprawling city like Managua. Granada's quite small and self-contained. It's
5 also the oldest colonial town in Latin America (founded in 1524) with beautifully preserved, elegant architecture. In some historic towns you feel like you're in a museum, but Granada's not like that; it's not scruffy, but it's not particularly smart either and I quite like that. It just feels
10 like a genuine working town, with farmers from the local countryside coming and going to sell their produce in the town's vibrant markets. Outside the commercial areas, life has quite a gentle rhythm and after dusk everything goes pretty quiet. That's changing a little
15 now as tourism in Nicaragua increases and Granada becomes a magnet for visitors. But you can see why they come; it's such an incredibly photogenic place.

Billund, Denmark

I moved to Billund in east Jutland, Denmark about ten years ago. It's a rather ordinary kind of town – except 20 in one respect. Almost everyone here has a connection with Lego. The town dates back to medieval times – it still has a few quaint streets with period buildings in the centre – but it boomed when the Lego factory started exporting its toys in the 1950s and 60s. Most 25 residents either work in the factory or the Legoland theme park, or they have some other business like a hotel or café that caters for the endless stream of visitors to the park. We live in a house that was built by the company (not out of Lego, in case you 30 wondered). Life's pretty good here, partly because it's such a family-friendly town – about thirty per cent of residents are couples with children – and partly because the company looks after its people. They charge us a fairly reasonable rent and they've built many amenities 35 for the town – a church, a library, the local park. My children even wear Lego-branded clothes.

Grammar qualifiers

> **QUALIFIERS**
>
> **1 QUALIFIER + ADJECTIVE**
> *quite, pretty, fairly* (usually with positive ideas)
> Life's **pretty/quite/fairly** good here.
> Life has **quite a** gentle rhythm.
> They charge us **a fairly/pretty** reasonable rent.
>
> *rather*
> It's **a rather** ordinary kind of town.
> It's **rather an** ordinary kind of town.
> The town is **rather** ordinary.
>
> *not very, not particularly*
> It's **not particularly/very** smart either.
>
> **2 QUALIFIER + VERB**
> *quite, rather, not particularly* (with *like, enjoy, want*)
> I **quite/rather** like that.
> I did**n't particularly** like that.
>
> *slightly, a little, a bit*
> It might be cheating **slightly / a little / a bit** …
> That's changing **slightly / a little / a bit** now.
>
> For further information and practice, see page 88.

4 Look at the grammar box. Answer the questions.
1 Do the qualifiers make the idea expressed:
    a much stronger?   b less strong?
2 What is the position of each qualifier when used with:
    a an adjective?
    b an article + adjective + noun?
    c a verb?

5 Put the qualifier in the right place in the sentence.
1 I always feel excited when I move to a new town. (pretty)
2 Liverpool used to be a busy port in the last century. (fairly)
3 We wanted to visit Verona, but there wasn't time. (quite)
4 Industry in the town has declined in the last thirty years. (slightly)
5 After moving to the country, we regretted our decision. (a bit)
6 The museum isn't interesting, if you don't like local history. (particularly)

6 Complete the conversations using the qualifiers given.

1 | a little   particularly   pretty   quite |

A: Do you like where you live now?
B: I ¹_____ like it, but it's not a ²_____ lively place. Don't get me wrong: the people are ³_____ friendly and they've welcomed us very warmly. We've just had to adapt ⁴_____ after living in a big city like London.

2 | a bit   fairly   slightly |

C: We've just moved into a new housing estate.
D: What's it like?
C: To be honest, it's ⁵_____ modern and characterless. I'm ⁶_____ confident it'll get better with time as more people move in. But at the moment we're struggling ⁷_____ to enjoy it.

7 Pronunciation *quite*, *fairly* and *pretty*

a ▶20 Listen to the conversations. Does the stress fall on the qualifier or the verb/adjective?

1 A: Is it far?   B: It's quite a long way.
2 A: How do you feel?   B: Pretty confident.
3 A: How's the water?   B: It's pretty cold.
4 A: Is it urgent?   B: Yes, it's fairly important.
5 A: Is she famous?
   B: Yes, she's quite a well-known actor.
6 A: How was the show?   B: I quite enjoyed it.

b ▶20 Listen again. Which stress pattern means 'but not *very*'? Which stress pattern doesn't change the meaning of the verb or adjective very much?

c Work in pairs. Practise saying the phrases. Choose which pronunciation pattern you use and see if your partner can guess the meaning that you intend.

Speaking and writing ⟨ my life ⟩

8 Work in pairs. Answer the questionnaire about your home town. Use at least one qualifier in each answer.

*It's a **pretty** mixed town really. **Quite** a lot of students live there, but it also has an industrial part. Guides on the internet usually describe it as a university town, but that doesn't really give the whole story.*

1 How would you describe your home town? How does this compare to descriptions of it you have read?
2 What's your home town known for – a famous person, a historical event, its produce?
3 Has your home town changed a lot in the time you've known it? If so, how?
4 I've got a day in your home town. What can I do?
5 Where is the best place to get a nice, reasonably-priced meal in your home town?
6 If you could change one thing about your home town, what would it be?
7 Would you be happy to live in your home town all your life? Why? / Why not?

9 Write a short description of what makes your home town special (up to 140 words). Use the descriptions in the article on page 34 to help you.

listening small homes • grammar intensifying adverbs • pronunciation stress in intensifying adverbs • vocabulary adverb + adjective collocations • speaking a bit of luxury

3b Compact living

Listening

1 Work in pairs. Ask and answer the questions.

1 How many different rooms are there in your home?
2 Do any of the rooms have more than one function?
3 If you had more space, what would you use it for?

2 ▶ 21 Look at the photos. Then listen to an interview with an architect who specializes in compact designs. Answer the questions.

1 Where are these two homes?
2 Why is the architect inspired by them?

A

B

3 ▶ 21 Read the sentences. Then listen to the interview again and choose the best option to complete the sentences.

1 Jonas Wilfstrand specializes in designing *compact holiday homes / small homes in general*.
2 There's a demand for compact living spaces because they are *cheaper / more practical*.
3 Dolgan homes consist of *one room / a shared space and a bedroom*.
4 The Dolgan need to move house regularly because of *the weather / their animals*.
5 In the ten-square metre cabin in California there is little room for *belongings / domestic appliances*.
6 In Gary Chang's apartment you can *move / remove* the walls.

Grammar intensifying adverbs

4 Look at these adjectives. Match each gradable adjective (i.e. not with a strong meaning) with an ungradable adjective (i.e. with a strong meaning) that expresses a similar idea.

Gradable	Ungradable
1 cold	a tiny
2 surprising	b stunning
3 important	c delighted
4 small	d brilliant
5 original	e freezing
6 pleased	f amazing
7 clever	g essential
8 attractive	h unique

5 Work with a partner. Take turns to ask questions using a gradable adjective. The other student should answer using the equivalent ungradable adjective.

A: *Is your apartment cold?*
B: *Yes, it's absolutely freezing.*

6 Look at these common spoken phrases. Which underlined words mean 'very' and which mean 'completely'?

1 Yes, you're absolutely right.
2 That's really kind of you.
3 Thanks. I'd be very grateful.
4 I'm sorry. It's totally out of the question.
5 Yes, I'm quite certain.
6 That's a completely different matter.

36

7 Pronunciation stress in intensifying adverbs

▶ 22 Work in pairs. Listen to the sentences in Exercise 6. Note where the stress falls. Then practise saying the sentences.

> **INTENSIFYING ADVERBS**
>
> **very, extremely, incredibly, really** + gradable adjective
> I'm **very** pleased to welcome …
> They are **extremely** basic.
>
> **absolutely, really, utterly, quite** + ungradable (extreme) adjective
> Some of them are **really** stunning.
> It's **absolutely** freezing there.
>
> **completely, entirely, totally, quite** + ungradable (absolute*) adjective
> Today we're looking at something **completely** different.
> * 'absolute' means adjectives which do not have a comparative or superlative form
>
> For further information and practice, see page 88.

8
Look at the grammar box. Turn to the audioscript of the interview on page 98 (track 21) and find:

a five more examples of intensifying adverbs with gradable adjectives
b two more examples of intensifying adverbs with ungradable (extreme) adjectives, e.g. *amazing, disgusting*
c two more examples of intensifying adverbs with ungradable (absolute) adjectives, e.g. *right, true*

9
Choose the correct intensifier to complete the sentences.

1 I prefer modern design because it's usually *absolutely / very* simple and neat. Having said that, my own house is *absolutely / incredibly* disorganized.
2 The outside of the house is old but the interior is *completely / utterly* new. They've done a *completely / really* incredible job of renovating it.
3 I saw an *absolutely / entirely* stunning penthouse flat for rent yesterday, but it's *utterly / extremely* expensive.
4 She's a(n) *incredibly / quite* talented architect. I'd be *totally / very* surprised if she isn't famous one day.
5 Cath is *very / quite* certain that there's a wasp nest under her roof. She's *entirely / utterly* miserable about it.
6 The price of houses in London is *extremely / absolutely* ridiculous. Even a one-bedroom flat is *absolutely / completely* unaffordable.

10
Complete these sentences in your own words. Use intensifiers where there is a highlighted space.

1 I would only eat … if I was _____ desperate.
2 I get _____ irritated by people who …
3 The last time I was _____ tired was …
4 It's _____ wrong to let children …
5 I think … are _____ gorgeous.
6 I'm _____ certain that good health is …

Vocabulary adverb + adjective collocations

11
Look at this example of an adverb + adjective collocation from the interview. What does *strongly* mean here: 'very' or 'a little'?

"I've also been **strongly influenced** by the architect Gary Chang."

12
Look at these other adverb + adjective collocations. In most cases the adverb has the meaning of *very* or *absolutely*. Find the two collocations where this is NOT the case.

bitterly disappointed	mildly amusing
closely associated (with)	painfully slow
deadly serious	patently obvious
desperately unlucky	perfectly reasonable
hopelessly in love	vaguely familiar
ideally suited to	wildly optimistic

13
Work in pairs. Think of examples that fit the descriptions of these things (1–5) or use your own ideas. Then discuss your situations with another pair.

1 something you learned where you found progress painfully slow
2 an ambition one of your friends has that seems wildly optimistic
3 a bad idea someone had, i.e. it was patently obvious that it wouldn't work
4 a sporting competition where someone was desperately unlucky
5 a job you are ideally suited to

Speaking my life

14
The architect in the interview designed 'a timber and glass vacation house with built-in sauna'. Work in pairs. Look at these luxury features of houses and say which three you would most like to have in your house and why. Try to use intensifying adverbs in your answer.

I'd absolutely love to have a home cinema, because there are so many films now with really amazing special effects that you can't appreciate on a small screen.

a conservatory	en suite bathrooms	a games room
a garage/workshop	a gym	a home cinema
a large kitchen	a library	a roof garden	a sauna
a walk-in wardrobe		

reading **Zaha Hadid** • critical thinking **summarizing** • word focus *ground* • speaking **how spaces affect you**

3c The paper architect

Reading

1 Look at the photos and answer the questions.
1 Do you like the designs? Why? / Why not?
2 Do you have a favourite modern building? What is it and what do you like about it? Have you been inside it?

2 Read the article about the architect Zaha Hadid. Choose the statement (a–c) that best summarizes her aims.

a to prove that women too can be successful architects
b to create original buildings that people like to be in
c to create buildings with unusual and complex forms

3 Read the article again and answer the questions.
1 Why was Hadid called 'the paper architect'?
2 What does it mean when it says Hadid became 'sought-after'?
3 What challenges did Hadid face when she entered the architecture profession in Britain?
4 How did Hadid begin when she wanted to create a new design?
5 Why were potential customers doubtful about Hadid's designs?
6 What was the most important thing for Hadid when designing a new building?
7 What is interesting about the inside of the Evelyn Grace Academy?
8 How does the author conclude that Hadid will be remembered?

Critical thinking summarizing

4 In order to check you have understood the main points of an article, it is useful to be able to summarize its message or arguments accurately. To help you summarize this article, underline adjectives or nouns that describe the following:
- Zaha Hadid's designs
- her character
- her buildings
- her position in the world of architecture
- the effect of her buildings on the user

5 Compare the words you underlined with your partner. Then together compose a short summary of Zaha Hadid's life and her contribution to architecture.

Word focus *ground*

6 Work in pairs. Look at the expression in bold from the article and discuss what you think it means. Then do the same for the other expressions in bold (1–5).

❝ But as with anyone who tries to **break new ground**, it was not easy to convince people to follow. ❞

1 It's a very clever design, but as a business idea it will never **get off the ground** unless they get some money to develop it.
2 The council decided to close the swimming pool **on the grounds that** it wasn't making money.
3 It was a great meeting. We **covered a lot of ground** in the two hours.
4 Even though she's going to appear on TV, it's important that she **keeps her feet on the ground**, because it may lead to nothing.
5 No one seemed to think his plan would work, but to his credit, he **stood his ground**.

7 From your own experience, think of an example of each of the following.
1 someone who always keeps their feet on the ground
2 a time when you stood your ground (despite opposition)
3 a company which is always breaking new ground with its products

Speaking my life

8 Public buildings or spaces can sometimes have bad associations for people. Look at these places which people in a survey said they didn't like being in. How do you feel in each of them? Why?
1 a dentist's surgery
2 a lift
3 an airport departure lounge
4 a classroom or lecture hall
5 a large open plan office

9 Work in small groups. Choose one of the public spaces in Exercise 8. Discuss how the design of this space could be improved to make people feel more comfortable. Think about the following:
- shape and size of the space
- lighting
- arrangement of furniture
- other additions (music, plants, etc.)

THE PAPER ARCHITECT

For a long time, Iraqi-born Zaha Hadid was known as 'the paper architect'. That was because very few of her bold and daring designs, though frequently praised for their imagination and originality, ever left the page to become real buildings. Between 1978, when she graduated, and 1998, just four of her 27 projects were actually realized. However, following the successful completion of two art galleries in Cincinnati and Denmark and a commission for BMW in Leipzig in 2005, Hadid's buildings began to appear everywhere. Within ten years, she had become one of the most sought-after architects in the world. So why did Hadid's architecture take so long to be accepted?

Firstly, she was one of the few women in a profession dominated by men. Today in Britain less than fifteen per cent of practising architects are women. A lot more enter the profession, but over half leave, either because of slow career progress or because they become disillusioned with the conservatism of most British architectural design. But in Hadid's case, this seems to have been a motivator. From an early stage, she was determined to challenge the establishment with her own new ideas. But it was never going to be an easy fight.

Secondly, even during her student days, Hadid was interested in pushing boundaries and in creating buildings that were new and different. She felt that 21st-century developments in materials science and computer modelling tools provided an opportunity to experiment with more complex curved forms than architects had attempted in the past. She would initially sketch out her ideas in the form of an artist's drawing. But as with anyone who tries to break new ground, it was not easy to convince people to follow – to believe that these sketches could be translated into functional structures. However, once people began to see the results – in buildings such as the Guangzhou Opera House in China and the MAXXI art museum in Rome – they began not only to believe, but also to start shouting her name.

The idea of the architect as an artist was something Hadid herself rejected. She did not want people to think that she had designed a building just so that they could stare and admire its beauty from the outside. 'Architecture,' she said, 'is not a medium of personal expression for me. It facilitates everyday life.' In other words, her aim was to create buildings that were not just innovative, but practical too. The internal space and how people interacted with it were the keys for her.

For this reason, she was attracted particularly to public projects: for example, the Aquatics Centre for the 2012 Olympics and the Evelyn Grace Academy, a large secondary school in south London. For the latter, Hadid designed a building with lots of natural light and dramatic angles, so that pupils could view the activity of other students from different perspectives within the structure. Right in the middle of the site, between buildings, she placed a 100-metre running track to celebrate the school's emphasis on sports. The idea of offering the viewer multiple viewpoints inside a building is a common theme in Hadid's work. Internal spaces interconnect cleverly so that the visitor is surprised and charmed at every turn.

Zaha Hadid died of a heart attack in 2016 aged 65, leaving behind a groundbreaking body of work. She remained all her life something of an outsider; or, if not completely outside, then on the edges of the architectural establishment. Yet her impact on architecture was enormous: it will never be the same again.

real life expressing opinions • pronunciation linking vowel sounds (intrusion)

3d A lot to recommend it

Real life expressing opinions

1 Work in pairs. Think about a public work of art in your town or area. Describe it to your partner, saying what you like or dislike about it.

2 Look at the photo and the caption and discuss the questions.
1 Do you like these public works of art? Why? / Why not?
2 What benefits do you think they might bring to the city (for both locals and visitors)?

3 ▶ 24 Listen to two people discussing a proposal for a public work of art in a city. Answer the questions.
1 What piece of work is being proposed?
2 Are the speakers in favour of or against it?

4 Work in pairs. Read the short text below. Then discuss which way of expressing opinions you most commonly encounter. How much does this depend on the person you are talking to?

> Different people express their opinions in different ways. Some people disagree briefly and bluntly, e.g. 'I don't agree,' or 'That's not correct.' Others disagree openly but politely, e.g. 'I'm afraid I don't share your opinion.' In some cultures, it is considered rude to disagree openly and people express disagreement by keeping silent or even by saying the opposite, e.g. 'Yes, I agree.'

5 ▶ 24 Listen to the discussion again. Complete the arguments that each speaker gives in favour of or against the idea.
1 Speaker A: I think it's _____.
2 Speaker B: Personally, I'd rather have something _____.
3 Speaker B: I'm also not convinced that it will _____.
4 Speaker A: I reckon people … will really like the fact that it _____.
5 Speaker B: I'm all in favour of something that's relevant …, but I'm afraid it just seems _____.
6 Speaker A: Well, for me, it's very important that it's _____.

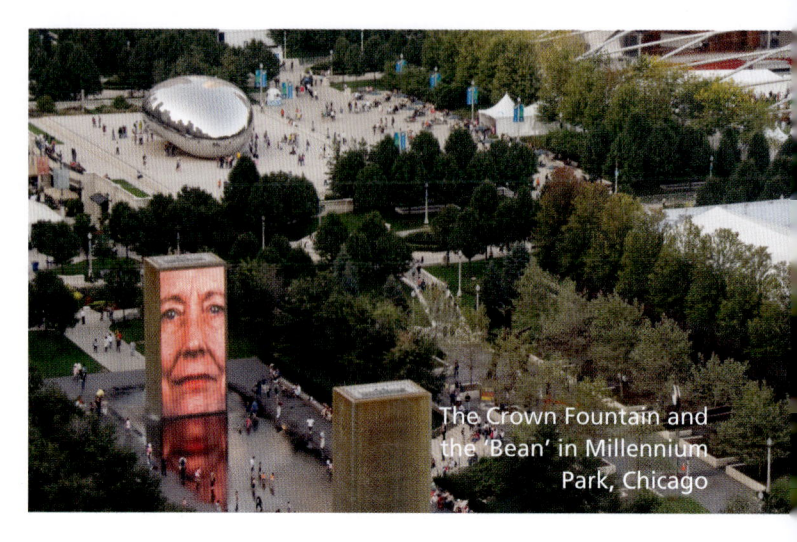

The Crown Fountain and the 'Bean' in Millennium Park, Chicago

6 Look at the expressions for expressing opinions. Say which expressions are used to agree, disagree politely, disagree or give an opinion.

▶ **EXPRESSING OPINIONS**
I think … / I reckon …
I have to say, …
Personally, I …
For me, … / If you ask me, …
It seems a bit … to me.
It's pretty obvious that … / It's fairly clear that …
I'm (all) in favour of …
I'm against …
I agree completely. / Absolutely.
I disagree. / I don't agree.
I don't think you should underestimate …
I can see that, but …
I'm not (entirely) convinced that …

7 Pronunciation linking vowel sounds (intrusion)

a ▶ 25 Listen to these phrases. Which consonant sounds (/w/ or /j/) are used to link the vowel sounds in each of these sentences (1–6)?
1 Have you seen the_artwork?
2 It's more likely to_attract people.
3 If you_ask me, …
4 I disagree_about the cost of it.
5 I_expect you're right.
6 I'm not so_interested in architecture.

b Work in pairs. Practise saying the sentences in Exercise 7a, linking the vowel sounds with /w/ and /j/.

8 Work in pairs or small groups. Look at the two proposals for a public work of art on page 82. Ask each other for your opinion of each proposal. Use expressions to agree or disagree.

What do you think of the LED screen idea?
Personally, I think …

my life ▶ YOUR HOME TOWN ▶ A BIT OF LUXURY ▶ HOW SPACES AFFECT YOU ▶ EXPRESSING OPINIONS ▶ AN OPINION ESSAY writing an opinion essay • writing skill discourse markers

Unit 3 Design for life

3e Old and new

Writing an opinion essay

1 Look at the photo of two buildings. Do these two buildings go well together? Why? / Why not?

2 Read the essay question and the essay. Answer the questions.

1 What is the writer's opinion?
2 What arguments does he give to support this?
3 What points against his own argument does he mention?

3 Look at the four key elements of an opinion essay. Find each element in the essay. What is the correct order?

a deal with opposing arguments
b give your opinion and present the arguments supporting it
c make your conclusion
d analyse the question and set out your starting point

4 Writing skill discourse markers

a The writer uses certain phrases to present his ideas. Look at the underlined discourse markers in the essay and match the discourse markers with the function (1–5).

1 introduce an opinion (1 adverbial phrase, 2 verb phrases)
2 qualify or make a concession to an opinion or argument (2 adverbial phrases)
3 reinforce a point or argument (2 adverbial phrases)
4 express the same point in another way (1 phrase)
5 sum up the argument (1 adverbial phrase)

b Complete this text. Use discourse markers from Exercise 4a.

1 _____, modern buildings that try to imitate older architectural styles do not work. 2 _____, they sometimes look worse than an unimaginative modern design. Despite this, some architects and planners insist on building in a 'traditional' style. 3 _____, their intentions are good: they do not want to spoil the overall look of an area, but 4 _____ they are mistaken. It would be much better if architects and planners considered a range of new designs. 5 _____, they need to be more adventurous.

Should we allow modern buildings to be built next to older buildings in a historic area of a city?

In order to answer this question properly, first we need to ask whether people actually want to preserve the historic character of an area. Not all historic buildings are attractive, but they may contribute to an overall feeling that makes the area attractive to people. What should we do then if a new building is needed?

In my view, modern architecture can fit perfectly well with buildings from another period. Indeed, there are many examples in my own home town of Tours where radical modern designs sit comfortably next to old buildings. As long as the new building is pleasing and does not dominate its surroundings too much, it should enhance the attractiveness of the area. Having said that, there must also be a limit to the number of new buildings if people want to preserve the area's historic feel.

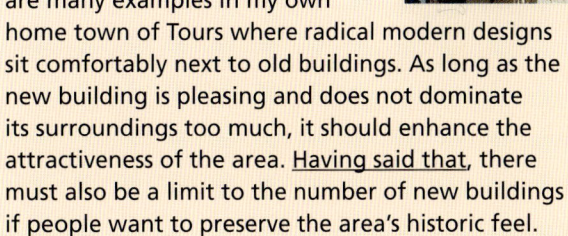

Admittedly, there are examples of modern buildings which have spoilt an area, but this is not an argument against putting new buildings among historic ones in principle. I suspect that the main reason for objections to such buildings is that people are conservative: in other words, they do not like change.

In conclusion, I believe that while we must respect the views of others, it is the duty of architects and planners to move things forward. After all, if we only reproduced what was there before, we would all still be living in caves.

5 Write an opinion essay about this question (200–250 words).

Should we create more socially mixed residential areas, where rich people live next to poorer people, instead of in separate communities?

6 Exchange essays with your partner. Use these questions to check your essays.

- Is their opinion clear and have they presented both sides of the argument?
- Have they followed the structure suggested in Exercise 3?
- Have they used discourse markers correctly to present the ideas?

my life ▶ YOUR HOME TOWN ▶ A BIT OF LUXURY ▶ HOW SPACES AFFECT YOU ▶ EXPRESSING OPINIONS
▶ AN OPINION ESSAY

3f A story of solutions

The new fire station in Newbern, Alabama, USA

Before you watch

1 Look at the photo. How does (or did) this building serve the community? Who works/worked there and what is their job like, do you think?

2 Look at this list of public buildings or buildings that serve the community. Add any others you can think of. Then answer the questions (1–2).

college   community centre   court house   fire station
hospital   museum   leisure/sports centre
post office   public library   theatre   town hall

1 Which buildings/amenities would you expect to find in a town of less than 500 people?
2 Which do you think are the most important buildings/amenities for residents?

While you watch

3 ▶ 3.1 Watch the first part of the video (0.00 to 0.14). Note down all the things you see. Compare notes with your partner. Then answer the questions.

1 What kind of town is Newbern?
2 Can you describe the buildings you saw in the town? What were they like?

4 ▶ 3.1 Watch the whole video. Give more details of what you saw by answering these questions.

1 What was the first fire engine you saw like?
2 What was the meeting about?
3 How would you describe the design of the new fire station?
4 What kind of fire did you see?
5 What did you see the architecture students doing?
6 Who did you see using the library?

5 ▶ 3.1 Watch the whole video again. Pause after each speaker and write in the words to complete the summary of each speaker's message. The first letter is given for you.

1 Sarah Curry: Having no local firehouse means houses b_____ d_____; so people can't get i_____ and they are h_____.
2 Andrew Freear: Community groups focused on the o_____ and we helped with the b_____.
3 Patrick Braxton: Our first call was to a grass fire and we took t_____-t_____ people with us.
4 Andrew Freear: Frances Sullivan came to us and said 'If you really want to help, build a l_____.'
5 Kesha Jones: I don't know how you c_____ Newbern, but I'm very g_____ you came.
6 Sarah Curry: This works because everyone is working towards the s_____ g_____ as a team.
7 Frances Sullivan: Architecture is part of the s_____, but it's the p_____ that really make the difference.

After you watch

6 **Vocabulary in context**

a ▶ 3.2 Watch the clips from the video. Choose the correct meaning of the words and phrases.

b Work in pairs. Complete these sentences in your own words. Then compare your sentences with a partner.

1 The sole reason that I learn English is …
2 … was a catalyst for …
3 The book, … , had a profound effect on me when I was younger.

7 Look at the viewer comments about the video. Which is closest to your impression after watching the film? Explain why.

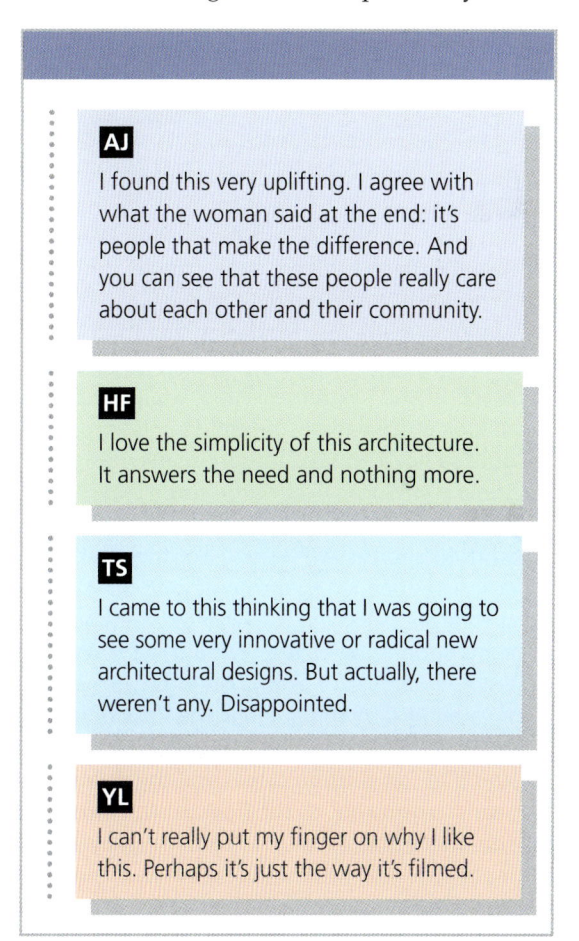

AJ
I found this very uplifting. I agree with what the woman said at the end: it's people that make the difference. And you can see that these people really care about each other and their community.

HF
I love the simplicity of this architecture. It answers the need and nothing more.

TS
I came to this thinking that I was going to see some very innovative or radical new architectural designs. But actually, there weren't any. Disappointed.

YL
I can't really put my finger on why I like this. Perhaps it's just the way it's filmed.

8 What new building would your community most benefit from? Present your idea to the class and explain your reasons.

UNIT 3 REVIEW AND MEMORY BOOSTER

Grammar

1 Look at the photo. What do you think this building is for? Read the text and check your ideas.

2 Choose the correct options to complete the text.

I ¹*really / completely* love the London Olympics Aquatics Centre. It's a great example of how to design a public building and actually it's ² *slightly / quite* rare for design and function to come together as successfully as this. It's both very practical and ³ *extremely / absolutely* pleasing to look at. Like many of Hadid's buildings, the outside has a ⁴ *quite / rather* organic feel to it. Some say it looks like a large turtle with its flippers outstretched. Hadid did not ⁵ *quite / particularly* want to add these 'flippers', but they were extra structures needed to accommodate the 15,000 spectators attending the Olympic swimming competitions. After the Olympics, 12,500 seats were ⁶ *completely / utterly* removed. If the exterior is ⁷ *a bit / pretty* remarkable, the interior is ⁸ *quite / entirely* spectacular. Bare concrete sweeps this way and that in beautiful curves and the diving boards seem to grow out of the floor. At floor level is the fifty-metre pool, which is ⁹ *totally / really* still and a deep, deep blue. The whole effect is ¹⁰ *entirely / incredibly* dramatic.

3 >> MB Work in pairs. Look at the adjectives which follow the modifiers or intensifiers in the text. Which are: a) gradable adjectives b) ungradable (extreme) adjectives and c) ungradable (absolute) adjectives?

I CAN

use adverbs to modify or intensify meaning ☐

Vocabulary

4 Complete the phrases. Then put the phrases into three categories: a feature of a house, a feature of a town and an adverb + adjective collocation.

1 a two-b_____ flat
2 b_____ly disappointed
3 a b_____ wall
4 a b_____-up area
5 a s_____ing suburb
6 a ten-s_____ block of flats
7 an en-s_____ bathroom
8 w_____ly optimistic
9 a w_____-in wardrobe

5 Which of these adjectives would you use to describe these places from Unit 3?

characterless	compact	imposing	lively
modern	quaint	run-down	sleepy	smart
spacious			

6 >> MB Work in pairs. Use the adjectives from Exercise 5 to describe a building, area or city that you know.

I CAN

use adverb + adjective collocations ☐
describe buildings and places ☐

Real life

7 Match the sentence beginnings (1–7) with the endings (a–g).

1 Personally,   a of public art works.
2 It seems a bit   b the benefits.
3 It's pretty clear that   c no one wants it.
4 I'm all in favour   d completely.
5 I can see that,   e I think it's a great idea.
6 I agree with you   f old-fashioned to me.
7 You shouldn't   g but I still think it's too
  underestimate   expensive.

8 >> MB Work in pairs. Give your opinions about an idea to create a small zoo in your local city where children can learn more about animals. Use the expressions in Exercise 7.

I CAN

express my opinions ☐
agree and disagree politely ☐

Unit 4 Innovation

'Cyborg' woman with a bionic eye

FEATURES

46 Shrink it, bend it, fold it
The future of bendable technology

48 The mother of invention
What drives new discoveries

50 The shoe giver
The story of a successful social entrepreneur

54 This man risked it all
A video about a social enterprise in Uganda

1 Look at the photo and caption. What do you think 'cyborg' and 'bionic' mean? Is this science fiction or something real?

2 ▶ 26 Listen to a news report about bionic body parts. Answer the questions.
  1 How badly damaged was the woman's sight before her operation?
  2 What could she see after the operation?
  3 Who are the ear buds designed for and what can they do?
  4 What question does this new technology raise?

3 ▶ 26 Work in pairs. Try to replace the verbs in bold with the more scientific verbs used in the news report. Then listen to the news report again and check.
  1 Surgeons **put** an electronic chip into her right eye.
  2 It'll probably take months for Lewis to **teach** her brain to see again.
  3 She can already **see** nearby objects …
  4 They can **cut out** the background noise …
  5 … or **make** surrounding sounds **louder** …

4 Discuss how bionic body parts (e.g. bionic legs, a bionic hand, a bionic eye, bionic skin) could be more 'effective' than biological body parts. What advantages or abilities could they have?

my life ▶ FUTURE SOLUTIONS ▶ HOW PEOPLE MANAGED IN THE PAST ▶ A SOCIAL BUSINESS ▶ MAKING A SHORT PITCH
▶ A PROPOSAL

reading bendable technology • wordbuilding -able • grammar future probability • speaking future solutions

4a Shrink it, bend it, fold it

Reading

1 Work in pairs. Answer the questions.

1 What everyday objects can you think of that you can shrink, bend or fold?
   You can shrink a jumper.
2 What other everyday things could it be useful to make smaller by shrinking, bending or folding?

2 Read the article. Make two lists of objects (a and b). Were these the same as your ideas in Exercise 1?

a objects we are already familiar with that can be shrunk, bent or folded
b objects we will see more of in the near future that can be shrunk, bent or folded

3 Read the article again and answer the questions.

1 How do 21st-century TVs and mobile phones compare with 20th-century ones?
2 Where will the next generation of solar cells be placed?
3 What is the author's prediction for bendable screens?
4 Who in future will be able to launch their own small satellite?
5 What are the benefits of the new specially coated 'super-pills'?

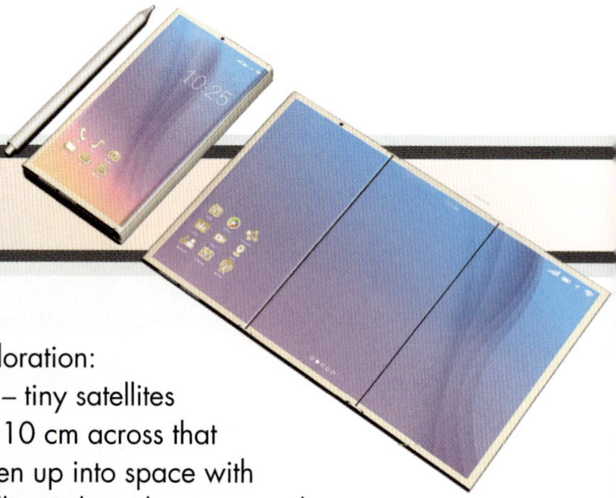

SHRINK IT, BEND IT, FOLD IT

▶ 27

There's always something rather satisfying about things that can be reduced in size and packed away: a folding bike you can take on the train; a raincoat you can roll up and pop into a carry bag; folding, unbreakable
5　sunglasses you can put in your back pocket. Now advances in electronics and materials science are pushing the boundaries of what is possible, helping manufacturers to make increasingly smaller or thinner or more flexible devices: you only have to compare a 21st-century
10　television or mobile phone with a 20th-century one to see that. What might the next ten years bring?

Energy: The idea of harnessing solar energy is nothing new, but we may well be about to see a revolution in the construction of solar cells which will allow them to
15　be incorporated into an ultra-thin transparent film. So instead of expensive solar panels on roofs or in solar farms, in future they could form part of the windows on our buildings.

Communications: Using screens as thin as a sheet of
20　paper, bendable technology is already here, but the chances are that it will become very widespread in the coming years: phones that wrap around your wrist, foldable computers that fit into your jacket pocket. Perhaps one day soon we will see TV screens that can be
25　rolled up and carried with us.

Space exploration: 'Cubesats' – tiny satellites measuring 10 cm across that can be taken up into space with larger satellites – have become much
30　more affordable: anyone can launch their own satellite now for as little as $3,000. This should increase our chances of making new discoveries in space.

Medicine: Doctors are already successfully repairing damaged eyesight with tiny electronic implants and
35　removing blockages in arteries with small foldable stents. Progress in bionics is likely to continue at a fast pace, although it will almost certainly raise difficult ethical questions along the way. The other area in which materials science is making huge progress is in
40　how drugs are delivered into the body. New types of coating around pills mean each pill needs to be taken just once and then the drug inside can be released over weeks and months, even years. It's likely that such 'super-
45　pills' will in future be inserted directly into the area needing treatment, such as cancer cells, increasing the drug's effectiveness enormously.

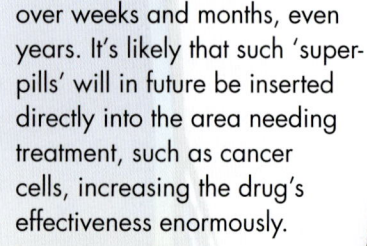

---

harness (v) /ˈhɑː(r)nɪs/ getting hold of and using
implant (n) /ˈɪmplɑːnt/ something that is put in your body during an operation
stent (n) /stent/ a small expanding tube used to replace damaged tubes in your body (e.g. in arteries)

Wordbuilding -able

> **WORDBUILDING -able**
>
> We can add the suffix *-able* to many verbs to form an adjective meaning something is possible. The prefixes *un-*, *in-* or *non-* can also be added to say that something is impossible.
> *foldable, removable, unbreakable, non-negotiable*
>
> For further practice, see Workbook page 129.

4 Look at the wordbuilding box. Then rewrite the sentences (1–6) using adjectives ending in *-able*. You will need to change other words in the sentence.

1. You can't **reuse** those cups: you're supposed to **dispose** of them.
   Those cups aren't reusable; they're disposable.
2. They said this camera could**n't** be **broken**. I hope they **refund** me the money.
3. Can I **wash** this jacket or does it have to go to the dry cleaners?
4. The car can be **repaired**. It's just a question of whether I can **afford** the repair.
5. I can't **excuse** his behaviour. All I asked was that I could **rely** on him.
6. You ca**n't imagine** how painful it was.

Grammar future probability

> **FUTURE PROBABILITY**
>
> **Modal verbs**
> *may (well) / could (well) / might (well), should*
> In future they **could** form part of the windows ...
> We **may well** be about to see a revolution in solar cells.
> It **should** increase our chances of making new discoveries ...
>
> **Adverbs**
> *perhaps, maybe, probably, almost certainly*
> It will **almost certainly** raise difficult ethical questions.
> **Perhaps** one day soon we will see TV screens that can be rolled up.
>
> **Adjective phrases**
> *It's possible/probable/(un)likely that; is likely to*
> It's **likely that** in future 'super-pills' will be inserted.
> Progress in bionics **is likely to** continue at a fast pace.
>
> **Noun phrases**
> *The likelihood is (that), The chances are (that), There's a good chance (that)*
> **The chances are** (that) it will become very widespread.
>
> For further information and practice, see page 90.

5 Look at the grammar box. Answer the questions.

1. How does *well* affect the meaning when it is used after *may*, *might* or *could*?
2. What are the usual positions of an adverb of probability?
3. Sentences with *(un)likely* have two possible grammatical forms. What are they? Transform each example in the grammar box using the other form.

6 Look at the expressions of probability again in the grammar box. Discuss which words or phrases mean the following:

1. something is possible (about 50% chance)
2. something is probable (about 70% chance)
3. something is not probable (about 20% chance)
4. something is very sure or almost certain (about 90% chance)

7 Look at the description of innovations. Rewrite the phrases in bold using the words in brackets.

> Smart textiles are already here but ¹ **we will probably see** (chances) a lot more of them in the coming years. Some innovations will just be cosmetic but others ² **are likely to have** (may well) practical uses. For example, scientists at Penn State University have created a self-repairing fabric. They believe that within the next ten years people ³ **will probably be wearing** (likely) clothes that mend themselves. ⁴ **It's possible this will mean** (could) the end of sewing as we know it. Meanwhile, researchers in China have made a fabric that generates electricity as you move. It ⁵ **is unlikely to produce** (probably) large amounts of power but ⁶ **it will probably be** (should) enough to recharge a phone.

8 Complete the conversation using one word in each space. There is sometimes more than one possible answer. Then discuss if you agree with the speakers' views.

A: Do you think that the problem of internet security ¹ _____ get worse in the future?
B: Well, there ² _____ be a technological solution, but I doubt it. I think what's more ³ _____ to happen is that we'll use the internet more and more and internet crime will almost ⁴ _____ increase.
A: I think you're right. Internet security may ⁵ _____ improve, but the criminals will ⁶ _____ get better at what they do too.

Speaking my life

9 Work in pairs. Choose two of the challenges (or your own ideas) that people face in the 21st century. Discuss whether technology will be able to solve them, and if so, how. Use expressions of probability.

- Traffic congestion and pollution
- The growing shortage of water
- Curing illness and disease

I think technology will almost certainly be able to solve traffic congestion and pollution problems. There's a good chance that ...

listening the inspiration for innovations • vocabulary phrasal verb *come* • grammar past modals • pronunciation weak forms in past modals • speaking how people managed in the past

4b The mother of invention

Listening

1 Work in pairs. Look at the saying below. Discuss what it means and if you think it is always true.

"Necessity is the mother of invention."

2 Look at the photo and the caption. What adjectives would you use to describe this invention? What do you think the inventor is trying to achieve?

3 ▶28 Listen to an interview about what inspires inventions. Choose the statement (a–c) that best summarizes the speaker's view.

a Most inventions are an answer to an urgent need.
b Most inventions are things that we didn't imagine we needed until we became used to them.
c Most inventions come from companies who want to make a commercial profit.

4 ▶28 Listen to the interview again and choose the correct option to complete the sentences.

1 People in their twenties probably can't imagine *doing research / following the news* without the internet.
2 Martha Kay is *a business woman / an academic*.
3 In the nineteenth century, British politicians said the telephone was *too expensive / of little use*.
4 The presenter uses the telephone as an example of a case where a need *was filled / didn't exist before*.
5 Most innovations make our lives *more satisfying / easier*.
6 The presenter suggests that women in the 1960s liked *going out to shop / staying in the house*.
7 The mobile phone and the personal computer are examples of innovations that were *very expensive at first / seen as unnecessary*.
8 *Literary Digest* predicted that the motor car would *remain a luxury / go out of fashion*.

Charles Steinlauf's invention: a four-position bicycle which also contains a built-in sewing machine

Vocabulary phrasal verb *come*

5 Look at the sentences. Choose the correct meaning (a–c) of each phrasal verb. The first three sentences are from the interview.

1 But how do such inventions **come about**?
  a succeed   b happen   c work
2 Entrepreneurs often **come up with** ideas to make our lives a little more convenient.
  a think of   b ignore   c search for
3 Over time, we **come to** rely on them.
  a start to   b try to   c have to
4 A researcher **came across** the material for post-it notes when looking for a new kind of glue.
  a thought of   b found by chance   c stole
5 Early experiments with flying didn't really **come off**.
  a succeed   b get noticed   c get taken seriously
6 Perrelet was so respected that when other watchmakers **came up against** a problem, they would consult him.
  a solved   b encountered   c analysed

6 Work in pairs. Write three sentences using the phrasal verbs from Exercise 5. Then read your sentences to your partner omitting the verb and see if they can guess the missing verb.

48

Unit 4 Innovation

Grammar past modals

▶ **PAST MODALS**

1 had to (do)
They felt they **had to find** a way to communicate at a distance.

2 needn't have (done) / didn't need to (do)
They **didn't need to have** phones.
We have so many things around us that we **needn't have acquired**.

3 must have, might/may/could have, can't have (done)
Life **must have been** very different before the invention of certain things.
You **might** never **have considered** how people searched for information before the internet.
It **can't have been** easy.

4 should have / ought to have (done)
They probably **should have been** more open-minded.

For further information and practice, see page 90.

7 Look at the grammar box. Match the past modal verb forms (1–4) with the uses (a–d).

  a to speculate on past events
  b to talk about an obligation
  c to say what was expected or advisable
  d to talk about a lack of necessity

8 Work in pairs. Complete the sentences with the correct past modal verb form.

1 | needn't have   didn't need to |

  a We use _____ to say something wasn't necessary but it was done anyway.
  b We use _____, to say something wasn't necessary whether it was done or not.

2 | may/might/could have   must have   can't have |

  a When we use _____, it means we are almost certain that something happened / was true.
  b When we use _____, it means we are almost certain it didn't happen / wasn't true.
  c When we use _____, it means we think it possibly happened / was true.

9 Choose the correct options to complete the conversation.
  A: I didn't hear you leave this morning. I ¹ *must / might* have been asleep.
  B: I left for work very early, actually. But I ² *didn't need to bother / needn't have bothered*. There was no traffic.
  A: I think it was a school holiday. That ³ *could / should* have been the reason. But you ⁴ *had to wake / should have woken* me. I got to work late in the end.
  B: Sorry. I was really focused on leaving in good time. I ⁵ *must have been / had to be* sure of getting to my meeting.

10 Complete the sentences. Use an appropriate past modal verb form with the words in brackets.

  1 Before cars were commonplace, it _____ (not / be) so easy to take your family for a weekend outing.
  2 In the 1940s, people _____ (not / own) a television, because radios provided news and entertainment.
  3 Before satellite navigation in cars, people _____ (depend) on printed maps.
  4 I never use this microwave oven. I _____ (buy) it.
  5 In the days before TV, it _____ (be) really exciting to go to the cinema!
  6 I'm not sure who invented the wristwatch. It _____ (be) a Swiss person.
  7 The inventor of 'cats eyes' in the road _____ (receive) more recognition. They've saved a huge number of lives.
  8 I think when Tim Berners-Lee invented the internet, he _____ (realize) that it would have negative as well as positive effects.

11 Pronunciation weak forms in past modals

  a ▶ 29 Circle the weak forms (words not stressed, including 'to') in these past modal verbs. Then listen and check.

  1 It should have worked, but it didn't.
  2 I had to wait half an hour.
  3 He must have forgotten.
  4 You needn't have worried.
  5 She may have left already.
  6 I didn't need to be there.

  b Practise saying the sentences in Exercise 11a.

Speaking my life

12 Work in groups. Use a range of past modals to speculate on the answers to these questions.

  How did people:
  • wake up on time before there were alarm clocks?
  • keep money safe before savings banks existed?
  • entertain themselves in the evenings before we had electricity in our homes?
  • deal with aches and pains without medicines?
  • contact each other in an emergency before the telephone existed?
  • clean their teeth without toothbrushes?
  • detect broken bones before x-rays existed?

13 Work in pairs. Think of two commonly used inventions: one that you couldn't live without and one that you find unnecessary. Discuss the inventions and the reasons you chose them.

I couldn't live without my electric kettle because I drink so much tea. I know in the past people used to boil water on the cooker, but it must have taken a long time.

reading a social entrepreneur • critical thinking finding counter arguments • word focus *give* • speaking a social business

4c The shoe giver

Reading

1 Work in pairs and discuss the questions.
   1 What are the main priorities of a business, in your opinion?
   2 Can you think of ways that a business could make money and help society at the same time?

2 Read the article on page 51. Then summarize how TOMS makes money and does good at the same time.

3 Read the article again. Are the sentences true (T) or false (F)?
   1 Blake Mycoskie's early career consisted of starting and then selling companies.
   2 Mycoskie immediately saw the Argentinian children's shoe problem as another business challenge.
   3 The main advantage of the one-for-one scheme is that Mycoskie doesn't have to keep asking people to donate money.
   4 The author suggests that in business, energy and enthusiasm is a very important factor.
   5 Mycoskie would like it if his customers became social entrepreneurs too.
   6 Podoconiosis is a disease that concerns developed countries as much as developing countries.
   7 Mycoskie thinks that any business could profit from making a similar one-for-one offer to its customers.
   8 The author thinks that Mycoskie should be proud that he has a successful business, not just one that helps people.

Critical thinking finding counter arguments

4 The author presents a positive picture of TOMS, but there are suggestions that there are also arguments against the initiative. Find possible criticisms in the text in these areas.
   a the price of the product
   b the business model
   c charitable giving

5 Work in pairs. Compare your answers from Exercise 4. Then write some questions for Blake Mycoskie that would challenge him on these points.

Word focus *give*

6 Work in pairs. Find these expressions with *give* in the article and discuss what they mean.
   a give it a break (line 11)
   b give it some thought (line 26–27)

7 Complete the expressions with *give* using these words. Discuss what each expression means.

| best | break | go | go ahead | thought | time |

   1 It's difficult to be in a new environment, but **give it some** _____ and you'll feel more at home.
   2 Don't worry if you don't win: just **give it your** _____ .
   3 I wasn't actually expecting him to like our business proposal, but he **gave us the** _____ .
   4 **Give him a** _____ . He's only been doing the job two months. He can't be expected to know everything.
   5 There's no need to tell me your answer now. **Give it some** _____ and then let me know.
   6 The only way to find out if you can mend it yourself is to **give it a** _____ .

8 Match these expressions with similar expressions from Exercise 7. Then make three sentences about your own experience using expressions with *give*.

| a chance | consideration | the green light | a try |
| a while | your all |

Speaking my life

9 Work in groups. Imagine these organizations come to you for financial help. Considering them both as businesses and as organizations with a social benefit, decide which you would help. Give reasons.

   A This organization collects food near its sell-by date from supermarkets and uses volunteers to distribute it free to homeless people. The company needs money for transport and administration costs.

   B This organization sells gardening and landscaping services to companies. The people it employs are all long-term unemployed people who get training, work experience and a little pocket money.

   C This organization collects unwanted clothing. Clothes in good condition are washed and given to people in need. Clothes in poor condition are recycled and made into fashion clothing to be sold.

10 Do *you* know a company with a social purpose?

The shoe giver

Blake Mycoskie is a self-confessed serial entrepreneur. He set up his first business, EZ Laundry, a laundry service for students, when he was still at college. Having built up the company to serve seven colleges in the south-west of the USA, he sold his share to his business partner and moved on to a media advertising business in Nashville. This again he sold on to Clear Channel, one of the industry's leading companies.

Three more businesses later, still only 29 years old, and feeling a bit 'burned out' from work, Mycoskie decided to give it a break for a while and headed down to Argentina for some rest and relaxation. But rest isn't really part of an entrepreneur's make-up and it wasn't long before Mycoskie had hit on another idea, one that would come to define him as perhaps the world's best-known social entrepreneur.

On a visit to a village outside Buenos Aires, he was shocked to see that many of the children didn't have any shoes; or if they did, the shoes were ill-fitting and badly worn. Since shoes – particularly the local farmers' canvas shoe, the alpargata – are relatively cheap in Argentina, Mycoskie's first instinct was to set up a charity to donate shoes to the children. But after giving it some thought, he realized that this probably wouldn't work: the shoes would quickly wear out and if he asked people to donate repeatedly every time more shoes were needed, their sympathy for the cause might also wear out pretty quickly.

So he came up with the idea of 'TOMS: one-for-one shoes'. He would take the alpargata to America, manufacture it and sell it as a high-end fashion item at around US$50 a pair. Quite a lot for a canvas shoe you might say, but for each pair he sold, another pair would be donated to village children. That way he could guarantee a continuing supply and also run the project as a business rather than as a charity, which was something he had no experience of.

Mycoskie knew nothing about manufacturing, let alone shoe manufacturing, but he understood that he had to learn fast. At first, by his own admission, he made 'a poor job of making shoes', so he brought in help from people with experience in the industry and soon his product was getting high satisfaction ratings from customers. The vital element that Mycoskie added was his own passion. It is a passion he wants others to share. TOMS encourages customers to become more involved by volunteering to hand-deliver the shoes to the children in need. It's an intimate giving experience and Mycoskie hopes it might inspire volunteers to develop similar projects.

Ten years on and with revenues of $392 million a year, the business is thriving, supplying shoes not only to children in Argentina but also other parts of the world where foot diseases are a problem. In southern Ethiopia, where a high concentration of silicone in the soil causes podoconiosis, a disease that swells the feet, 300,000 people suffer simply because they have no shoes. The same type of soil exists in parts of France and Hawaii, but people there are unaffected.

But is the one-for-one model repeatable with other products? TOMS is a for-profit business, but for a long time it didn't show a profit. Mycoskie says it is not like a sales promotion you can just add to your existing business model; you have to build it in from the beginning. He now diverts a lot of his profits into other innovative social ventures. He is conscious that 'giving' alone is not the answer and that educating people to improve their own lives is the real key. Yet he still loves 'TOMS: one-for-one', calling it his 'greatest hit'. And why shouldn't he? It has made a difference to millions of poor children around the world and brought him great entrepreneurial satisfaction.

Changing a life begins with a single step

real life making a short pitch • speaking skill making key points • pronunciation word stress

4d An elevator pitch

Real life making a short pitch

1 Read the definition of an elevator pitch. Then work in pairs. What information do you think you should include? What don't you need to talk about?

> An elevator pitch is where you imagine you are in an elevator with someone you want to sell your new (business) idea to. You only have the time until the doors open again to convince this person.

2 ▶31 Listen to someone giving advice about making an elevator pitch. What three points does she make? Compare the three points she makes with your ideas from Exercise 1. Did you agree with what she said? Why? / Why not?

3 ▶32 Listen to a short pitch for a new phone app and complete the notes in the table.

Name of app	1
What is does	Links people who want to volunteer to 2
Problem it solves	People don't volunteer because they can't commit to a 3
Competition	Doodle and 4
Why it's different	Has a database of volunteers' 5 and 6
Developers' qualifications	Team of 7 with experience of 8
Needs	9 to bring it to market

4 Speaking skill making key points

▶32 Look at the expressions for making key points. Listen again and tick the rhetorical questions and sentence adverbs the speaker uses. Can you remember what the speaker said directly after each question?

▶ **MAKING KEY POINTS**

Rhetorical questions	Sentence adverbs
What is it?	Basically, …
How does it work?	Essentially, …
What does it do exactly?	Clearly, …
Why is it/that necessary?	Obviously, …
So what, you say?	Of course, …
Won't that be expensive?	Honestly, …
How do we achieve this?	To be honest, …
What are we asking for?	Financially, ….
What's our ambition for …?	Practically, …

5 Pronunciation word stress

a ▶33 Mark where you think the stress falls in each adverb or adverbial phrase in the box. Then listen and check.

b ▶33 Work in pairs. Practise saying the words with the same stress patterns. Then listen again and check.

6 Work in pairs or groups of three. Present your own elevator pitch for a new social enterprise. Follow these steps.

Student A: Turn to page 81 and read the notes.

Student B: Turn to page 82 and read the notes.

Student C: Turn to page 82 and read the notes.

- Prepare your pitch carefully. Use the expressions for making key points to help you (use no more than three rhetorical questions).
- Speak for no more than a minute.
- Write down the main message of each pitch and at the end compare your answers.
- Vote on who you think gave the most persuasive pitch.

my life ▶ FUTURE SOLUTIONS ▶ HOW PEOPLE MANAGED IN THE PAST ▶ A SOCIAL BUSINESS ▶ MAKING A SHORT PITCH ▶ A PROPOSAL

writing a proposal • writing skill making recommendations   Unit 4 Innovation

4e Problem or solution?

Writing a proposal

1 Work in pairs. Read the proposal and answer the questions.

1 Does the author think the rise in the use of digital devices is a negative trend? How do you know?
2 Why does the author think the declining trend in book reading needs to be reversed?
3 Do you think the author's suggestions are good ones? Why? / Why not?

Introduction
This proposal suggests ways teachers can use technology to get children reading.

Current situation
It is a fact that children are now spending more time on digital devices, browsing on the internet, messaging friends, etc. It is also a fact that they are reading fewer books. This matters because reading books is known to help your ability to:

- focus and remember
- expand your vocabulary
- improve communication skills
- develop analytical thinking.

So how can we use students' enthusiasm for digital devices to encourage them to read more?

Possible solutions
First of all, we suggest that teachers actively encourage students to use the internet in class: either to research new subjects or to compare their conclusions with other people's. Secondly, we recommend using student blogs or learning diaries as a way of sharing ideas. Lastly, we think technology could help make reading a pleasure rather than a duty. One idea would be to put interesting short stories with visuals on screens in a quiet part of the classroom that students could read as a reward for finishing other work.

Recommendations
These are just a few examples of how technology could be an aid to reading. We strongly recommend teachers to explore similar ideas. Unless we begin to see technology as part of the solution, rather than part of the problem, we are unlikely to reverse the trend.

2 Look at how the proposal is organized. Answer the questions.

1 How is it divided into different sections? How are different points listed?
2 Underline the sentences in the proposal which do the following.
   a state the proposal's aim
   b state the problem that needs addressing
   c summarize the writer's opinion

3 Writing skill making recommendations

a Look at the forms used with the verbs *suggest* and *recommend*. Which forms are used in the proposal?

> 1 *recommend / suggest* (that) someone (should) do something
> 2 *recommend / suggest* something or doing something
> 3 *recommend* + someone to do something

b Complete these recommendations using appropriate verb forms.

1 I strongly recommend that _____ (people / follow) this advice.
2 We suggest that _____ (people / save) their money.
3 He recommends you _____ (wait) until after the summer.
4 We are not suggesting that _____ (teachers / always teach) this way.
5 I recommend that _____ (the company / look) into these options.

4 Write a proposal that each school child should be given a tablet computer at the age of five. Include the following points.

- different uses for these tablet computers
- the benefits they could bring
- why this is an opportunity not to be missed

5 Exchange proposals with your partner. Use these questions to check your proposals.

- Is your partner's proposal organized in the same way as the proposal in Exercise 1 (with sub-headings and bullet points)?
- Has your partner used the language to make recommendations correctly?
- Is it a persuasive proposal? Does your partner's proposal include any points you wish you'd included?

my life ▶ FUTURE SOLUTIONS ▶ HOW PEOPLE MANAGED IN THE PAST ▶ A SOCIAL BUSINESS ▶ MAKING A SHORT PITCH
▶ A PROPOSAL

4f This man risked it all

Women and children carrying firewood, Uganda

Unit 4 Innovation

Before you watch

1 Look at the photo and caption. How do you think this activity affects:
a the children's lives?   b the environment?

2 Key vocabulary

a Read the sentences. The words in bold are used in the video. Guess the meaning of the words.

1 I was **on the verge of** giving up my university course, but my parents persuaded me to carry on.
2 I don't know why I continued to believe him. It was as if I was **under a spell**.
3 We sell some products direct, but mostly, they are sold through high street **retailers**.
4 We supply over ten million **households** in the UK with gas and electricity.
5 The island has experienced terrible **deforestation** because the construction industry needs wood as a building material.

b Match the words in bold in Exercise 2a with these definitions.

a shops that sell to individual customers
b large-scale cutting down of trees
c just about to
d influenced by a powerful (often magical) force
e homes

While you watch

3 ▶ 4.1 Watch the video and check your ideas from Exercise 1. What benefits did Sanga Moses' business bring to the community?

4 Describe the following things you saw in the video.

- the tool used to cut wood
- the buildings in the villages
- the 'clean' cooking fuel he produced
- the transport farmers were using

5 ▶ 4.1 Watch the first part of the video (0.00 to 1.50) again. Answer the questions.

1 What part of his sister's situation particularly inspired Sanga Moses to act?
2 What did his boss think about his decision to quit his job?
3 How many of the university students wanted to help him with his new business venture?
4 How did he raise the funds for his new business?
5 What was his girlfriend's reaction?

6 ▶ 4.1 Watch the second part of the video (1.51 to the end) again. Complete the facts and figures.

- Eco Fuel Africa turns farm ^{1} _____ into clean cooking fuel.
- The fuels burns cleaner and ^{2} _____, and is ^{3} _____ cheaper.
- Eco Fuel Africa has a network of 2,500 farmers and ^{4} _____ women retailers.
- It supplies ^{5} _____ households.
- Its ambition is to supply 16.6 million households in the next ^{6} _____ years.
- Eco Fuel Africa prevents ^{7} _____ and ^{8} _____ air pollution.
- It provides a living for farmers and ^{9} _____ and makes sure children get an ^{10} _____.

After you watch

7 ▶ 4.2 Watch the clips from the video. Choose the correct meaning of the words.

8 Complete the sentences in your own words. Then compare your sentences with a partner.

1 The news that … hit people hard.
2 It's important to have a good network of friends because …
3 I have an idea to … but I don't know if I should act on it.

9 Work in pairs. First summarize the benefits of Eco Fuel Africa's service and then discuss if you see any potential drawbacks of this system.

10 Sanga Moses described himself as an 'everyday community guy', meaning that he had identified a problem in his community and tried to solve it. What problem have you seen in your community and what could be done about it, do you think? Think about these areas or one of your own. Then prepare a short talk to describe the problem and possible solution.

- Crime/safety
- Transport
- Pollution
- Lack of shops
- Noise
- Lack of public/recreation space
- Jobs

husk (n) /hʌsk/ the outer shell of an edible seed, e.g. in wheat or coffee
sugar cane (n) /ˈʃʊɡə(r) keɪn/ a tall thick grass from which sugar is extracted

UNIT 4 REVIEW AND MEMORY BOOSTER

Grammar

1 Read the article and complete it using these words. There are four extra words.

> can't   certainly   chances   had   likelihood
> likely   might   must   needn't   possible
> probably   unlikely

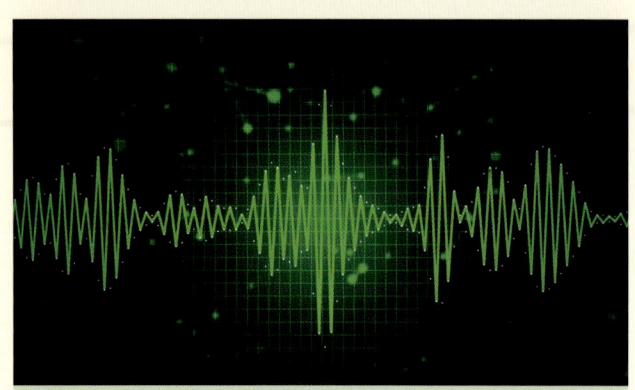

The problem of knowing what information to trust ¹_____ just have got harder. That's because a Canadian company has recently developed a computer program that can mimic people's voices. The program does not just copy words, it analyses speech patterns to create new sentences in the same voice. So, the person whose voice is being imitated ²_____ actually have said the words. The program is already very good at doing this and the ³_____ are that it will get better very quickly. Although the company developed the program for good reasons – for use in games and audio books – it is now worried that, in the wrong hands, the program is ⁴_____ to be used for identity theft. For example, it's ⁵_____ that someone could pretend to be a politician or a diplomat and use this ability to learn important secrets. The company felt it ⁶_____ to inform people about how powerful the technology is, because it thinks others ⁷_____ have developed similar programs. Their spokesperson said the development of these programs means that we will almost ⁸_____ not be able to trust audio evidence in future.

2 >> MB What is the probability (on a scale of 1–10) of these things happening, according to the article?

1 people using voice software to steal other people's identities
2 similar programmes already existing elsewhere
3 audio evidence no longer being useable

I CAN	
talk about future probability	
use past modals to express obligation or necessity	

Vocabulary

3 Replace the underlined parts of each phrase with an adjective ending in -able. Some of the adjectives need to use the negative form.

1 A table that can be extended.
2 A coat that can't be washed.
3 A mistake that can be forgiven.
4 A car that can't be relied on.
5 A cover that can be removed.
6 A deposit that can't be refunded.
7 A bag that can be used again.
8 A cost that can't be avoided.

4 >> MB Look at the phrases (1–4). Think of a situation when you would use each of these phrases. Then compare answers with a partner. How similar were your situations?

1 'Give it some thought, anyway.'
2 'Give her a break.'
3 'Sure. I'll give it a go.'
4 'We came up against a lot of opposition.'

I CAN	
use words with the -able ending	
use expressions with give and phrasal verbs with come	

Real life

5 Look at the statements from a short product pitch. Complete the rhetorical questions.

1 So, what _____? It's a vacuum cleaner that can clean any type of floor surface.
2 Why _____? Because there's no other machine that can perform all these functions.
3 How _____? At the base, there's a rotary brush which cleans as it sucks up the dirt.
4 Won't _____? Despite its sophistication, we're hoping to keep the cost down.
5 How _____? By making it in China, where manufacturing costs are much lower.

6 >> MB Think of a product that you use frequently. Then work in pairs. Take turns to present your product as if it was a new product. Use at least three rhetorical questions.

I CAN	
give a short presentation for a new product	
use rhetorical questions in a presentation	

Unit 5 The magic of travel

A street at sunset in one of the world's most famous cities
© TOUR EIFFEL – Illuminations PIERRE BIDEAU

FEATURES

58 How we travel
Different approaches to travelling

60 Magical mystery tour
Trips to unknown places

62 The adventures of Hergé
Travel through the eyes of a comic book hero

66 On the road: Andrew McCarthy
A video about a memorable travel experience

1 Work in pairs. Look at the photo. Discuss what you know about this place (its character, its landmarks, its people, etc.).

2 ▶ 34 Look at the questions and discuss them with your partner. Then listen to a travel writer's opinion and compare your answers.
  1 What different factors (time of year, reason for travel, etc.) influence how we experience a place when we travel?
  2 What makes a good travel writer?

3 ▶ 34 Look at these adjectives. Which ones normally describe people (P), places (PL) or a time (T)? Then listen to the travel writer again and say what the speaker uses each adjective to describe. Did you use any of the same adjectives to describe Paris?

| romantic | cosy | officious | lazy | elegant | affable |
| wary | grand | lively |

4 Work in groups. Use adjectives to describe a place you have enjoyed visiting. Use words from Exercise 3 if helpful.

my life ▶ HOW YOU TRAVEL ▶ A MYSTERY TOUR ▶ KNOWING PLACES ▶ TELLING AN ANECDOTE ▶ A REVIEW

57

reading a travel blog • vocabulary repeated word pairs • grammar emphatic structures • pronunciation *do*, *does* and *did* • speaking how you travel

5a How we travel

Reading

1 Work in pairs. Discuss the questions about travel.

1 Why do you think most people travel?
2 Where and when do you travel? What is your reason for travelling?
3 What do you enjoy / not enjoy about travelling?
4 Do you think the concept of travel and holidays differs from culture to culture? If so, how?

2 Look at the blog post about how we travel. Answer the questions.

1 How was the writer's experience of travel as a young boy typical of his culture?
2 What is his father's attitude to travel? In what ways does the writer agree with him?
3 What does the writer want from travel?
4 Which of these attitudes (the writer's and his father's) is closest to your own?

3 Find words or expressions in the second paragraph of the blog with these meanings.

1 without worries
2 a fixed list of places to visit
3 burning slowly with smoke but no flame
4 very still and shiny
5 bordered
6 a steep valley

▶ 35

Going on holiday when I was a young boy meant going to spend the summer with my grandparents in my parents' home town in the north of India. For many Indians who live or work in a big city, that is still what travel is. For my father it was the same: escaping the heat of Kolkata to visit uncles and aunts in the cooler hills of Darjeeling. He is well off now and can afford to travel abroad to see the world, but instead he prefers to stay at home. On the few occasions he does travel, it's to visit my sister in Delhi or me in San Francisco, because he'd rather see us face to face than on a computer screen. But he doesn't behave like other tourists and visit the sights. What he enjoys is sitting and reading the newspaper with a good cup of coffee and wandering down to the local market to buy some food. Most people are pretending when they travel, he says, doing things they don't really want to do because they are on the traveller's checklist.

In some ways I understand his point of view. The thing we all value as travellers is that feeling of being carefree and open to experiences as they happen, just taking life day by day. But in other ways I disagree with him. Because it's exciting and unusual experiences that I want. Last month I had the trip of a lifetime in Chile. It was a guided trip with a strict itinerary, but it did fulfil my expectations of what travel should be, and more. We explored a volcanic cave under the smouldering Villarrica Volcano. We hiked through a forest of 1,000-year old monkey-puzzle trees and found ourselves looking down on the glassy Huinfuica Lagoon, flanked by majestic mountains. We stayed at a lodge in the Huilo Huilo Biological Reserve, a sustainable-tourism playground complete with walking trails, mountain-biking and kayaking. And we zip-wired across a 100-metre deep gorge called El Abismo.

I know what I like about travel; my father does too. It's just how we travel that's different.

How we TRAVEL

Unit 5 The magic of travel

Vocabulary repeated word pairs

4 Work in pairs. Look at the expressions in bold (a–b) from the blog. Discuss what they mean. Then discuss the meanings of the other expressions in bold (1–6).

a He'd rather see us **face to face**.
b … just taking life **day by day.**

1 I saw Layla last night. She's just back from holiday. She went **on and on** about how terrible the hotel was.
2 A country's success in sport goes **hand in hand** with how much it invests in promoting it.
3 I couldn't predict the winner of the election. They've been **neck and neck** all the way.
4 We both recognized the problem, but we don't really **see eye to eye** on the solution.
5 They started their travel website in 2015 and it's just gone from **strength to strength.**
6 Writing is a process that you need to approach **step by step.**

5 Think of examples of the following things. Then work in small groups and compare your ideas.

- an experience that went on and on
- a subject you don't see eye to eye with your parents (or someone you know) about
- a person whose career has gone from strength to strength
- something that you (or someone else) are taking step by step (or day by day) to reach a goal

Grammar emphatic structures

> **EMPHATIC STRUCTURES**
>
> **Cleft sentences**
> 1 **It's** relaxation **that** I want.
> 2 **What** I enjoy **is** sitting and reading the newspaper.
> 3 **The thing** we really value **is** being carefree.
>
> **do, does, did (in affirmative sentences)**
> 4 When I **do** travel now, I avoid the 'sights'.
> 5 I **did** take my laptop on my last holiday too.
>
> For further information and practice, see page 92.

6 Look at the grammar box. Notice the word order in the sentences. Rewrite the sentences (1–5) using a non-emphatic form.

  1 I want relaxation.

7 Rewrite this sentence in four different ways. Use emphatic forms, starting with the words given.

  'I love the unpredictability of travel.'

  1 It's …
  2 What …
  3 The thing …
  4 I …

8 Rewrite the parts of these sentences in italics using emphatic forms. Use the words given in brackets.

1 The destination is not important. *The journey matters.* (it)
2 I didn't miss my home town. *I missed my friends and family.* (what)
3 Colombia was full of surprises. *I read up a lot about it before I went*, but nothing really prepares you for it. (did)
4 When I went to Bali, *I was really struck by how relaxed the people were.* (what)
5 People always talk about how fascinating travel is. *But they never tell you how boring it can be too.* (the thing)
6 He's not normally a food lover, *but he likes to eat well when he's on holiday.* (does)
7 Our family holidays were hilarious. *I'll never forget the seven of us travelling through France in a tiny car.* (thing)
8 *I didn't mind the disruption*; it was the fact that they didn't apologize for it. (it)

9 Pronunciation *do, does* and *did*

a ▶ 36 Listen to these sentences and write in the missing emphatic auxiliaries. Note how the auxiliary verbs are stressed.

1 I _____ regret not stopping there.
2 She _____ travel a lot.
3 We _____ miss home sometimes.
4 I _____ spend a lot of time at the beach.

b Practise saying the sentences in Exercise 9a with the same stress.

Speaking my life

10 Work in small groups. Make a list of statements about how to travel (what's important, what you like, how you feel, etc.). Use emphatic structures in your ideas. Then compare your statements with your partner. Are your views similar or different? How?

- planning your journey
- things you always take with you
- avoiding stress when travelling (esp. flying)
- eating when travelling
- getting around from place to place
- holiday activities
- language and culture

*Try not to plan too much, because **it's** always the unexpected things **that** happen on a holiday that are the most memorable.*

my life ▶ HOW YOU TRAVEL ▶ A MYSTERY TOUR ▶ KNOWING PLACES ▶ TELLING AN ANECDOTE ▶ A REVIEW

wordbuilding synonyms • listening a mystery tour • grammar avoiding repetition • pronunciation stress in short responses • speaking a mystery tour

5b Magical mystery tour

Wordbuilding synonyms

▶ **WORDBUILDING synonyms**

We often use synonyms in English as a way of avoiding repetition. It is important to remember that few words are exact synonyms. They often differ slightly in meaning or in the grammar that surrounds them:
holiday and *break*, *succeed in* and *manage to*, *popular* and *well-liked*

For further practice, see Workbook page 143.

1 Work in pairs. What synonyms or close synonyms can you think of for these words? How similar or different in meaning is each word you thought of?

| hotel | relax | travel around | trip |

2 Look at these words which are used in the interview you are going to hear. Match the words (1–9) with the correct synonyms (a–i).

1 trip	a swimming costume
2 spot	b wonderful
3 head for	c expectation
4 thrilling	d journey
5 spoil	e location
6 swimsuit	f set off
7 start out	g make your way to
8 anticipation	h exhilarating
9 magical	i ruin

Listening

3 ▶37 Listen to an interview about a 'mystery tour' that a reporter went on. Complete the information.

Company name	1 _____ Adventures
Company based in	2 _____
Things to take	a³ _____ , a⁴ _____ , a dry bag
Length of trip	5 _____ days
Type of cycling	6 _____
Destination	7 _____ on the river
Night accommodation	slept in ⁸ _____
Return journey	By ⁹ _____
Cost of trip	10 _____

4 ▶37 Listen to the interview again and answer the questions.

1 Who started the fashion for mystery tours?
2 What kind of companies organize mystery tours nowadays?
3 How did Maggie describe her experience?
4 Why does the interviewer agree that it was better not to ask for too much pre-trip information?
5 What did the guide do as they travelled to their destination to add to the excitement?
6 How did Maggie feel about swimming to her 'accommodation' for the night?
7 How did she feel when she got back into London?
8 What lesson did the trip teach her?

Grammar avoiding repetition

> **▶ AVOIDING REPETITION**
>
> **one, that, it, so**
> 1 It was a magical experience … definitely **one** I'd recommend.
> 2 Did you know how far you would have to swim? Yes, I did ask **that**.
> 3 [She] went on one of the trips and talked to me afterwards about **it**.
> 4 Is that our island? I don't think **so**.
>
> **Ellipsis (omitting words)**
> 5 I thought about asking … but then I decided not **to**.
> 6 A few people were screaming and gasping – I know I **was**.
>
> **synonyms**
> 7 **a mystery tour** → a journey to an unknown destination
>
> For further information and practice, see page 92.

5 Look at the grammar box. Answer the questions.

  1 What do the words in bold refer to in sentences 1–4?
  2 Which of the words in bold in sentences 1–4 substitutes for:
    a a thing (i.e. a noun)?   b a phrase, clause or sentence?
  3 What verbs have been omitted after the words in bold in sentences 5 and 6?

6 Look at the audioscript on page 99–100 (track 37). Answer the questions.

  1 What synonym of 'idea' is used (para 1) and of 'track'?
  2 What does 'that' refer to in the sentence 'And that gave us the chance …'?
  3 What does 'it' refer to in the sentence '… but it was fine'?
  4 What verb phrase has been omitted after 'had' in 'actually it had'?
  5 What does 'one' refer to in the sentence 'it depends which one'?
  6 What verb phrase has been omitted after 'to' in 'you really don't need to'?

7 Read the review of a Secret Adventures holiday. Rephrase the words in bold in the review to avoid repetition. Use appropriate forms from the grammar box, including synonyms where necessary.

> Four days in the freezing wilderness with no electricity. You might ask why you would do ¹ **four days in the freezing wilderness with no electricity**. Well, I just returned from an amazing holiday with Secret Adventures Arctic and it's the best ² **holiday** I've been on. ³ **Returning** to work after such ⁴ **an amazing** adventure is really hard. We spent four days in northern Sweden and each ⁵ **day** was magical. We rode on sleds pulled by dogs – we had to ⁶ **ride on sleds** because it's the only way to get around. We stayed in a simple log cabin, drank hot lingonberry juice and we went cross-country skiing. ⁷ **Cross-country skiing** was great fun too. Often it was dark and I thought I'd hate ⁸ **that it was dark**, but I ⁹ **didn't hate it**. The highlight was seeing the Northern lights. ¹⁰ **Seeing the Northern lights** is an experience everyone should have once in their lives – at least I think ¹¹ **they should have that experience**.

8 Put an appropriate word into each sentence to avoid repetition.

  1 He said he wasn't going to take the car, but I think he _____, because I can't see it outside.
  2 She said, 'Good things come to those who wait.' What do you think she meant by _____?
  3 We need to set off early. So, shall we _____ at 7.30 a.m.?
  4 I'm so tired that I might fall asleep during the film, but I'll try _____.
  5 Sorry, this pen isn't working. Do you have _____ that I can borrow?
  6 I had an amazing childhood. I'm going to write a book about _____ one day.

9 Pronunciation stress in short responses

a Work in pairs. We often use substitution in spoken exchanges. Complete the answers to each question using one word in each case.

  1 A: You have to be careful not to get overcharged in the local markets.
    B: Yes, I know _____.
  2 A: Would you like to drive?
    B: No, I'd rather you _____.
  3 A: Did he take warm clothes with him?
    B: I hope _____.
  4 A: Do you mind travelling alone?
    B: No, I actually prefer _____.
  5 A: Are there many good guidebooks about this region?
    B: Yes, there are some excellent _____.
  6 A: Did she enjoy visiting Russia?
    B: Yes, she loved _____.

b ▶ 38 Listen and check your answers. Underline the stressed words in each response. Then work with a partner and read the exchanges aloud using the same pronunciation patterns.

Speaking my life

10 Work in small groups. Design your own mystery tour. The tour should be a reasonable price, take participants to an unknown destination and involve activities that bring people together. Then present it to the class. When you present the tour, try to use at least three expressions for avoiding repetition.

5c The adventures of Hergé

Reading

1 Work in pairs. Look at the photo and discuss the questions.

1. What comics or cartoon books did you read when you were a child?
2. What did they contain that appealed to you: adventure, humour, interesting facts, life stories?
3. Do you still read any comics or graphic novels now?

2 Read the article. Are the sentences true (T) or false (F)?

1. Tintin is a writer who travels around the world in search of adventure.
2. The author Hergé loved to travel.
3. The artwork in *The Adventures of Tintin* is remarkable for its precise detail.

3 Read the article again. Choose the best option to complete the sentences.

1. The author *read / daydreamed* a lot about foreign lands as a child.
2. The author compares *Tintin* books to reading *thrillers / National Geographic*.
3. Hergé made multiple *drawings / models* of objects like cars and planes before putting them in his pictures.
4. Hergé's methods have been an inspiration to *other illustrators / movie makers*.
5. Visitors to Petra see the tall Treasury *at the last moment / from a long way off*.
6. The author thinks *Destination Moon* and *Explorers on the Moon* are Herge's *best / most ambitious* books.

4 Find words in the article with the following meaning.

1. distant (para 1)
2. looked in amazement (para 1)
3. extremely careful (para 3)
4. truly and precisely (para 3)
5. very strange (often of a coincidence) (para 4)
6. talent (para 5)

Critical thinking evaluating sources

5 What sources (research, experts, first-hand experience) does the author mention to show that the following things were accurately represented by Hergé? NB For one item no real source is mentioned.

a. the scientific expedition to the Arctic
b. cars, planes, ships and bridges
c. the Treasury at Petra
d. sending a rocket to the Moon

6 Were you persuaded that Hergé represented things accurately for his readers? Do you think it's important that writers do this? Why? / Why not?

Word focus *matter*

7 Look at the expression in bold from the article. Choose the correct definition (a or b).

[The books] were a kind of *National Geographic* for children – and adults, **for that matter**.

a. of course (but you know that)
b. also (now that I think of it)

8 Complete the expressions with *matter* using these words. Then discuss with your partner what you think about each statement.

| course | laughing | mind | principle | time |
| way | | | | |

1. With new technology, I think **it's only a matter of** _____ before people are taking virtual holidays from their own living rooms.
2. Getting lost in a big city might seem like an adventure, but believe me, **it's no** _____ **matter** when it happens to you.
3. I think you can put up with a lot of discomfort when you're travelling. It's just a question of _____ **over matter**.
4. When I'm abroad, I use public transport **as a matter of** _____. You discover much more that way.
5. **No matter which** _____ you look at it, not speaking the language of the country you are visiting is a disadvantage.
6. I don't fly on planes **as a matter of** _____; they create too much pollution.

Speaking my life

9 Work in small groups. Make a list of four places you all know about in one or other of the ways listed below (e.g. New York). Then compare what you know about these places. Do you have a similar view of each place? Would you like to go there? Why? / Why not?

- from visiting yourself
- from what friends or family have told you
- from what you have seen in the TV news or a documentary
- from what you have read in a magazine, book or online
- from photos you have seen

Unit 5 The magic of travel

THE ADVENTURES OF HERGÉ
▶ 39

I spent a lot of my childhood travelling to far-off places and learning about their history and geography. I went to Peru and saw the Sacsayhuaman fortress of the Incas and the citadel of Machu Picchu. I visited the ancient rose-red city of Petra in Jordan and marvelled at the grand buildings carved out of the rock. I journeyed on a ship to the Arctic Ocean with a scientific expedition that was investigating a meteorite that had fallen to Earth. I even travelled to the Moon and learned what it was like to experience gravity six times weaker than I was used to.

I saw all these things not in person, of course, but through the eyes of the investigative journalist, Tintin, in the pages of the graphic novels of Hergé, the Belgian author and cartoonist. I was not the only one. In the days before full-colour television documentaries, Hergé's *Adventures of Tintin*, twenty-three books written between 1929 and 1976, were a kind of *National Geographic* for children – and adults, for that matter. These were not just great detective stories; they were learning adventures.

The amazing thing about the books is that their creator never travelled to these places either. They were all the result of painstaking research done from his studio. Hergé and his team of illustrators and researchers scoured libraries, museums and photographic archives to provide as accurate a representation, both in the drawings and the storylines, as they could. This included examining catalogues of cars and planes, and technical drawings of ships and bridges. Hergé made numerous sketches of these objects seen from different angles and sometimes created models of the characters and other items so as to be able to construct a particular scene and capture it more faithfully – a technique that has since been used by many film animators, such as Pixar.

Actually, I can personally attest to the incredible accuracy of Hergé's representations of foreign places because a few years ago, I visited Petra with my family. We rode on horses down the long narrow passage called *the Siq*, just as Tintin and his companion Captain Haddock do in *The Red Sea Sharks*. At the end, we came out from between the tall rock walls that frame the passage and caught our first sight of the magnificent forty-metre tall Treasury, sculpted from the pink sandstone. I was looking at a view straight from the pages of the book: the colours, the play of the sun on the walls, the dusty earth, the Bedouin guides with their keffiyehs wrapped around their mouths. It was uncanny.

Perhaps Hergé's greatest triumph is the two-part story *Destination Moon* and *Explorers on the Moon* which, considering the books were written in 1955, gave, according to commentators at the time, an extraordinarily realistic account of what would be involved in sending a manned rocket to the Moon. As well as the smaller drawings that carry the narrative, from time to time the reader turns the page to discover a stunning full-page image: a rocket on its launch-pad, complete with gantry, a mountainous moonscape, the Earth below as the rocket leaves the atmosphere. Few people in those days could imagine what it was like to be looking down at our planet from outer space. But that was Hergé's true gift: to understand and communicate what a place was like without ever having travelled there.

archives (npl) /ˈɑː(r)kaɪvz/ historic records or documents
citadel (n) /ˈsɪtəd(ə)l/ a fortress or castle, usually on a hill
gantry (n) /ˈɡæntri/ a bridge-like metal supporting structure
meteorite (n) /ˈmiːtiəraɪt/ a piece of rock or metal that falls from outer space
scour (v) /ˈskaʊə(r)/ to search intensively

my life ▶ HOW YOU TRAVEL ▶ A MYSTERY TOUR ▶ KNOWING PLACES ▶ TELLING AN ANECDOTE ▶ A REVIEW

real life **telling an anecdote** • speaking skill **linking events** • pronunciation **long sounds**

5d To my amazement

Real life telling an anecdote

1 Look at the photo. Answer the questions.

1. Where do you think the photo was taken?
2. Can you name four things in the photo that you associate with a beach holiday?
3. Would you choose to go on a beach holiday somewhere like this? Why? / Why not?

2 ▶ 40 Listen to a travel story. Make notes about the main details of the story.

1. Issue that the story highlights
2. The speaker's background and setting for the story
3. Main events
4. The speaker's conclusion

3 Work in pairs. Retell the story to each other using your notes from Exercise 2.

4 ▶ 40 Look at the expressions for telling an anecdote. Tick (✓) the expressions the speaker uses in the travel story. Then listen again and write down what followed the expressions the speaker used.

> ▶ **TELLING AN ANECDOTE**
>
> It's a (well-known) fact that …
> We all know that …
> These days, …
> It's famous for …
> Consequently / Because of that …
>
> A few years ago, … / Last summer, …
> The following day/morning …
> As luck would have it, …
> By chance, I happened to …
> By coincidence, …
> To my amazement/surprise/horror/delight/relief, …

5 Speaking skill linking events

a Look at these expressions. Which are used to signal the time of an event (T) and which are used to indicate the speaker's feelings about an event (F)? Which expressions add a sense of drama?

a A few years ago, …
b As if by magic, …
c Worryingly, …
d A little while later, …
e To my relief, …
f Just at that moment …
g Amazingly, …
h By sheer luck, …
i The following week, …
j As soon as … , …

b Work in pairs. You are going to link events in a story. Start with the sentence below. Take turns to suggest a linking phrase to continue the next sentence in the story.

> *A few years ago*, I was travelling on my own in Australia.
> A: *By sheer luck*, …
> B: *By sheer luck*, I bumped into a friend in Sydney, whom I hadn't seen for years.

6 Pronunciation long sounds

▶ 41 Look at these expressions. How do you think the underlined vowel sounds are pronounced? Then listen and check. Which two are NOT long vowel sounds?

1 to my am<u>a</u>zement
2 to my rel<u>ie</u>f
3 to my surpr<u>i</u>se
4 to my h<u>o</u>rror
5 to my dism<u>a</u>y
6 to my del<u>i</u>ght
7 to my frustr<u>a</u>tion
8 to my emb<u>a</u>rrassment

7 Work in pairs You are going to develop a story. Follow these steps.

- Look at the main elements of the story.
- Discuss what extra details could be added and how you can link the ideas and events.
- When you have finished, work with a new partner and retell your stories.

1	Issue that the story highlights	When abroad, you can forget you are not at home and be surprised by something different
2	The speaker's background and setting for the story	Newly-wed couple, Theo and Eleni, on holiday in Cyprus; walking in the mountains
3	Main events	Long walk, stop at village café, look out at view, Theo feels Eleni's hand on his, looks down, not her hand but a huge insect
4	The speaker's conclusion	Eleni still laughs

8 Work in small groups. Tell a story of your own using the same structure as in Exercise 7.

my life ▶ HOW YOU TRAVEL ▶ A MYSTERY TOUR ▶ KNOWING PLACES ▶ **TELLING AN ANECDOTE** ▶ A REVIEW

writing a review • writing skill using descriptive words

Unit 5 The magic of travel

5e Book of the month

Writing a review

1 Work in pairs. Which of these ways of choosing a book to read or film to watch is most reliable or useful? Why? Discuss your answers.

   a personal recommendation
   b a book/film review in the press
   c the blurb on the back cover or a film trailer
   d choosing a book that has been made into a film or vice versa

2 Read the book review. What is the reviewer's opinion of the book? Explain why.

Book of the month

THE BRIDGE OF SAN LUIS REY
by Thornton Wilder

In 1714 a rope suspension bridge in Peru snaps and the five people on the bridge fall to their deaths. By chance Brother Juniper, a Franciscan monk, witnesses this tragedy. He is not only troubled by what he has seen but also troubled by why this should have happened. Why at this precise moment? Why these five people? Accordingly, he sets out to find out something about the lives of each person and so to make sense of the tragedy.

This short novel (only 124 pages long) is a beautiful reflection on the subject of destiny. It is not a true story, but some of the characters are based on real people. Written in elegant prose, each chapter describes the life of one of the five people on the bridge: from the aristocratic Marquesa de Montemayor, who longs to be back in her native Spain to the wise Uncle Pio, whose lifelong ambition to make a star of a young actress is in the end frustrated. Our interest is not kept alive by the mystery of their deaths, but by the compelling characters that Wilder has drawn so vividly: each eccentric in their own way, and each very human in their virtues and in their faults.

I cannot recommend this thought-provoking book highly enough.

3 Read the review again and answer the questions.
   1 What type of book is it?
   2 What is the main theme?
   3 What tense is used to describe the plot?
   4 What words describe the style of writing in the book?

4 Look at the different ways (a–e) to begin a book review. Which way does the reviewer use in the review in Exercise 2?

   a give your opinion about the book directly
   b talk about the writer's background
   c describe the opening of the story
   d give a short summary of the whole story
   e discuss the topic of the book

5 Writing skill using descriptive words

a Underline the adjectives and adverbs in paragraphs 2 and 3 of the review. What does each describe? Which two are compound adjectives?

b Complete these compound adjectives.

| breaking | fetched | going | moving | packed |
| provoking | willed | written | | |

   1 thought-_____ (book)
   2 far-_____ (plot)
   3 heavy-_____ (book)
   4 well-_____ (book)
   5 action-_____ (adventure)
   6 heart-_____ (ending)
   7 fast-_____ (plot)
   8 strong-_____ (character)

c Match the compound adjectives from Exercise 5b with their opposites below.

convincing	easy-to-read	happy	indecisive
poorly written	slow-moving	uneventful	
uninspiring			

6 Write a review of a novel you have read or a film you have seen (approx 200 words). Follow this plan.

   • Describe the setting and give a brief summary of the plot.
   • Say what the theme of the book/film is.
   • Describe the style of writing/filmmaking.
   • Give your opinion or recommendation.

7 Exchange reviews with your partner. Use these questions to check your reviews.

   • Is the review organized into clear paragraphs?
   • Does it NOT reveal the whole story?
   • Are you persuaded by the recommendation?

my life ▶ HOW YOU TRAVEL ▶ A MYSTERY TOUR ▶ KNOWING PLACES ▶ TELLING AN ANECDOTE
▶ A REVIEW

5f On the road: Andrew McCarthy

Walkers on the Camino de Santiago, Spain

Before you watch

1 Look at the photo and answer the questions.

1. Where is this place?
2. What kind of trip do you think these travellers are on?

2 Key vocabulary

a Read the sentences. The colloquial expressions in bold are used in the video. Guess the meaning of the words.

1. I just **sort of went** … 'that's **kind of weird**'.
2. I read your book. It was **so cool**.
3. And he **was like**: 'You read my book?'
4. I called him **pretty much** every day.
5. … **truth be told**, I was a gold-card traveller.

b Match the words in bold in Exercise 2a with these definitions.

a	thought to myself	d	said
b	almost	e	really good
c	rather strange	f	to be honest

While you watch

3 5.1 You are going to watch an interview with travel writer Andrew McCarthy. Watch the video and answer the questions.

1. What was the trip that changed Andrew McCarthy's life?
2. In what way did it change him?

4 5.1 Work in pairs. Watch the first part of the interview (0.00 to 2.09) again, where McCarthy describes how he became interested in this trip. Look at the words (a–e) and note why they are significant in the story. Then, with your partner, reconstruct the story.

a. a bookstore
b. a plane
c. the internet
d. Harper's magazine
e. home phone number

5 5.1 Watch the second part of the interview (2.10 to 3.10) again and answer the questions.

1. What adjectives does McCarthy use to describe:
   a. this travel experience?
   b. his feelings while on the trip?
   c. what the experience was not?
   d. what he felt for the first time when travelling?
2. What was the reason for the trip that he didn't know at the time but now realizes?

6 5.1 Watch the third part of the interview (3.11 to the end) again and answer the questions.

1. What makes McCarthy unsure about going again with his children?
2. How long was the trip?
3. Where did he stay?
4. Complete this description of himself: 'a _____ pilgrim'. What does he mean?
5. How did he justify not being this kind of traveller on this occasion?

7 Complete the summary of Andrew McCarthy's story using one word in each space.

About eighteen years ago, I was in a ¹ _____ and I picked up a book by a guy who had ² _____ the Camino de Santiago in ³ _____ . It sat on my bookshelf for months and one day I ⁴ _____ it when I was looking for something to read on the plane. And having read it, I decided I wanted to do that. There was no ⁵ _____ to research places in those days so I called the ⁶ _____ up and said, 'Hey, I read your book,' and I asked him questions about how to go about doing this trip.

I went to Spain for a month and I had a ⁷ _____ experience. I felt ⁸ _____ and frightened but then something happened that ⁹ _____ my life. And for the first time I felt ¹⁰ _____ in the world. I stayed in little pilgrim ¹¹ _____ and to be truthful it wasn't very comfortable, so I sometimes stayed in *pensiones* instead and I justified it by saying that this is the way to meet the ¹² _____ .

After you watch

8 Vocabulary in context

a 5.2 Watch the clips from the video. Choose the correct meaning of the words and phrases.

b Complete these sentences in your own words. Then compare your sentences with a partner.

1. Often for lunch I just grab …
2. Sometimes I feel like I can't take … anymore
3. I didn't mind … . It was just one of those things.

9 Work in small groups. Discuss the questions.

1. What things do you think made Andrew McCarthy uncertain about travelling alone?
2. What do you think the event was that changed this (when he said 'then something happened and I had, sort of, one of those experiences that you have')?
3. Make a list of five things that make people nervous about travelling abroad. Which things make *you* nervous? What could you do to overcome this feeling?

Unit 5 The magic of travel

67

UNIT 5 REVIEW AND MEMORY BOOSTER

Grammar

1 Read a travel writer's description of the Fiji islands in the South Pacific. Answer the questions.

1 In what ways is Fiji an exclusive destination? In what ways is it not?
2 Why does the writer suggest you might prefer to visit the main island?

Fiji is a collection of over a hundred islands in the South Pacific. Most are the image of what a perfect desert island should be like. So it's no surprise to find upmarket hotels catering for rich tourists and
5 honeymooners. I went there hoping to experience this paradise more simply and wondering if it was possible to do so on a limited budget.
I shouldn't have worried. The Fijian's experience of dealing with different types of tourists means they
10 have provided for this by offering less expensive youth hostel-style accommodation for backpackers like me in places like Yasawa. Here, hospitable locals will help you to feel part of their lives, inviting you to see their fishing villages – and even take you fishing
15 with them, if you want to.
But beautiful and relaxing though these islands are, the feeling of being a tourist remains. It's not an uncomfortable sensation, but if what you value is seeing the country's true way of life, then perhaps
20 you should visit the main island of Viti Levu. This is the cultural hub of Fiji, where most of the population live: it's here that you can experience real Fijian culture.

2 Look at the description again. What do these words refer to?

a most (line 2)   d Here (line 12)
b do so (line 7)   e want to (line 15)
c this (line 10)   f sensation (line 18)

3 **» MB** Find two emphatic structures in the third paragraph (with 'what' and 'it'). Rewrite them as non-emphatic structures.

I CAN	
use substitution to avoid repetition	☐
recognize emphasis to statements	☐

Vocabulary

4 Make repeated word pairs using the words in brackets. Then rewrite the underlined words using the repeated word pairs. Sometimes you need to change the verb. Then use the word pairs in your own sentences.

1 We met for the first time yesterday. (face)
2 We don't really agree on many issues. (eye)
3 He talked a lot about his new car. (on)
4 I'm just taking things as they come. (day)
5 Hard work and success go together. (hand)

5 Complete the words using the synonyms in brackets to help you.

1 It was a mag_____ experience. (wonderful)
2 We found a co_____ restaurant. (warm and comfortable)
3 The coast has been rui_____. (spoiled)
4 It's a very scenic sp_____. (location)
5 The buildings are very gr_____. (large and impressive)
6 I was wa_____ of travelling alone. (cautious)
7 The doorman was offi_____. (self-important)
8 We hea_____ for the mountains. (went towards)

6 **» MB** Use each of the words in Exercise 5 to describe a travel experience you have had.

I CAN	
use repeated word pairs	☐
describe places and journeys	☐

Real life

7 Match the words (1–8) with words (a–h) to make phrases for telling anecdotes.

1 It's a well-known fact   a ago …
2 Because   b luck ….
3 Well, a few years   c day …
4 By chance, I happened   d relief …
5 Just at that   e to …
6 So the following   f that …
7 By sheer   g of that …
8 To my   h moment …

8 **» MB** Use the phrases in Exercise 7 to make a story about finding something you wanted to buy, thinking you had missed your opportunity and then finding you could get it after all. Tell the story to your partner.

I CAN	
use expressions for telling an anecdote	☐

Unit 6 Body matters

FEATURES

70 Exercise around the world
Different exercise regimes

72 No pain, no gain
How to avoid sports injuries

74 The enigma of beauty
What is beauty and why is it important to us?

78 The art of parkour
A video about the history of free running

1 Work in pairs. Write a short caption to accompany the photo.

2 ▶ 42 Listen to a woman discussing health and exercise with her friend, Rashmi, who is a doctor. What does Rashmi say about the following?
   1 intensive exercise versus gentle exercise
   2 the kinds of exercise that she does

3 ▶ 42 Look at the expressions to do with exercise and health. Four of the expressions need a preposition to complete them. Write in the prepositions. Then listen and check your answers.

   1 keep _____ shape
   2 take _____ exercise
   3 go _____ a walk/run/ride
   4 watch _____ your weight
   5 go _____ a diet
   6 stay _____ fit
   7 work _____ at the gym
   8 stretch _____ your legs
   9 keep _____ active

4 Work in groups. Ask each other questions about your fitness. Use the expressions in Exercise 3.

   A: What do you do to stay fit?
   B: I walk a lot and I go swimming a couple of times a week.
   C: Don't you find swimming boring?
   B: Just doing lengths is a bit dull, but it keeps me in reasonable shape.

my life ▶ EXERCISE TRENDS ▶ DESCRIBING AN INJURY ▶ DOES BEAUTY SELL? ▶ DISCUSSING PROPOSALS ▶ A FORMAL REPORT

reading exercise regimes • wordbuilding compound words • grammar phrasal verbs • speaking exercise trends

6a Exercise around the world

Reading

1 Look at the quotation by swimmer David Walters. What point was he making about exercise? Do you have any similar experiences?

"An hour of basketball feels like fifteen minutes. An hour on a treadmill feels like a weekend in traffic school."

David Walters, professional swimmer

2 Read the sentences (1–6). Then quickly read the article. Match the sentences with the exercise routine it describes: Radio Taiso (RT), swogging (S) or yoga (Y).

1 It's a fashionable form of exercise.
2 It benefits the mind and the body.
3 It doesn't need a lot of effort or practice.
4 Your body feels as if it is under attack.
5 People have been doing this form of exercise for centuries.
6 It's an enjoyable way to exercise.

3 Work in pairs. Write a suitable heading for each paragraph. Then discuss whether any of these forms of exercise appeal to you. Give reasons.

Wordbuilding compound words

▶ **WORDBUILDING compound words**

We form certain nouns and adjectives using verb/noun/adjective + preposition. The combination can be a whole word or a hyphenated word.
breakdown, follow-up

For further practice, see Workbook page 151.

4 Look at the wordbuilding box. Find one similar compound adjective and compound noun in the article.

EXERCISE AROUND THE WORLD ▶ 43

Here are a few of our readers' experiences.

KEVIN

Not many people outside Japan have come across Radio Taiso. Each day at 6.30 in the morning you hear this tinkly piano sound coming from the radio and everywhere people start doing callisthenics – gentle warm-up exercises – to get ready for the day ahead. They're group exercises that everyone can join in with – at home, in the park. The group principle is a very Japanese thing. People say the idea was copied from US factories in the 1920s. It's fantastic, because it's good fun and it's not too strenuous: they're simple movements that anyone can do, old or young. Also, they get the brain working as well as the body.

JO

I do something called 'swogging': a mixture of swimming and jogging. The inspiration came from a book about people in the Caucasus mountains, who often live to well over a hundred and remain mentally and physically fit. The book puts this down to their practice of walking down steep slopes to swim in cold mountain streams – something they've been doing for generations. Then they dry off and climb back up the mountain. The idea of freezing cold water might put a lot of people off, but it's scientifically proven to help your circulation and boost your immune system, because it triggers your body's self-defence mechanisms. I do the same thing in North Wales where I live, but I jog two miles to a lake. It's very exhilarating, but I've a little way to go before I get to 100!

NICKY

I went on a group yoga retreat last year in Tamil Nadu. To an outside observer, yoga doesn't look demanding – just slow stretching and holding certain positions. Yoga practitioners came up with their own version of the saying 'Don't just sit there, do something' which is 'Don't just do something, sit there'. But actually, it's a very good workout. Like a lot of eastern exercise, it offers a more holistic approach to health by combining bodily fitness with mental well-being. The idea is to concentrate on your breathing to make movement easier and reduce tension. Although it started out in India, only a relatively small proportion of the population still practise yoga seriously. In the West, it's an increasingly trendy form of exercise, but Indian traditionalists say that the versions practised by many Westerners are far removed from the original form.

5 Complete the phrases with these compound words. Then try to put each word in a sentence.

| backup   break-in   drive-through   far-off |
| stop-off |

1 a _____ of computer files
2 a _____ on the way to Australia
3 a house _____
4 a _____ land
5 a _____ restaurant

Grammar phrasal verbs

6 Look at these two verb + preposition(s) combinations (a–b) from the article. Which is a phrasal verb? Which isn't? Give reasons.

  a come across
  b coming from

> **PHRASAL VERBS**
>
> 1 **Intransitive phrasal verbs**
>   It **started out** in India.
>
> 2 **Separable phrasal verbs**
>   The idea of freezing cold water might **put** a lot of people **off**.
>   The idea of freezing cold water might **put off** a lot of people.
>   The idea of freezing cold water might **put** them **off**.
>
> 3 **Inseparable phrasal verbs**
>   Not many people have **come across** Radio Taiso.
>   Not many people have **come across** it.
>
> 4 **Three-part phrasal verbs**
>   Yoga practitioners **came up with** their own version.
>   Yoga practitioners **came up with** it.
>
> 5 **Three-part phrasal verbs with two objects**
>   The book **puts** this fact **down to** their practice of walking …
>   The book **puts** this **down to** their practice of walking …
>
> For further information and practice, see page 94.

7 Look at the grammar box. Notice the position of the noun and pronoun objects for each type of phrasal verb. When do we have to put the object between the verb and the preposition?

8 Read the sentences. Identify the words that make up the phrasal verbs in both options (a and b). Then say whether the position of the object(s) is correct or not. Sometimes both options are correct.

1 a When did you set up the company?
  b When did you set the company up?
2 a I'll catch you up with in a moment.
  b I'll catch up with you in a moment.
3 a I think you should definitely go for the job.
  b I think you should definitely go the job for.
4 a A lot of children look up to sport stars.
  b A lot of children look up sport stars to.
5 a I'd like to take up on you your offer.
  b I'd like to take you up on your offer.

9 Read the description of other exercise routines. What do the phrasal verbs in bold mean? Then put the objects of the phrasal verbs in the correct position.

Sickness as a child left Joseph Pilates, born in Germany in 1880, frail and weak. To ¹ **get over** (this), he developed exercises to build core muscle strength. Some of his early students then opened studios using his methods, ² **setting up** (them) in various cities. Pilates is now practised by millions all over the world.

The idea for Zumba **came about** by accident in the 1990s. Alberto Perez ³ **hit on** (it) when he was taking an aerobics class in his native Colombia. Having forgotten his usual music for the class, he ⁴ **fell back on** (some Salsa dance music) he had with him. Zumba, a routine combining aerobics with Latin dance moves, was born. Since then it has **taken off** and become an international exercise craze.

Most people think Tai Chi is a form of meditation. In fact, it's an old Chinese martial art based on the idea of ⁵ **getting out of** (dangerous situations) by turning an attacker's force against him. The most common form of Tai Chi today is a routine of slow movements. You often see people ⁶ **trying out** (them) in parks and public spaces.

10 Put the words in the correct order to make sentences using phrasal verbs.

1 I'm thinking / of / up / Pilates / taking
2 I hurt my back playing tennis. It took / it / me / over / ages / to get
3 At school we had to exercise twice a week. We / of / it / get / couldn't / out
4 The doctor / out / some tests / is going / to carry / on my knee
5 How / come / that idea / with / did you / up ?
6 She / hard work / puts / to / down / her success
7 Playing hockey / me / takes / back / my childhood / to

Speaking my life

11 Work in pairs. Read the questionnaire and check you know the meanings of the phrasal verbs. Interview your partner using the questionnaire.

> **1** How much time do you set aside for exercise each week?
> **2** What kind of exercise do you go in for mainly?
> **3** Have you taken up any new forms of exercise in the last twelve months?
> **4** Do you keep up with trends in exercise routines?
> **5** Do you prefer to exercise alone or to join in with others?
> **6** What puts you off exercising more?

12 Compare your findings with another pair. What conclusions can you draw about attitudes to exercise?

vocabulary injuries • listening sports injuries • idioms health • grammar verb patterns • pronunciation stress in two-syllable verbs • speaking describing an injury

6b No pain, no gain

Ultrarunner on the 161 km *Ultra-Trail du Mont-Blanc* annual race, France

Vocabulary injuries

1 Match verbs and nouns from each box to make collocations about typical injuries. There is sometimes more than one possible answer. Then with a partner mime each injury to explain its meaning.

graze your knee

Verbs		Nouns	
break	bruise	your ankle	your arm
bump	chip	your back	your head
graze	lose	your knee	a muscle
pull	sprain	your ribs	your toe
strain	stub	your tooth	your voice

2 Answer the questions. Use the collocations from Exercise 1.
 1 What injuries do you think the runner in the photo risks?
 2 Which injuries in general are:
  a the most common?
  b the most painful?

Listening

3 ▶ 44 Listen to an interview with ultrarunner Ben Newborn about sports injuries. Answer the questions.
 1 How does Ben define ultrarunning?
 2 What was his main concern about doing the Ultra-Trail du Mont Blanc?
 3 What mistake do many sports people make?
 4 How does Ben avoid getting sports injuries?

4 ▶ 44 Complete the descriptions of injuries and problems that Ben talks about. Then listen to the interview again and check your answers.
 1 He had to overcome _____ and the things that make you feel _____ .
 2 A lot of sports people try to ignore a small muscle _____ or _____ in a joint.
 3 Minor problems can develop into more _____ injuries.
 4 His exercises have prevented him from getting ankle _____ , lower _____ pain and runner's _____ .

Idioms health

5 Work in pairs. The ultrarunner used this idiom in the interview. What do you think it means?

"I'm not talking about when they're **in a** really **bad way**"

6 ▶ 45 Complete the idioms using these prepositions. Then listen and check your answers. Discuss the meanings of the idioms with your partner.

| down | in | off | on | out | under | up |

 1 A: I heard Sarah came off her bicycle. Is she *in* **a bad way**?
  B: Luckily she didn't break anything; she was pretty **shaken** _____ though.
 2 A: Is it true that Jack nearly cut his finger off?
  B: Yes, he practically **passed** _____ when he saw what he'd done … but he's _____ **the mend** now, I think.
 3 A: You look a bit _____ **colour**. Are you feeling _____ **the weather**?
  B: No, I'm not ill. I'm just **run** _____ from working too much.

Grammar verb patterns

> **VERB PATTERNS**
>
> **verb + to + infinitive**
> They **tend to take** some painkillers.
>
> **verb + object + to + infinitive**
> A race which **requires runners to run** 161 kilometres ...
>
> **verb (+ object) + infinitive**
> ... the things that can **make you feel** sick ...
>
> **verb + -ing**
> It could **mean running** 100 kilometres in a single day ...
>
> **verb + preposition + -ing**
> Didn't you **worry about doing** yourself real damage?
>
> **verb + object + preposition + -ing**
> ... that shouldn't **discourage us from doing** exercise.
>
> For further information and practice, see page 94.

7 Look at the grammar box. Try to remember what verb patterns these verbs (1–10) take. Then check your answers in the audioscript on page 100 (track 44).

1. afford
2. avoid
3. carry on
4. involve
5. let
6. prevent
7. succeed
8. try
9. urge
10. warn

8 Pronunciation stress in two-syllable verbs

a Look at these verbs. Which syllable is stressed in each of these verbs?

| afford | attempt | avoid | complain | convince |
| insist | involve | prevent | rely | succeed |

b ▶ 46 Listen and check your answers. Then practise saying the words again.

9 Complete the sentences about sports injuries using the correct verb patterns. You need to add prepositions in some of the sentences.

1. These people often complain _____ (suffer) 'pink eye' from the chlorine in the water. They also tend _____ (be) susceptible to shoulder problems.
2. These people risk _____ (damage) the joints in their legs. But they can avoid _____ (get) long-term injuries by wearing the right shoes.
3. Since their sport relies so heavily _____ (use) the arm, these people tend _____ (have) problems with their elbow and wrist.
4. Because these people pull muscles so often, they are encouraged _____ (warm up) properly before a match to prevent such injuries _____ (occur).

5. Neck pain is common among these people. Because they insist _____ (bend) low over the handlebars, they are forced _____ (raise) their heads to see ahead.

10 Which of these sportspeople are being referred to in each sentence in Exercise 9? Discuss with your partner.

| cyclists | footballers | runners | swimmers |
| tennis players |

11 Often verbs that express a similar idea are followed by the same verb pattern. Look at the sentences (1–8). Replace the verbs in bold with these verbs without changing the verb pattern.

| appear | blame | convince | decide | expect |
| mean | postpone | stop |

1. We can't **prevent** people from having accidents.
2. The organizers were **criticized** for not having paid enough attention to track safety.
3. If the job **involves** straining my back in any way, I'm afraid I can't risk it.
4. I've **made up my mind** to get fit.
5. She **seemed** to pull a muscle as she stretched to reach the ball.
6. Don't **delay** going to the doctor. If you do, it'll take longer to recover from the injury.
7. I **hope** to be playing again in a few weeks.
8. The doctor **persuaded** him to take it easy for a while.

12 Complete this short description. Use the correct verb pattern of the verbs in brackets.

I remember ¹_____ (have) to play rugby at school when I was fourteen or fifteen. At that age, kids seem ²_____ (develop) at very different rates and so sometimes they'd ask you ³_____ (play) a match against people twice your size. One time I attempted ⁴_____ (tackle) a huge boy running with the ball. His knee struck me in the face, making me ⁵_____ (fall) back and I hit my head on the ground and passed out. The sports teacher never apologized ⁶_____ (for / put) me in that situation, so the next time he asked me ⁷_____ (play) for the team, I refused ⁸_____ (do) it!

Speaking my life

13 Work in pairs. Choose one of the following incidents and describe what happened. Try to use at least two verb patterns in your answer.

1. a time when you or a friend were injured doing a sport or in some other situation
2. a time when you or a friend narrowly escaped being injured

my life ▶ EXERCISE TRENDS ▶ DESCRIBING AN INJURY ▶ DOES BEAUTY SELL? ▶ DISCUSSING PROPOSALS ▶ A FORMAL REPORT

reading what is beauty? • critical thinking author influence • word focus *face* • speaking does beauty sell?

6c The enigma of beauty

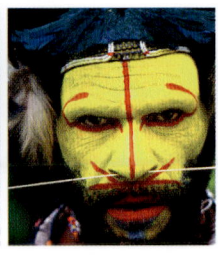

Reading

1 Work in groups. Look at the photos. Which faces do you find beautiful or handsome? Can you explain why? How many do you agree on? Discuss your findings.

2 Read the sentences. Do you think each one is true? Then read the article and find out the author's views.

 1 There are no universally agreed characteristics of human beauty.
 2 Perceptions of a person's beauty can be connected to their social position.
 3 Your character can have an influence on whether people think you are beautiful or not.
 4 The search for beauty is superficial and vain.

3 Read the article again. Find the phrases from the article. Choose the best meaning (a or b).

 1 beauty is **in the eye of the beholder** (para 2)
    a subjective
    b related to how someone looks at you
 2 a **glowing complexion** (para 2)
    a healthy skin   b smiling face
 3 a **symbol of status** (para 4)
    a a sign of great wealth
    b a sign of a high social position
 4 has **preoccupied** (para 4)
    a dominated the thoughts of   b worried
 5 a **shallow quest** (para 5)
    a a pointless search   b a trivial search
 6 **fussed over** (para 6)
    a made to feel special b made to feel comfortable

Critical thinking author influence

4 Look at these topics from the article. How did you personally feel about each one? Read the article again and discuss with a partner.

 1 the experience of the women wanting to be models
 2 the practice of extending your neck using copper coils
 3 the way that our idea of an ideal body shape has changed
 4 the fact that the author's grandmother still cared about her looks at 100 years old

5 What was the author's opinion about the topics (1–5) in Exercise 4? Did this influence your reaction to any of them? How?

Word focus *face*

6 Find two expressions with *face* in the article with these meanings:

 a unhappy expressions (para 1)
 b to be honest (para 6)

7 Work in pairs. Look at the expressions with *face* in these sentences and explain the meaning of each phrase.

 1 He couldn't admit he was wrong. He didn't want to **lose face** in front of the boss.
 2 She was disappointed not to be picked for the team, but she **put a brave face on** it.
 3 I **took** her offer of help **at face value**. I don't think she had any hidden motive.
 4 The actors had trouble **keeping a straight face** when Jon fell off the stage.
 5 You should tell her that you scratched her car, because sooner or later you will have to **face the music**.
 6 **On the face of it,** it seems like a good idea, but I wouldn't rush into making a decision.

8 Make two sentences of your own using expressions with *face* from Exercises 6 and 7.

Speaking my life

9 Work in pairs. You are going to design an advertising campaign. Read your role cards and prepare ideas. Then act out the meeting to agree on the advertisement you will run.

Student A: Turn to page 81.

Student B: Turn to page 82.

10 Discuss which view is closest to your own. Give reasons.

The ENIGMA of BEAUTY

▶ **47**

Sheli Jeffry is searching for beauty. As a scout for Ford, one of the world's top model agencies, Jeffry scans up to 200 young women every Thursday afternoon. They queue up and one by one the line shrinks. Tears roll and there are long faces as the conclusion 'You're not what we're looking for right now' puts an end to the conversation – and to hope. Confronted with this, one poor hopeful, Rebecca from Rhode Island, asks: 'What are you looking for? Can you tell me exactly?' Jeffry simply replies, 'It's hard to say. I'll know it when I see it.'

Define beauty? Some say you might as well analyse a soap bubble; that beauty is only in the eye of the beholder. Yet it does seem that across different cultures we can agree on certain points. Psychologists have proven this by testing the attractiveness of different faces on children. Symmetry is one characteristic that wins general approval; averageness is another: we seem to prefer features that are not extreme. Things that suggest strength and good health – a glowing complexion and full lips in women, a strong jaw in men – are also universal qualities. Scientists say that this is the true definition of beauty, because ultimately we are influenced not by aesthetic but by biological considerations: the need to produce healthy children.

At the same time, we can also observe cultural differences in how beauty is defined. The women of the Padaung tribe in Myanmar put copper coils around their necks to extend them because in their culture, very long necks are considered beautiful. In cultures where people's skin is of a dark complexion, it is often seen as desirable to have a fair skin. Conversely, in the northern hemisphere among the naturally fair-skinned, people want a tanned skin.

Perceptions of beauty also change over time. Historically, in northern Europe, a tanned skin belonged to those who were forced to work outside – agricultural workers or other poorer members of society – and so a white skin was a symbol of status and beauty. But in the late 20th century, a tan reflected status of a different kind: those that could afford beach holidays in the Mediterranean or the Caribbean. Our idea of the perfect body shape is also different from 200 years ago. In almost all cultures a little fat was formerly seen as a positive trait, a sign of wealth and well-being. Nowadays, a very different image stares out at us from the pages of fashion magazines: that of a long-limbed, impossibly slim figure. Whatever the perception of ideal beauty may be, the search for it has preoccupied people of all cultures for centuries, from ancient Egypt to modern China.

Is it a shallow quest? We say that beauty is only skin deep; that personality and charm contribute more to attractiveness than superficial beauty. Certainly, as we grow older, the more generous our definition of beauty seems to become. Experience teaches us to look for the beauty within, rather than what is on the outside.

But let's face it, most of us still care how we look. Until she was a hundred years old, my grandmother had a regular appointment at the beauty salon down the street. A month before she died, I took her there in my car. I stayed and watched as she was greeted and fussed over by the hairdresser and manicurist. Afterwards, I drove her back to the nursing home. She admired her bright red nails every few minutes, patted her cloud of curls and radiated happiness. She is not alone in getting satisfaction from looking nice. It seems the quest for beauty goes deeper than vanity – maybe it fulfils a deep need in all of us.

real life discussing proposals • speaking skill proposing and conceding a point • pronunciation toning down negative statements

6d A bold initiative

Real life discussing proposals

1 Work in pairs. Read about the different methods governments around the world use to encourage their populations to keep fit and healthy. Answer the questions.

1 What do you think are the pros and cons of each method?
2 Which initiative would work best, do you think? Why?
3 Are there any similar initiatives in your country?

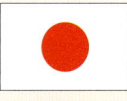

1 JAPAN: Broadcast a daily exercise routine on national radio each day.

2 WASHINGTON STATE, USA: Fast-food chains must publish the number of calories in each item on the menu.

3 QATAR: Get companies to install gyms at work so workers can exercise before or after work or during breaks.

4 UK: Run public health campaigns promoting exercise activities that are quick and easy to do.

5 SOUTH KOREA: Make good grades in Physical Education a qualification for university entrance.

6 PHILIPPINES: Promote sports like karate in school that combine exercise with self-defence skills.

2 ▶48 Listen to a discussion at a large insurance company about ideas to promote health and fitness among their employees. Answer the questions.

1 Why is promoting health and fitness among their employees important to the company?
2 What different ideas are proposed? Are any of them similar to the ideas in Exercise 1?
3 Which idea got approval from another member of the group? Which idea was rejected?

3 Speaking skill proposing and conceding a point

▶48 Look at the expressions for proposing and conceding a point. Then listen to the discussion again and say which phrases are used to propose and concede these points.

1 Spending money on a workplace gym – may not be a budget for this
2 Dance classes – people do these things in their free time
3 Group exercises in the morning – not an original idea
4 Give people incentives to do things on their own – don't know the details

▶ **PROPOSING and CONCEDING A POINT**

Proposing points
One possibility is / would be to …
Another alternative/idea is / might be …
You could …
It would be better to …
What about …?

Conceding points
Having said that, …
I realize/admit that …
Admittedly, …
I know that isn't really …
It's not (a) particularly … , I admit. / I'll grant you.
I haven't thought it through exactly, but …

4 Pronunciation toning down negative statements

a ▶49 Listen to these statements where an adverb is used to tone down (reduce the impact of) a negative statement. Underline the words most strongly stressed in each sentence.

1 It's not a particularly original idea.
2 It wouldn't be so easy to monitor …
3 I know that isn't really the intention …

b ▶50 Work in pairs. Practise saying these sentences where a negative sentiment has been toned down. Then listen and compare your pronunciation.
1 I know it's not a very practical solution.
2 It wouldn't be so simple to convince people.
3 I'm not entirely confident about the result.

5 Work in groups. Each person should think of another idea to promote the health and well-being of company employees. Then present and discuss your ideas. Concede any points against your proposal.

my life ▶ EXERCISE TRENDS ▶ DESCRIBING AN INJURY ▶ DOES BEAUTY SELL? ▶ DISCUSSING PROPOSALS ▶ A FORMAL REPORT

writing a formal report • writing skill avoiding repetition Unit 6 Body matters

6e A controversial plan

Writing a formal report

1 Read the report about a public health issue and look at the questions. Underline the parts of the report that answer the questions.

1 What is the aim of the report?
2 What is the main finding?
3 What action is proposed?

2 Read the description of reports in general. Which of the features in bold appear in the report in Exercise 1?

> Formal reports present the **findings** of an investigation and make **recommendations** based on these findings. The reader should be able to scan a report quickly for key information, so **bullet points**, **subheadings**, and **short paragraphs** are all useful. Reports present **objective facts**, often using **passive verb forms**, but some internal reports can also offer more **subjective comments**.

3 Find formal phrases in the report that mean the following:

1 because (para 2)
2 if you follow (para 2)
3 so (para 3)
4 concerning (para 3)
5 in general (para 4)
6 in view of this (para 4)
7 on the other hand (para 4)

4 **Writing skill** avoiding repetition

a When writing reports, you often have to find ways of repeating the same idea using different words. Find these words (1–6) and then find the different ways that the writer used to describe these things.

1 the interviewees (two ways)
   those questioned
2 took the … view (that)
3 assistance
4 quit smoking (two ways)
5 insurance company
6 period

INTRODUCTION

This report examines a proposal to make smokers pay higher health insurance premiums. Over 100 people of different ages and social backgrounds were interviewed about the proposal, which was based on a straightforward evaluation of risk: that if a person smokes, their chances of becoming ill increase.

RESULTS

30% of the interviewees objected to the proposal on the grounds that it was discriminatory. One common argument was that, according to this principle, higher premiums should also be paid by people who overeat.

18% of those questioned agreed that the habit of smoking was often beyond an individual's control. However, 55% took the opposite view: that smokers make a personal choice to smoke and therefore should pay for the consequences. With regard to assistance to quit smoking, 74% of respondents believed free help should be given to smokers.

RECOMMENDATION

Overall, interviewees were in favour of some change to insurance companies' current practice of treating smokers and non-smokers similarly. Accordingly, we recommend that a pilot scheme should be set up where smokers are given free help by their insurer to stop smoking over a six-month period. During this time, they will be offered various solutions to give up. If they succeed, they will be rewarded with a discount of 5% on their insurance premiums for as long as they remain non-smokers. Conversely, if they fail, their insurance premiums will rise by 20%.

---

b Replace the words in bold in these sentences to avoid repetition.

1 This report examines the results of a survey on health, describing the main **results** and making some recommendations.
2 260 members of staff were asked for their views on the proposal and they responded with a range of **views**.
3 87% agreed that more exercise would be good for their physical health, while 54% said it would **be good for** their mental health.
4 We recommend that a fact-finding team should be set up. We also **recommend** that the leader of this **team** is someone from outside the company.

5 Write a short report on a survey of employees about how a company can help to improve employees' health. Use your own ideas or the ideas you discussed in Exercise 5 on page 76. Write 200–250 words.

6 Exchange reports with your partner. Use these questions to check your reports.

- Have they presented their aims, findings and recommendations?
- Does the report use formal language, including passive forms?
- Is the report divided into clear sections?
- Is the overall result a clear, concise and easy-to-read report?

---

my life ▶ EXERCISE TRENDS ▶ DESCRIBING AN INJURY ▶ DOES BEAUTY SELL? ▶ DISCUSSING PROPOSALS
▶ A FORMAL REPORT

6f The art of parkour

A parkour athlete, Vienna, Austria

Unit 6 **Body matters**

Before you watch

1 Work in pairs. Look at the categories (a–e). Try to name a different sport for each category. Then compare your ideas with the rest of the class.

A sport that is:
a very dangerous
b creative
c very expensive
d urban / played in the street
e growing in popularity

2 Look at the photo and the caption on page 78. What does this sport involve? Which of the categories in Exercise 1 does it fall into, do you think?

3 Key vocabulary

a Read the sentences. The words in bold are used in the video. Guess the meaning of the words.

1 The documentary contains some **footage** of the two climbers reaching the summit.
2 He went into the army when he was eighteen. He had to – it was the official **draft** age.
3 I think some birds have made a nest on the **ledge** above my window.
4 He didn't jump from the bridge in the film. It was done by a **stuntman**.
5 We'd like to get more students involved in university decisions, but up to now they've shown complete **apathy**.

b Match the words in bold in Exercise 3a with these definitions.

a a narrow shelf or surface, usually made of stone or rock
b someone who does dangerous things in place of the actor in a film
c an official order to serve time in the armed forces
d lack of interest or concern
e (short) film of a particular event

While you watch

4 **6.1** Work in pairs. Answer the questions. Then watch the video and compare your answers.

1 What is parkour?
2 Who does parkour and why do they do it?
3 What kind of moves do parkour artists do?
4 Can you make a career out of parkour, do you think?

5 **6.1** Watch the first part of the video (0.00 to 0.50) again. Complete the facts about the footage of John Ciampa.

1 Date of film:
2 His job:
3 His age:
4 His abilities:

6 **6.1** Look at the questions. Then watch the second part of the video (0.51 to 1.26) again. Discuss the answers with your partner.

1 Where and when did the modern craze for parkour start?
2 What is a better description than 'sport' for parkour, according to the speaker?
3 What is the essence or fundamental principle of parkour?
4 Why has it been especially popular in places where opportunities are limited?

7 **6.1** Watch the last part of the video (from 1.27 to the end) again. Then complete this description.

These two young men from Khan Younis in Gaza both practise parkour. In this part of the world, for example, ^{1} _____ is over 40 per cent and 35 per cent live in poverty. But there is no sense of ^{2} _____ amongst the young: they are focused on staying ^{3} _____ and they like ^{4} _____ themselves.

Abed's mother feels ^{5} _____ of him, even though he has had injuries like a broken ^{6} _____. Injuries, like sprains, are common so it is important to learn how to ^{7} _____ without hurting yourself. Mohammed says it took time to ^{8} _____ people around him about the sport. But now they both feel a great sense of personal ^{9} _____ and hope that one day they might be asked to perform in a competition or a ^{10} _____.

After you watch

8 Vocabulary in context

a **6.2** Watch the clips from the video. Choose the correct meaning of the words and phrases.

b Complete these sentences in your own words. Then compare your sentences with a partner.

1 I don't think … will ever really catch on.
2 I have a friend who has an uncanny ability to …
3 Once I fell awkwardly when I was … and hurt my …

9 Work in groups. Discuss these questions and give reasons for your answers

1 Do you think parkour should become an official Olympic sport?
2 Do you think more sports should be just amateur sports, like parkour, and not professional sports?
3 Do you think street sports like parkour should be regulated (i.e. rules about where you are allowed to do it, what you are allowed to do, etc.)?
4 Would you like to try parkour yourself? Why? / Why not?

UNIT 6 REVIEW AND MEMORY BOOSTER

Grammar

1 Read the blog. Who in the world suffers from back pain? What can be done about it?

Back pain is an extremely common health problem, which affects eighty per cent of Americans at some time in their lives. It prevents people ¹_____ (work), causes people ²_____ (become) depressed and affects general wellbeing.
You could be forgiven ³_____ (think) that lower back pain is a result of our sedentary habits: working at computers, etc. But in fact, back pain is something that everyone around the world seems ⁴_____ (suffer) from, whether they spend their days ⁵_____ (sit) at a desk or ⁶_____ (work) in the fields.

Scientists believe that back pain is an inevitable result of being bipedal – standing up on two feet. So, unless you ⁷ *go in for* regular posture training or are not susceptible to it, you will suffer from back pain at some point.
What to do about it is another question. You can ⁸ *look into* exercise classes such as yoga or Pilates, which help to build core muscle strength, but these are mainly preventive. Most treatment for chronic pain consists of taking painkillers, either synthetic or natural, as in Madagascar, where Baobab tree bark is used. Another possibility is manipulation, but it can be months before the practitioner can ⁹ *turn around* the situation. It seems that for the time being, we will just have to ¹⁰ *put up with* back pain.

2 Complete the first part of the blog by putting the verbs (1–6) in the correct form: infinitive, *to* + infinitive, *-ing* form or preposition + *-ing* form.

3 Look at the phrasal verbs (7–10) in the blog. Find the noun objects of each phrasal verb and replace these with a pronoun. Think carefully about the position of the pronoun.

4 **» MB** Work in pairs. What kind of phrasal verbs are used in the blog: intransitive, separable, inseparable or three-part? Explain the difference.

I CAN

use correct verb patterns (verb + *-ing* or infinitive)

use different kinds of phrasal verbs

Vocabulary

5 Complete the sentences with the missing verbs. You have been given the first letter.

1 Shall we g_____ o_____ for a quick walk? I need to s_____ my legs.
2 How do you k_____ in such good shape? Do you t_____ a lot of exercise?
3 I think I p_____ a muscle when I was w_____ out at the gym.
4 I wasn't badly hurt. I just g_____ my knee and b_____ my ribs.
5 She only c_____ her tooth, but she was s_____ up by the experience.
6 I try to s_____ aside a couple of hours a week for exercise.

6 **» MB** Work in pairs. When did you last do these things? Describe what happened.

a passed out
b felt off colour
c stubbed your toe
d lost your voice
e went on a diet
f sprained your ankle

I CAN

talk about exercise, health and injuries

Real life

7 Look at the proposal for workplace gyms. Complete the proposal with these words.

| admittedly | alternative | having | grant | out |
| particularly | possibility | through | | |

Workplace gyms are not a ¹_____ original idea, I'll ²_____ you, but I think they could be very popular with our employees. I haven't thought ³_____ all the details but the basic idea is to get people exercising during the working day. ⁴_____, it's not a cheap option, but, ⁵_____ said that, there are ways to lessen the cost. One ⁶_____ would be to make employees pay a small contribution. Another ⁷_____ would be to open it to the public. I'm just thinking aloud here - I haven't worked it ⁸_____ exactly.

8 **» MB** Work in pairs. Look at these points. After each point make another point that concedes an argument against it.

1 It's always good to try out new food.
2 Team sports are great fun.
3 Walking is the best form of exercise.

I CAN

propose and concede points in a discussion

Communication activities

UNIT 1c Exercise 11, page 14
Group A
1 **misgiving** (n) /mɪsˈɡɪvɪŋ/ doubt or apprehension about something
2 **spurn** (v) /spɜːn/ reject
3 **zany** (adj) /ˈzeɪni/ eccentric and unconventional, even a little crazy

Example:
If the word was 'immortal', a true definition could be: '*Immortal* means living forever, never dying. So we say, for example, "the immortal words of Shakespeare" or "Shakespeare has achieved immortal fame".'
A false definition could be: '*Immortal* means behaving in a way which is not right. So we say, for example, "Earning that much money when others earn very little is immortal."'

UNIT 2a Exercise 1, page 22

SEA FACTS

1 **Over 70%** of the Earth's surface is covered by water.
2 About **50%** of the world's population live in coastal regions.
3 **90%** of the world's goods are transported by sea.
4 **90%** of the world's animals live in the sea.
5 The average consumption of fish per person per year is **20 kg**.
6 Fish is the main source of protein for **1 billion** people.
7 The average time someone can hold their breath underwater is **30–40 seconds**.

UNIT 2c Exercise 10, page 26

Quiz

How would you feel in the following situations? Read the questions and answer A, B or C for each one. Then look at the key on page 82 to find out what your comfort zone is. Discuss if you agree with the answers.

A comfortable and keen on the idea
B a little uncomfortable, but willing to try
C uncomfortable and reluctant to do it

1 At a Karaoke club, a friend forces you to go on stage to sing Frank Sinatra's 'My Way'.
2 You are asked to give a 45-minute talk about your organization to a group of 250 pre-university students next month.
3 A famous person you admire is sitting near you on a train reading a book. You would love to speak to them and get their autograph.
4 A friend, who is a cycling fanatic, has invited you to go on a cycling holiday with them in the mountains.
5 A group of your friends has organized an adventure weekend, involving canoeing in white water rapids, rock climbing and caving in underground caves.
6 You are asked if you would mind being filmed at work by a TV crew who are making a fly-on-the-wall documentary about your organization.
7 You are unexpectedly offered a promotion to a job with more pay, but also much more responsibility and less security (you will be judged by your results).
8 Your next-door neighbour's daughter practises the violin for two hours every evening and the sound is very distracting. You need to speak to them directly about it.

UNIT 4d Exercise 6, page 52
Student A
A typical coffee shop selling fresh coffee produces over two tonnes of waste coffee grounds each year. Your idea is to use these coffee grounds to grow mushrooms, which you can then sell to shops and supermarkets. Currently, cafés throw away the used coffee grounds into the general waste. By using them to grow mushrooms, you would be a) recycling the waste coffee and b) reducing the cost of the compost you need to grow your mushrooms.

UNIT 6c Exercise 9, page 74
Student A
You are a marketing manager. Your company has developed a face cream for women in their 40s. It moisturizes the skin, protects against the sun, and helps to prevent wrinkles forming.
Because women in their 40s are keen to remain looking young, you want the advertisements to feature a single young model in her 30s who is fair-skinned and very beautiful: a universally recognizable image of beauty. It will also encourage men to buy the product for their wives. Beauty sells, as far as you are concerned.

Communication activities

UNIT 1c Exercise 11, page 14

Group B
1 **howl** (v) /haʊl/ let out a long cry like a dog or wolf
2 **jaded** (adj) /ˈdʒeɪdɪd/ bored with something, lacking enthusiasm
3 **reprieve** (n) /rɪˈpriːv/ a delay in a punishment

Example:
If the word was 'immortal', a true definition could be: 'Immortal means living forever, never dying. So we say, for example, "the immortal words of Shakespeare" or "Shakespeare has achieved immortal fame".'
A false definition could be: 'Immortal means behaving in a way which is not right. So we say, for example, "Earning that much money when others earn very little is immortal."'

UNIT 3d Exercise 8, page 40

By Francesca Martelli: A children's carousel powered by wind and solar power. The carousel will have little carriages in the shape of historic cars made over the decades by the city's car manufacturer. Francesca hopes the project can be part-funded by the car manufacturer.

By Rana Suweilah: A giant LED screen mounted on a black granite wall (granite being the rock found in the nearby mountains). In front of the wall will be a large paved area, where people can skate or play games, with seating around it. The screen will show video footage of construction workers in the 1950s, building skyscrapers in the city centre.

UNIT 4d Exercise 6, page 52

Student B
Your idea is to make it easier for people to scrap their old cars. Currently, the owner has to pay a scrap metal dealer £100 to collect the old car from their house. You would offer to collect people's scrap cars for free. You will then a) try to recycle as many parts as possible before b) taking it to the scrap metal dealer to get money for the remaining metal or parts.

UNIT 2c Exercise 11, page 26

Answers to quiz

Mostly 'A's: You feel confident with new challenges and are happy to be in the spotlight. That's great, but be careful not to over-extend yourself.

Mostly 'B's: You are careful, but want to expand your comfort zone by doing things that challenge you.

Mostly 'C's: You are someone who likes to stay well within their comfort zone. That's OK, but remember that leaving your comfort zone now and then can be empowering.

UNIT 4d Exercise 6, page 52

Student C
It is very annoying to return home in the evening and find the postman has been unable to deliver a package because no one was at home. Your idea is to provide an evening redelivery service for parcels and big letters. Currently, if no one is at home, the package is returned to a depot on the outskirts of town, which people have to visit in person to collect their post. Using your system, people would pay an annual fee for you to collect these packages and redeliver them at a more convenient time.

UNIT 6c Exercise 9, page 74

Student B
You are a sales manager. Your company has developed a face cream for women in their 40s. It moisturizes the skin, protects against the sun, and helps to prevent wrinkles forming.
You think that women don't want to see an impossibly beautiful model in the advertisements, but women that they can identify with: that are average, with some wrinkles and blemishes, and that represent diverse ethnic backgrounds. You think you could even use members of the public in the advertisements.

82

GRAMMAR SUMMARY

UNITS 1–6

GRAMMAR SUMMARY UNIT 1

Time phrases

There are particular time words and phrases that we often use with each different tense.

Tense	Time phrases
present simple I *often read* books about history.	*often, never, every week/month/year, nowadays, generally*
present continuous I*'m currently working* in South America.	*now, at the moment, while, currently, this week/summer/year*
past simple I *saw* Jack *three days ago*.	*three days ago, a few years ago, last week, at the time, in (+ year), once, when*
past continuous I once visited Berlin. I *was living* in Germany *at the time*.	*while, at the time*
present perfect simple I'm quite fit because I*'ve been working* out a lot *recently*.	*just, recently, so far, in recent years, over the last two years, how long, for, since (2010 / I left school), already, yet, ever, never*
present perfect continuous I*'ve recently started* to learn to play the piano.	*how long, for, just, recently, since (2010 / I left school), for some time*
past perfect simple and continuous They asked me to dinner but I*'d already eaten*.	*already, before that / the 1990s, up to then, prior to the 1990s*
will, going to, present continuous (for future) *In the long term*, I believe the plans *will fail*.	*next week, in three days / in three days' time, soon, in the long term, from now on, on Friday*

Note that some time words and phrases can be used with more than one tense.
> I was four *when* Nelson Mandela was released from prison.
> The Prime Minister will make an announcement *when* she arrives back in the country.
> I lived in Mexico City *for* five years.
> I've been living in Mexico City *for* five years.

▶ Exercises 1, 2 and 3

The continuous aspect

We use the continuous aspect to describe actions that happen over a period of time. They are often temporary or incomplete, and in some cases are repeated. We don't normally use the continuous aspect with stative verbs (e.g. *belong*, *prefer* and *seem*).
> Does this jacket belong to you? (not *Is this jacket belonging to you?*)

We use the present continuous to describe:
- an action in progress at the time of speaking
  I*'m just finishing* some work – I'll call you back later.
- an action around the time of speaking
  Laura*'s looking* for a new job.
- a current trend
  More and more people *are doing* voluntary work.
- a situation which happens regularly and is irritating, especially with the adverb *always*
  My boss *is always asking* me to stay late after work.

We use the present perfect continuous to talk about:
- an action that started in the past and is still continuing
  I*'ve been waiting* here for over an hour.
- an action that was repeated in the past and continues to be repeated now
  We*'ve been going* to that theatre for over ten years.
- a continuous past action that has an effect on the present
  I'm hot because I*'ve been running*.

We use the past continuous to describe an action that was the background to another more important event in the past. The background action may continue after the more important event, or be interrupted by it.
> She *was working* as a teacher when her book was published.

We don't normally use the past continuous to describe repeated past actions. Use past simple, *used to* or *would*.
> When I was ten, I *used to play* football almost every day. (not *I was playing*)

We use the past perfect continuous to talk about:
- something that was in progress up to a point in the past
  She*'d been hoping* to move abroad for years when the offer came.
- an action that was repeated up to a point in the past
  We*'d been complaining* about the problem for days but nobody wanted to help us.

We use the future continuous to describe:
- something we expect to be happening at a particular time in the future
  This time next week, we*'ll be lying* on the beach!
- something we expect to be repeated around a particular time in the future
  I don't work on Thursday evenings any more, so I*'ll be coming* to football practice every week.

We also use the future continuous to make a guess or prediction about an action in progress now.
> Colin *will* probably *be driving* to work now.

▶ Exercises 4, 5 and 6

Exercises

1 Choose the correct time word or phrase(s) to complete the sentences. Sometimes two words or phrases are correct.

1. People *often / at the time / sometimes* like to read on trains and buses on their way to work.
2. My home town has completely changed *when / since / for* I was a little girl.
3. He's moving house *next month / soon / recently*.
4. Henry bought a flat when he was thirty-five. He'd been living with his parents *already / up to then / in the long term*.
5. The course is going to start late *last week / next week / before that*.
6. The two companies are *currently / recently / soon* trying to negotiate a deal.

2 Complete the sentences with the correct tense of the verbs in brackets. Use the time phrases to help.

1. So you're learning Japanese! How long _____ it? (you / study)
2. She _____ a new computer when the sales start in two days' time. (buy)
3. Finding a secure job _____ harder for young people in recent years. (become)
4. The film _____ already _____ when they arrived at the cinema. (start)
5. I _____ at the moment so I'll have to call you back. (drive)
6. She found somebody's wallet on the pavement while she _____ to work. (walk)

3 Complete the text with these words and phrases.

| currently | from now on | in the long term |
| nowadays | recently | up till then |

My son is ¹_____ doing a project at school about changes in the last seventy years. I couldn't answer his questions, so I suggested that he ask his grandparents. ²_____, my son had just been using the internet. Afterwards I started to think about it more. ³_____, we get most of our information from the internet, not from speaking to other people. ⁴_____, I've been doing some DIY at home and I always search the internet for instructions. We don't ask other people for advice as much as we used to. ⁵_____, I think we'll lose a lot of knowledge if we carry on like this. ⁶_____, I'm going to encourage my children to talk to their grandparents as much as possible.

4 Read the sentences. Then choose the correct explanation (a or b) for each one.

1. Joe's always calling me to talk about his girlfriend.
   a. I enjoy his phone calls.
   b. I find his phone calls annoying.
2. More and more young people are staying in education for longer.
   a. The situation described is changing.
   b. The situation described hasn't changed for a long time.
3. I didn't go to the cinema because I was studying.
   a. I was studying at one particular time.
   b. I was studying every day.
4. They've been living in Russia for six years.
   a. They still live in Russia.
   b. They don't live in Russia any more.
5. Jennifer will be working from home on Thursday afternoon.
   a. She does this every Thursday.
   b. I'm just talking about Thursday this week.

5 Choose the correct words to complete the sentences.

1. I can't meet you at the same time next week as I *'ll be doing / 'll do* an exam.
2. My sister *is always / had always been* borrowing my clothes without asking me!
3. More and more people *were / are* becoming vegetarians these days.
4. He *hasn't been / wasn't* attending his lessons for the last few months.
5. They *had been / have been* driving for hours when they decided to stop for a break.
6. Sorry, I *was having / have been having* a shower when you called me.
7. A: Has Tina woken up yet?
   B: No, she *is still / has still been* sleeping.
8. A: Why are you so dirty?
   B: I've *been cleaning / cleaned* out the garage.

6 Complete the conversation with the correct form of the verbs in brackets. Use a continuous form when possible.

A: What's all that noise? Is that the workmen?
B: Yes. They ¹_____ (build) a new community centre at the end of our road.
A: How long ²_____ they _____ it for? (do)
B: For six months. They said it would be finished by now, but I think they ³_____ still _____ on it this time next year! (work) But we need something like that here. I ⁴_____ (live) on this street for ten years but I only say hello to a few people I ⁵_____ (know) since I first moved here.
A: Well, more and more people ⁶_____ (move) to big cities so you're less likely to know your neighbours. The other day I ⁷_____ (walk) down my street and I saw a neighbour on his way to work. I said hello but he was in such a rush that he just walked past me!

GRAMMAR SUMMARY UNIT 2

Perfect forms

Perfect verb forms link two periods of time. We use them to look back at an event that has an impact on a later time. They can be used in the active or passive.

We use the **present perfect simple** to describe:

- a completed event or action that might be repeated or continued and has a present connection
  Carlo **has broken** his arm and won't be able to come to work for a week. (= Carlo can't come to work now because of his broken arm.)

- a situation or state that started in the past and is not finished
  I've always **loved** working as a doctor. (= I still love it now.)

We don't use the present perfect with a finished time period. We use the past simple instead.
  We **had** a really good time last night. (not We've had)

We use the **present perfect continuous** to describe:

- a continuous completed action that has a present connection
  Sara **has been studying** all day so she's really tired. (= She's tired now because she studied for so long.)

- an event or action that started in the past and is not finished
  We've **been living** here for five years. (= We still live here.)

We don't use the continuous aspect with stative verbs.
  I've **owned** my car for ten years so I think it's time to buy a new one. (not I've been owning)

We use the **past perfect simple** (had + past participle):

- to describe a completed action before another action in the past
  By the time we got to the station, the train **had** already **left**.

- in a narrative, to talk about an action that happened before the main events of a story
  I'd always **wanted** to visit Australia, so when I saw the competition in the newspaper, I decided to enter.

There is a **past perfect continuous** form (had + been + -ing):
  They'**d been searching** for gold for six months before they found any.

We use the **future perfect simple** (will + have + -ing) to describe a completed event or action at a point in the future.
  Call me at six thirty – I'**ll have finished** work by then.

There is a **future perfect continuous** form (will + have been + -ing):
  I'**ll have been learning** to play tennis for a year in May.

▶ Exercises 1, 2 and 3

Passive forms

We form the passive with a form of the verb *be* + the past participle of the verb.

We can form the passive in any tense, although we do not normally use it with present perfect continuous and past perfect continuous.
  Over 10,000 calls **are made** to the police every day.
  Three cars **were stolen** in our neighbourhood last week. (past simple)
  A new hospital **is being built** near here.
  When I opened the parcel, I saw that contents **had been damaged**.
  The safety rules **were being explained** to us when the fire alarm went off.
  The diamond **has been kept** locked away for fifty years.

The passive can be used with modal verbs, and there are also gerund and infinitive forms.
  The work should **be completed** by next week.
  I hate **being woken** up in the middle of the night.
  She hopes **to be promoted** this year.

In informal English, we also form the passive with *get* instead of *be*. We don't normally use *get* in present perfect simple or future perfect simple passives, and we only use it to describe actions, not states.
  Sorry I'm late – I **got delayed** in the traffic.
  What time does lunch **get served** in the canteen?

When we use the active form of a verb, the focus of the sentence is on the 'agent' – the person or thing that does an action. When we use the passive form, the object of the active sentence becomes the subject and the focus changes.
                          OBJECT
  A team of authors wrote this book. (focus on agent)
  SUBJECT
  This book **was written** by a team of authors. (focus on 'this book')

We often use the passive:

- when the agent is obvious, unknown or not important
  Your essays **will be returned** to you next month.
  Because of the snow, drivers **were asked** to avoid all unnecessary journeys.

- when we are following a series of actions that happen to the same subject
  La Gioconda is one of the most famous paintings in the world. It **was painted** in the 16th century by Leonardo da Vinci and **has been displayed** in the Louvre museum in Paris since 1797.

We also use the passive when we want to give extra emphasis to the agent. We do this by using the passive, and putting the agent at the end of the sentence (after the preposition *by*).
  The child was rescued **by the fire service**.

▶ Exercises 4, 5 and 6

86

Exercises

1 Correct the mistake in each sentence.

1. I was a hairdresser since 2005.
2. He hasn't been on holiday last year.
3. We don't need to go to the station because her train won't be arrived yet.
4. I've been having this car for a long time.
5. She couldn't pay for our coffees because she'd leave her wallet at home.
6. I'm wearing glasses since I was child.
7. Last week was the first time I saw Marion since we were students.

2 Complete the sentences with the correct perfect form of the verb in brackets.

1. I'm really hungry! I _____ since this morning. (not eat)
2. We didn't want to watch the film because we _____ already _____ it. (see)
3. How long _____ at this company? (you work)
4. I think by the year 2050, a lot of animals _____ extinct. (become)
5. I _____ Ella for two years. (know)
6. She arrived late but luckily the lesson _____ yet. (not start)

3 Complete the text with the correct form of the verbs in brackets. Sometimes you do NOT need a perfect form.

I ¹_____ (live) on a boat for fifteen years now, and I love it. Before moving to London, I ²_____ (not live) on a boat before, so when I first ³_____ (tell) people about my plan to live on the River Thames, they thought I was crazy. When I arrived in London, I realized I ⁴_____ (cannot) afford a normal flat, so I decided to buy a boat, and I ⁵_____ (be) here ever since. The best thing about living like this is that you see a different side to London – one that's closer to nature. However, I don't have much storage space so I ⁶_____ (be able to) buy a lot of things since I moved here. In fact, I'm hoping that by the end of this year, I ⁷_____ (save) enough money to buy a bigger boat.

4 Rewrite the sentences using the passive.

1. The prime minister announced the tax increase.
   The tax increase _____ by the prime minister.
2. The local council are building a new bridge.
   A new bridge _____ by the local council.
3. You must finish this report by the end of the day.
   This report _____ by the end of the day.
4. The manager has cancelled the football match because the pitch is flooded.
   The football match _____ because the pitch is flooded.
5. The speaker will give the lecture in French.
   The lecture _____ in French.
6. The other guests had eaten all the food by the time we arrived.
   All the food _____ by the time we arrived.
7. You need to pass the written theory test first.
   The written theory test _____ first.

5 Complete the conversation with the active or passive form of the verbs in brackets. Use *get* where possible.

A: Did you see that documentary about dangerous jobs? I never ¹_____ (know) cutting down trees was so dangerous! Every year, a lot of loggers – they're the people who cut down trees – ²_____ (kill) by falling trees or by the equipment they are using.

B: I wonder if they ³_____ (tell) about the dangers before they start working.

A: Well, I expect they must know. But why does anyone choose to do it if it's so dangerous?!

B: Maybe they ⁴_____ (like) working outdoors and they ⁵_____ (pay) well. Which other jobs were mentioned?

A: Fishermen! Especially the ones that fish for crabs. Apparently, crabs can only ⁶_____ (catch) during winter in places like Alaska. So the water is really cold and people can die from hypothermia if they ⁷_____ (hit) by heavy equipment and fall into the water. They said that they ⁸_____ (earn) a lot of money, but I'm happy working in an office!

6 Rewrite the sentences using the passive to emphasize the agent.

1. A teenager from our street broke into our car.
   _____.
2. Dr Taylor can't see you today.
   _____ today.
3. Astronomers have discovered a new planet.
   _____.
4. A fast food company is going to buy the old cinema.
   _____.
5. He got lost because the app on his phone didn't give him the right directions.
   He got lost because _____.
6. Our actions are destroying the environment.
   _____.

GRAMMAR SUMMARY UNIT 3

Qualifiers

We use qualifiers such as *quite*, *pretty* and *rather* to make adjectives and verbs less strong.

Qualifier + adjective

We use *quite*, *pretty* and *fairly* before adjectives to make them less strong. We use them with both positive and negative adjectives, but it is most common to use them with positive adjectives.

*It's a **fairly** interesting city to visit, but I wouldn't spend more than a day there.*
*I thought the film was **quite** good, but not great.*

When we use *quite* with *a/an* + adjective + noun, we normally place it **before** the article.

*We had **quite a good trip** but the weather was disappointing.*

We also use *quite* in the phrases 'quite a lot' and 'quite a few' to talk about an amount or number when we want to be vague.

Rather has a similar meaning to *quite*, but it is slightly stronger. We can place it before the indefinite article, like *quite*, or after it.

*I waited **rather a long time** for the bus to arrive.*
*There's **a rather nice** restaurant by the river.*

We use *not very* and *not particularly* before adjectives to give them the opposite meaning.

*It was**n't very** difficult. (= It was easy.)*
*They weren't **particularly** impressed. (= They were unimpressed.)*

▶ Exercise 1

Qualifier + verb

We use *quite* before the verbs *like*, *enjoy*, *understand* and *agree*. We often use *quite* to mean 'a bit':

*I **quite** enjoyed the film. (= But I've seen much better films.)*

We can use *quite* before the verbs *understand* and *agree* to mean 'completely'.

*I **quite** agree with you. (= I completely agree.)*
*He didn't **quite** understand what to do. (= He didn't completely understand.)*

However, we also use *quite* + verb when we are disagreeing with someone or to show surprise. In this case it doesn't change the meaning or strength of the verb.

A: *I thought the food here wouldn't be very good but actually it's OK.*
B: *Yes, I'm **quite** enjoying it. (= I'm enjoying it.)*
A: *I really don't like this kind of music?*
B: *Really? I **quite** like it. (= I like it.)*

We use *rather* in this way before the verbs *like*, *enjoy* and *hope*.

*Our hotel had received very bad reviews online, but we **rather** enjoyed it.*

We use *not particularly* before *like*, *enjoy* and *hope* to give them the opposite meaning.

*We did**n't particularly like** what she cooked for us. (= We disliked what she cooked for us.)*

We also use *slightly*, *a little*, *a bit* and *rather* after verbs to mean 'a bit'.

*I'm going off rock music **slightly** now that I'm getting older.*
*He annoys me **a little** with his constant moaning.*
*She cooks **a bit** but her husband usually prepares the meals.*

▶ Exercises 2 and 3

Intensifying adverbs

We use intensifying adverbs before adjectives to make them stronger.

*When I got my exam result, I felt **extremely** relieved.*

The choice of intensifying adverb depends on whether the adjective is gradable or ungradable. Most adjectives, e.g. *cold*, *surprising*, are gradable. This means we can make them stronger or weaker with adverbs like *very*, *a bit*, *incredibly*, *really* or *extremely*.

*I'm **a bit** / **very** / **extremely** cold.*
*The new flats they're building look **incredibly small**.*

Other adjectives, e.g. *freezing*, *amazing* are ungradable. We cannot make them stronger or weaker in this way. Adjectives like *freezing*, *essential* and *amazing* already contain the idea of 'very' in their meaning. We use *absolutely*, *really* and *utterly* with ungradable adjectives.

*It's **very cold** today. = It's **freezing** today. (freezing = very cold)*
*I like Jann's new house, but it's got an **absolutely tiny** garden.*

Ungradable adjectives can also be 'absolute' adjectives. Adjectives like this do not have a comparative or superlative form, e.g. *right*, *wrong*, *unique* and *true*. With absolute adjectives, we use the intensifying adverbs *completely*, *entirely* and *totally*.

*I'm not going to pay them until all the work is **totally finished**.*

We can use the adverb *quite* with ungradable adjectives, including absolute adjectives. When we do this, the meaning is 'very'.

*I'm **quite** interested in that period of history. (quite = a bit)*
*I think this painting is **quite** stunning. (quite = really)*

Often, the choice of adverb and adjective combination is a question of collocation. For example, we prefer to say 'absolutely freezing' rather than 'utterly freezing', even though both are grammatically correct. There are also some exceptions, for example, we sometimes say *very/really different* (even though 'different' is an absolute adjective).

▶ Exercises 4, 5 and 6

88

Exercises

1 Choose the correct option to complete the sentences. In one case, both options are correct.

1. The food in that restaurant *wasn't very good / was quite good*. I won't be going there again.
2. There's *quite a / a quite* big queue in that shop. Let's go somewhere else.
3. This car *is quite / isn't particularly* cheap. We should buy it.
4. It was *a fairly / fairly a* difficult test.
5. She's had *rather a / a rather* relaxing day.
6. He'd had *pretty a / a pretty* tiring day so he decided to go straight home.

2 Read the sentences. Then choose the best explanation (a–b) for each one.

1. I quite agree with what you're saying.
   a. I agree with everything.
   b. I only agree with a few things.
2. It was freezing this morning but the weather's improving a little now.
   a. The weather is much better now.
   b. The weather is slightly better now.
3. Martina: I hate this kind of music.
   Isabella: Really? I quite like it.
   a. Isabella only likes this kind of music a little.
   b. Isabella enjoys this kind of music.
4. I don't particularly enjoy this kind of food.
   a. I dislike this kind of food.
   b. I sometimes enjoy this kind of food.
5. I rather hoped that the party would be cancelled because I'm so tired.
   a. This was my wish.
   b. I only hoped this a little bit.

3 Complete the texts with the qualifiers given. Sometimes more than one answer is possible.

| fairly | not particularly | quite | rather |

I grew up in the countryside in Poland. I suppose it was ^{1} _____ a nice place to grow up – there weren't many people in the village but I had a ^{2} _____ big group of friends and we always played a lot outside. But it was ^{3} _____ exciting and I used to dream about living in a big city. But now I live in one, I think I'd ^{4} _____ enjoy living in the countryside again!

| not very | pretty | slightly |

My home town is a ^{5} _____ big place, but it's not huge. It's very close to London but this means the facilities are ^{6} _____ limited because most people go to London for entertainment and shopping. It's ^{7} _____ cheap to live there, because it's so close to the city.

4 Correct the mistake in each sentence. Not all the sentences contain an error.

1. It's very freezing outside today.
2. This room is incredibly small.
3. I was utterly surprised to see Matt at the party last night.
4. I found the exam really difficult.
5. It's absolutely important that you listen to the safety instructions.
6. We've just watched an extremely amazing film!
7. You're utterly right. We needed to turn left after the traffic lights.

5 Complete the sentences with these adjectives.

| cold | exhausted | freezing | small | stunning |
| stylish | tiny | tired |

1. You should put a coat on. It's absolutely _____ outside.
2. Silvia's extremely _____ and wants to stay at home and rest.
3. That's a very _____ necklace you're wearing. It looks great on you.
4. Our hotel room is absolutely _____ ! I'm going to ask for a bigger one.
5. It was a very _____ winter and most of the plants died.
6. The views from the tower are quite _____ . You should take a camera when you go.
7. I felt utterly _____ yesterday after our long run.
8. They've just bought a very _____ flat in the city centre. They don't have much space for furniture.

6 Choose the best options to complete the conversation.

A: How was your weekend?
B: Not great. We were flat hunting! It was ^{1} *very / absolutely* frustrating because the estate agent made the flats sound ^{2} *really / very* amazing but when we looked at them, they weren't what we'd been promised.
A: Oh no! How many flats did you look at?
B: Five. The first two were in a nice area but were ^{3} *utterly / incredibly* small! I just couldn't live in them! Then we saw another small flat in the town centre but it was on a ^{4} *very / totally* busy road, and I didn't like that. The fourth flat was in an ^{5} *extremely / absolutely* terrible state! We'd have to do a lot of work on it.
A: So what about the fifth one?
B: It was great – new and modern, in a lovely neighbourhood. And it has a(n) ^{6} *incredibly / very* huge garden.
A: But …
B: Well, it was ^{7} *completely / extremely* expensive, so we can't really afford it.

GRAMMAR SUMMARY UNIT 4

Future probability

Modal verbs

We use the modal verbs *may*, *could*, *might* to say that something is possible in the future (about a 50% chance).

*In the future, we **may / might / could** find solutions to many environmental problems.*

We can add the adverb *well* after *may / could / might* to make the event sound more probable.

*Driverless cars **may / could / might well** become available sooner than people expect.*

To say that it is possible that something will not happen in the future, we use *may not* or *might not*.

*They **may / might not** be able to fix the problem.*

We use *should* or *shouldn't* to say that something is probable in the future (about a 70% chance).

*We **should** arrive before 7 p.m. if there is no traffic.*

We don't use *should* to talk about something bad that we think will happen.

*I think climate change **will** be a disaster for many countries.* (not *I think climate change should be*)

Adverbs

We use *perhaps* and *maybe* to say something is possible (a 50% chance). We normally put *perhaps* and *maybe* before the subject.

***Perhaps / Maybe** the weather will improve tomorrow.*

We use *probably* (*not*) to say something is probable (a 70% chance). We normally put *probably* between *will* and the main verb.

*Shin will **probably** arrive late again.*

We use *almost certainly* (*not*) when we are almost certain that something will happen (a 90% chance). We put *almost certainly* between *will* and the main verb.

*There will **almost certainly** be an election this year.*

Adjective phrases

We use the adjectives *possible*, *probable*, *likely* and *unlikely* in the structure *it's* + adjective + *that* + clause.

***It's possible that** we will create colonies on Mars this century.* (about 50% certainty)
*Unfortunately, it's **probable / likely** that there will be a delay with your order.* (about 70% certainty)
*In my opinion, **it's unlikely that** the new plans will cut traffic in the city centre.* (about 20% certainty)

We also use *likely* and *unlikely* with a subject and *to* + infinitive.

*The journey is **likely to take** over ten hours.*
*The work is **unlikely to be finished** today.*

Noun phrases

We use some noun phrases + *be* + (*that*) + clause to say something is probable in the future (a 70% chance).

***The likelihood is that** he will leave the company.*
***The chances are (that)** they'll offer me a promotion.*
***There's a good chance (that)** our team will win.*

Note that when we use 'there's a good chance that', the future event isn't necessarily something good.

There's a good chance that it will rain later.

▶ Exercises 1, 2 and 3

Past modals

To talk about **past obligation** we use *had to*. We cannot use *must* to refer to past obligation.

*Yesterday, I **had to** be at work at 7 a.m.*

For negative past obligation we use *couldn't*, *wasn't / weren't allowed to*.

*We **couldn't** leave the room during the exam.*
*Women in the USA **were not allowed to** vote until 1920.*

To talk about a lack of necessity in the past, we use *needn't have* + past participle or *didn't need to* + infinitive. This means the action happened but wasn't necessary.

*I **needn't have gone** to the meeting.*
*You **didn't need to cook** dinner.*

We can use *didn't need to* or *didn't have to*, but not *needn't have*, when the unnecessary action in the past didn't occur.

*We went by train so we **didn't need to find** somewhere to park.*

▶ Exercise 4

To speculate on past events (to make deductions or guesses about them), we use *must have*, *might / may / could have* and *can't / couldn't have* + past participle.

*Luke **must have had** to stay late at work – he's normally home by now.* (= I think it's probable that he had to stay late at work.)
*I **may / might / could have got** a few questions wrong in the exam.* (= I think it's possible that I got a few questions wrong.)
*They **can't have got** lost – they've been here lots of times!* (= I think it isn't probable that they got lost.)
*A: Did Joan just drive by? B: No, it **couldn't have been** her. She drives a much bigger car.*

We also use *could have* when we know that something didn't happen but we want to say it was possible.

*Why were you so careless? You **could have been** killed!*

We use *should(n't) have* + past participle when:

- we think something was advisable but didn't happen, or was inadvisable but did happen
  *You **should have called** me as soon as you knew you were going to be late.*
  *I **shouldn't have gone** to the job interview in a T-shirt.*

- we expect that something happened in the past, but we're not sure if it did
  *Luca's train **should have arrived** by now.*

We use *ought to have* + past participle when we think something was advisable but didn't happen. It is more formal than *should have*.

*We **ought to have** booked seats.*

▶ Exercises 5 and 6

90

Exercises

1 Choose the correct option to complete the sentences.

1. Matt said he *might / will / is likely to* come to the football game with us tonight but he's not sure.
2. We *probably won't / won't probably / maybe won't* know the results of the election till tomorrow.
3. In ten years, we *couldn't / may not / shouldn't* be using smartphones any more.
4. It's *likely / possible / probably* that the heating system will have to be replaced soon. It's broken down three times already this month.
5. Philip and Ruth *might / should / could* be here at 8.00 p.m. They set off at 7.30 p.m. and the journey takes half an hour.
6. There's *almost certainly / maybe / a good chance* that your flight will be delayed.

2 Rewrite the sentences so they have the same meaning. Use the words in brackets.

1. It's very probable that our train will be late today. (chance)
   _____ today.
2. He might well not come to our party this evening. (probably)
   _____ this evening.
3. In the future we might all be driving electric cars. (perhaps)
   _____ in the future.
4. Space travel will probably be a lot cheaper in the future. (likely)
   _____ in the future.
5. The government might raise interest rates this year. (possible)
   _____ this year.

3 Complete the text with these words and phrases.

| almost certainly | certainly | chances | could |
| possible | should | unlikely |

Air pollution causes millions of premature deaths throughout the world every year, and this number will ¹_____ increase in the future. As a result, we ²_____ start to see more interesting solutions for this problem. One idea to deal with pollution is Daan Roosegaarde's 'Smog Free Tower' – a tower that sucks in polluted air and blows out clean air. Roosegaarde believes that in the future, towers like this ³_____ be used to improve the air quality in polluted cities. Roosegaarde says it's ⁴_____ to build 'Smog Free Towers' the size of buildings, for an even bigger impact. Although the towers are ⁵_____ to solve the problem of air pollution completely, the ⁶_____ are that we will need to develop many innovative ideas to keep pollution under control.

4 Choose the correct option to complete the sentences. Sometimes both options are possible.

1. I was late to work this morning because I *had to / must* stop for petrol.
2. They *didn't have to / weren't allowed to* pay to enter the museum because it was free.
3. Thank you for the flowers! You *didn't have to buy / needn't have bought* me anything!
4. I *needn't have worn / didn't need to wear* this jumper. It's so hot today!
5. We *didn't have to / weren't allowed to* speak during the exam.
6. She *didn't need to go / needn't have gone* to work so she spent the day relaxing in her garden.

5 Complete the conversation with these modal forms.

| could have | couldn't have | might not have |
| must have | should have | shouldn't have |

A: I'm so tired! Some friends came for dinner last night. I spent all day cooking, and then they didn't leave until 2 a.m.! It's my fault – I ¹_____ invited them to come during the week. It's better to invite friends round at the weekend.
B: Oh dear! You ²_____ just got a takeaway!
A: Oh, I ³_____ done that! But you know, I'm sure I ⁴_____ spent an hour just cutting up vegetables!
B: You should buy a food processor. I've got one that cuts up vegetables really quickly. I ⁵_____ lent it to you!
A: It's a good thing you didn't. You ⁶_____ ever got it back from me!

6 Complete the conversations with *must, can('t), could(n't), might(n't), should(n't)* and *ought (not)* and the correct form of these verbs. You don't need to use all the modal forms.

| buy | drive | eat | leave | open | see |

1. Maia _____ to work. Her car is still outside her house.
2. I have a stomach ache. I _____ so much food earlier!
3. Oh no! We've missed our train. I told you we _____ the house earlier!
4. I thought I just saw Steve, but I _____ somebody who looks like him because Steve's on holiday in Peru.
5. I can't remember where I got this dress. I _____ it from that new shop on the High Street.
6. The bank _____ by now. It's 9.15 and it opens at 8.30.

GRAMMAR SUMMARY UNIT 5

Emphatic structures

We use various sentence structures to make a sentence more emphatic or to give emphasis to a certain part of a sentence.

Cleft sentences

A cleft sentence emphasizes a particular part of a sentence by splitting it into two parts. There are two patterns.

We use *it + be + emphasized phrase + that* to emphasize the subject, object or an adverbial phrase. The information we want to emphasize comes at the beginning of the sentence, after *be*.

In Thailand, the beaches are the most popular places to visit. → *In Thailand,* **it's the beaches that** *are the most popular places to visit.* (emphasizing subject)

I most want to see Mexico City. → **It's Mexico City that** *I most want to see.* (emphasizing object)

Most people go to Greece in summer. → **It's in summer that** *most people go to Greece.* (emphasizing adverbial phrase)

Note that we can use a relative pronoun instead of 'that'.

It's Jenny that / who I want to see.

We use *what* or *the thing (that) + subject + verb + be* to emphasize a subject, object, a clause with *that* or a clause with a *wh-* word. The information we want to emphasize comes at the end of the sentence, after *be*.

I hate airports most. → **The thing that I hate most is** *airports.* (emphasizing the object)

We need to decide which dates we can travel on. → **What we need to decide is** *which dates we can travel on.* (emphasizing a *wh-* clause)

I hope that our train isn't delayed. → **What I hope is** *that our train isn't delayed.* (emphasizing a clause with *that*)

We can also emphasize a whole clause with *what + subject + verb + to do + be + (to) + infinitive*.

My country needs to invest in tourism. → **What my country needs to do is (to)** *invest in tourism.*

▶ Exercises 1 and 2

do, *does*, *did* in affirmative sentences

We can add a form of *do* to affirmative sentences to add emphasis. We always stress the form of *do*.

We hope you enjoy your stay with us. → *We* **do** *hope you enjoy your stay with us.*

We don't add *do* when a sentence already contains an auxiliary (*be* or *have*) or a modal verb. In this case, we just stress the auxiliary to add emphasis.

We have enjoyed our trip.
The train service can be rather unreliable.
He is rude sometimes. (We use the full form, not the contraction.)

▶ Exercise 3

Avoiding repetition

We can use synonyms, e.g. *loss – defeat*, or words such as *one, that, it, so* and ellipsis (leaving out words) to avoid repetition.

one, that, it, so

We use *one* in place of a singular countable noun and *ones* in place of a plural countable noun.

Which top do you prefer? The blue **one** *or the red one?*
Here are your shoes. Are these the **ones** *you wanted?*

When we use an adjective before *one*, we always use the indefinite article or another determiner.

A: This hotel's great! B: I know! And just think that you wanted to book **that** *cheap* **one***!*

We always add an adjective when we use *ones* after numbers or determiners.

A: Did you bring any biscuits? B: Yes, I brought **some chocolate ones** *and* **some plain ones***.*

We use *that* to replace a phrase, clause or sentence.

A: Ask Juan to come at 8 o'clock. B: I've already asked him **that***.* (*that* = 'to come at 8 o'clock')
A: Why don't we get a takeaway tonight? B: **That***'s a great idea.* (*that* = 'get a takeaway')

We use *it* to replace a noun phrase.

Has anyone seen my bag? It's not where I left it.

We use *so* after verbs like *say, think, hope* and *expect* to replace a clause, especially a short answer.

A: Is it going to rain today?
B: I think **so***.* (*so* = 'it's going to rain today')

▶ Exercise 4

Ellipsis

Sometimes we omit words to avoid repetition, when the context is clear which words we have omitted. We can omit words:

- when we have two verbs together, and the second verb is a *to* + infinitive form. In this case, we can omit everything after *to*.
A: Why don't we just book a beach holiday? B: **I don't want to** *[book a beach holiday]. I hate the beach!*

- after verbs and phrases like *hope, suppose* and *be afraid*, when what comes after is negative. In this case, we omit everything apart from *not*.
A: Do you think we're going to miss the flight? B: I **hope not***.* (= I hope that we don't miss the flight.)

We can also omit a whole clause after a subject and auxiliary or modal verb.

I've never been to Asia, and most of my friends haven't either. (= Most of my friends haven't been to Asia.)
Most of my friends can speak Spanish, but I can't.

When the clause that we are replacing contains a verb in the present or past simple, we use a form of *do*.

Magda wanted to spend the day hiking but we **didn't***.*
(= We didn't want to spend the day hiking.)

▶ Exercise 5

Exercises

1 Rewrite the sentences to emphasize the underlined word or phrase.

1. <u>Francis</u> called Ben last night.
   It _____.
2. I'd like <u>more free time not money</u>.
   It _____.
3. She doesn't like <u>the way her manager speaks to her</u>.
   It _____.
4. The hotel we stayed in was expensive but <u>the flights cost us the most</u>.
   The hotel we stayed in was expensive, but it _____.
5. The report is going to focus on <u>the reasons why the project failed</u>.
   It _____.
6. The students find out their results <u>in January</u>.
   It _____.

2 Rewrite the sentences to emphasize the underlined phrases.

1. In winter I hate <u>the cold weather</u>.
   The thing that _____.
2. We forgot <u>to lock our front door</u>.
   What _____.
3. I loved <u>being able to relax on a beach</u>.
   The thing that _____.
4. She liked <u>the film's ending</u> the most.
   What _____.
5. The airline won't <u>refund our tickets</u>.
   The thing that _____.
6. You're now going to see <u>a summary of the research</u>.
   What _____.

3 Rewrite the underlined parts of the sentences to make them more emphatic, using a form of *do*. When it is not possible to add a form of *do*, circle the word that needs to be stressed.

1. <u>I thought</u> the tourist office would be a bit more helpful. _____
2. <u>These snakes will bite</u> you if they get the chance. _____
3. <u>She seemed to be ignoring</u> everything the tour guide was saying. _____
4. <u>They have already paid</u> for their meal.
   _____
5. <u>They offered</u> to exchange the faulty item, but she wanted a refund. _____
6. <u>She works</u> in a bank, doesn't she?
   _____

4 Choose the correct (a–c) option to replace the underlined parts of the sentences.

1. Shall we go to the restaurant by the sea or <u>the restaurant</u> near the castle?
   a that   b the one   c it
2. A: Is the film festival starting this weekend?
   B: Yeah, I think <u>the film festival is starting this weekend</u>.
   a it   b that   c so
3. A: I had to wake up at 4 a.m. to get to the airport on time.
   B: <u>Waking up at 4 a.m.</u> must have been hard!
   a so   b that   c one
4. A: The suitcases you bought are too small!
   B: They were the biggest <u>suitcases</u> they had in the shop!
   a ones   b one   c it
5. A: What time does the tourist office open?
   B: I think <u>the tourist office</u> opens at 9 a.m.
   a one   b that   c it
6. A: Will there be a lot of people at the meeting?
   B: I expect <u>there will be a lot of people at the meeting</u>.
   a it   b so   c ones

5 Find six phrases in the email that can be deleted to avoid repetition.

> Hi Alex
>
> How's it going? Samira and I arrived on Koh Chang island a week ago and it's amazing! We'd thought about going to one of the busier islands but we decided not to go to one of the busier islands. And I'm glad because it's perfect here! On the day we arrived we'd arranged to go on a jungle hike but in the end we couldn't go on a jungle hike because it was raining! It's been sunny and hot since then – I've just felt like relaxing on a beach and Sally has felt like relaxing on a beach too! But now I'm getting bored. Tomorrow I'd like to go elephant trekking but Samira doesn't want to go elephant trekking. I think she's a bit scared! So instead we're going to visit a waterfall, and go snorkelling with a group of friends we've made. They've all been snorkelling before but I haven't been snorkelling before. (Have you?) I'm really looking forward to it! Sally thinks we should stay longer on the island. I'd like to stay longer on the island too, but there are so many other places to see!
>
> Hope to see you when we get back.
>
> Renata

93

GRAMMAR SUMMARY UNIT 6

Phrasal verbs

There are some verbs that are often followed by prepositions, and the preposition doesn't change the meaning of the verb.

*It is believed that chess originally **comes from** India.*

Other verb + preposition combinations have an idiomatic meaning. You cannot predict the meaning from the individual meanings of the verb and the particle.

*Can you **look after** my bag for a minute? (look after = take care of)*

Verb + adverb combinations almost always have an idiomatic meaning.

*I had to **give up** tennis after I injured my elbow. (give up = stop doing)*

Verb + adverb

Verb + adverb combinations can be transitive or intransitive. Intransitive phrasal verbs do not have an object.

*She **grew up** in Los Angeles.*

Transitive phrasal verbs are **separable phrasal verbs**. We can put the object after the adverb or before it, with no difference in meaning.

*Can you **turn the radio down**? = Can you **turn down the radio**?*

However, when the object is a pronoun, we always put it before the adverb.

*Can you **call me back** later? (not: Can you call back me later?)*

Verb + preposition

Verb + preposition combinations always have an object. They are **inseparable phrasal verbs**. We always put the object, including pronouns, after the preposition.

*It took two months for me to **get over the injury**. = It took me two months to **get over it**.*

Verb + adverb + preposition

Three-part phrasal verbs are made up of a verb + adverb + preposition. We always put an object after the preposition.

*He doesn't **get on with** some of his colleagues at work.*

A small number of three-part phrasal verbs take two objects. We put the first object after the verb, and the second object after the preposition.

*I've decided to **take you up on** the job offer.*

▶ Exercises 1, 2 and 3

Verb patterns

When we use two verbs together in a sentence, the form of the second verb depends on the first verb.

- **verb + *to* + infinitive:** *(can/can't) afford, agree, allow, arrange, ask, begin, choose, continue, decide, expect, fail, help*, hope, intend, learn, manage, need, offer, plan, pretend, promise, refuse, seem, start, tend, threaten, want, would like, would love, would prefer*
  *I **need to finish** my work before I go to the gym.*

- **verb + object + *to* + infinitive:** *ask, get, help, need, require, tell, urge, warn*
  *I **asked Luke to lend** me his bike.*

- **verb (+ object) + infinitive:** *help, let* and *make*
  (Sometimes we do not include the object.)
  *They **made me do** a medical test before I could enter the race.*

- **verb + -ing:** *adore, avoid, begin, can't help, can't stand, consider, continue, describe, enjoy, fancy, finish, imagine, involve, keep, mention, mind, miss, practise, recommend, risk, spend (time/money), start, suggest*
  *I **avoid running** on hard surfaces as it hurts my knees.*

- **verb + preposition + -ing:** e.g. *carry on, worry about, succeed in*
  *Do you **worry about injuring** your body?*

- **verb + object + preposition + -ing:** e.g. *discourage from, prevent from*
  *Injuries **prevented her from competing**.*

Verb + -ing or to + infinitive

After *start* and *continue*, we can use the *-ing* form or *to* + infinitive, with no difference in meaning. Some verbs change their meaning depending on whether we use the *-ing* form or *to* + infinitive.

*I'm starting a new job soon, which will **mean earning** a lot more money. (mean + -ing = involve)*
*I **meant to go** to the supermarket but I forgot. (mean + to + infinitive = intend)*

*Mia **regrets not doing** more sports when she was younger. (regret + -ing = feel sorry about something)*
*I **regret to inform** you I have decided to cancel my membership. (regret + to + infinitive = feel sorry that you have to tell someone about a situation)*

*Do you **remember playing** football here? (remember + -ing = have memories of an earlier event)*
*Did you **remember to call** the doctor? (remember + to + infinitive = not forget to do something)*

*She **stopped running** when her foot started to hurt. (stop + -ing = finish doing an action)*
*She **stopped to drink** some water. (stop + to + infinitive = finish an action to do another action)*

*I **tried training** late in the evening but I didn't like it. (try + -ing = do something to see what happens)*
*I **tried to call you** but your phone was switched off. (try + to + infinitive = make an effort)*

*I've never **forgotten swimming** in the lake at midnight. (forget + -ing = not having a memory of doing something in the past)*
*Sorry, I **forgot to bring** your present. (forget + to + infinitive = not remember to do something)*

Exercises 4, 5 and 6

Exercises

1 Correct the mistake in each sentence.

1. Please pay back me the money you owe as soon as you can.
2. At 8.34 a.m., took the plane off.
3. He's been looking his phone for all morning but he hasn't found it yet.
4. If you're not watching the TV, can you turn off it please?
5. His teacher won't put up his bad behaviour with any longer.
6. They let in Adam on the plans for the surprise birthday party.

2 Choose the correct option to complete the sentences. Sometimes both options are correct.

1. His cousin is an expert in cars so he *turned to him / turned him to* for advice.
2. They arranged the meeting for tomorrow but now they've decided to *put it off / put off it*.
3. She *takes after her father / takes her father after*.
4. They've *fallen out their neighbours with / fallen out with their neighbours* because of the party.
5. I told them to *come over / come over our house* at around 9 p.m.
6. You should *throw away these old clothes / throw these old clothes away* if you never wear them.
7. I hadn't seen Michele for years but I *ran into her / ran her into* yesterday at the shops.
8. Can you *fill this form in / fill in this form* now?

3 Match the phrasal verbs in Exercise 2 with these meanings (a–h).

a be similar to an older relative
b complete
c delay (postpone)
d have a serious argument with
e meet somebody by chance
f put into the rubbish bin (dispose of)
g visit somebody in their home
h ask for support or help

4 Choose the correct verb form to complete the sentences.

1. Would you consider *doing / to do* a yoga course?
2. I told him *to wait / wait* for me outside the gym.
3. He tried *ringing / to ring* the door bell but no one answered.
4. The world champion has failed *finishing / to finish* the race.
5. We need to hurry up! I'm worried about *miss / missing* our train.
6. She regretted not *wearing / to wear* a warmer jacket. It was quite cold outside.
7. Rita made me *wake / to wake* up early to go for a run.
8. I remember *to watch / watching* this cartoon when I was a child. I used to love it!

5 Complete the second sentences so they mean the same as the first sentences. Use the correct form of the verbs in brackets.

1. Stefan doesn't play squash any more because of his injury. (stop)
   Stefan _____ because of his injury.
2. He said, 'I won't be late for the meeting.' (promise)
   He _____ late for the meeting.
3. I don't want to put you off doing the race, but it's very demanding. (discourage)
   I _____, but it's very demanding.
4. They said they really wanted us to decide by the end of the week. (urge)
   They _____ by the end of the week.
5. Julia allowed me to borrow her racing bike while she was away. (let)
   Julia _____ while she was away.
6. Are you sad now that you don't live by the sea? (miss)
   Do _____ by the sea?

6 Complete the conversation with these words and the correct form of the verbs in brackets. Add an object if necessary.

| ask | decide | help | make | start | stop |
| think about |

A: Guess what? I've ¹_____ (do) a marathon!
B: Wow! Where are you going to do it?
A: In Berlin. It's in September but I've ²_____ (train) already. I even have a personal trainer. She ³_____ (exercise) really hard for an hour every day!
B: I'm not exercising at all these days.
A: I thought you went to the gym every morning.
B: No, I've ⁴_____ (go). It just wasn't ⁵_____ (get) fit.
A: You should come and train with me! I often go running outdoors with my trainer. I could ⁶_____ (work) with you, too.
B: Thanks, that'd be great.
A: Have you ever ⁷_____ (do) a marathon?
B: I think I should start exercising again regularly before thinking about races!

Audioscripts

Unit 1

1

Speaker 1
I think the most valuable lesson I've learned was when I was starting a business at the age of 25. I used to get very frustrated with my business partner, a guy called Giles. We'd set up our own web design business and Giles would always take ages making a first design to show the customer. He was trying to get it perfect when actually, it didn't need to be. When I told my dad about it – that it was driving me crazy – he said, 'Look, you can't change other people; you can only change the way that you behave towards them.' So, from then on I just tried to accept that Giles was a perfectionist and to see it as a positive thing. And since then we've got on much better. And that's become a sort of guiding principle for me in life – not to try to change other people.

Speaker 2
I think a good rule of thumb is: 'Never get too attached to things.' But it's a lot easier said than done and sometimes it takes a big event to make you realize how true this is. Our house was flooded a few years ago and because my bedroom was on the ground floor, I lost a lot of my most valued possessions: my laptop with all my photos on it; my favourite books; all my shoes were ruined and some of my best clothes too. But in fact, what mattered at the time was knowing that everyone was safe – my parents and my little brother. We've actually moved to a new house now, and it's not nearly as nice as the old one, but it doesn't matter. You need to move on. Now, I always make a point of not getting too attached to places or things. It's just stuff.

3

How many times have you been asked the question, 'So, what do you do?' when you first meet someone? It's the classic way in which people start a conversation in order to form an idea of a person's identity, by trying to fit them into an easy-to-understand category. But while some people might like to define themselves by their job – because it's what they live for – actually for many people, their work is not their identity, and the question can make you feel as if people are always judging you by your position in society, or worse, by how much you earn.

There are of course other ways we identify people. By their background: 'Sally was brought up on a farm in Wales, not in London like the rest of her friends.' By their values: 'John's a family man, really.' Or by their hobbies or interests: 'Frank's a keen photographer.' Or sometimes by their character: 'Jack's a free spirit,' or 'Kate's always the life and soul of the party.' We also define people by their beliefs: 'Anne's a campaigner for healthy eating.' And yes, sometimes too by their work: 'Sarah's a medical researcher – she's spent most of her life looking for cures for tropical diseases.' What do these identifying characteristics have in common? Well, identity really seems to be about the experiences that shape us. Take John, our 'family man'. When his children were born, he was working as a carpet salesman. It was a secure job – not very well paid – but it kept him and his family comfortable. At one point he'd been intending to leave the company and start up his own business, but when he thought about it he realized that it would be a risk and also would take up too much of his time – time that he'd rather spend with his two boys.

What about Jack? People call him a free spirit because he's 44 and hasn't settled down yet. He fell in love when he was 25, but the relationship ended and he hasn't had another one since. He travels a lot and lives in different places, picking up bits and pieces of work as and when he can. He keeps saying that in a few years, he won't be moving about anymore – that he's had enough of that life – but actually he's been saying that since he was 35.

Anne works for a big legal firm. She's quite a driven person. A few years ago, her flatmate introduced her to a new vegetarian diet and it made her feel great and gave her more energy. It also made her think about all the bad food she had eaten in her life, particularly at school, and so she joined a campaign to provide healthier food for school kids. It has attracted a lot of interest and is now becoming a national movement. So while there are many ingredients that go into making us what we are, it seems that what defines people first and foremost is experience.

4

1 I need peace and quiet to concentrate.
2 They all came back from their canoeing trip safe and sound. No one was injured, but most of them had a few aches and pains.
3 Try not to give a long talk. By and large, it's better to keep it short and sweet.
4 People come from far and wide to see Stonehenge. There are busloads of tourists coming to and fro all day.
5 You think my job is all fun and games, but actually now and then we do some serious work too!

6

1
A: Hi. Is it your first day at college too?
B: Yes, it is.
A: How's it going? Is it as you expected?
B: It's great, actually. I was a bit nervous before, but the teachers have been really welcoming.

2
A: So, what do you do?
B: I work for an IT company, sorting out people's computer systems.
A: Oh, really? How did you get into that?
B: By accident. I got a temporary job with a company selling laptops – one of those 'no experience necessary' ads – and then they trained me in computer networks.

3
A: Hi, I don't think we've met. I'm David.
B: Oh, hi David. Good to meet you. I'm Tara. I'm an old school friend of Kate's.
A: Oh, yeah – what school was that then?
B: Langley Secondary. It wasn't a great school, actually, but a few of us have kept in touch over the years.

4
A: Hey, I like your jacket.
B: Oh, thank you. I bought it in the sales yesterday. It was only £18.
A: £18? You wouldn't know it – it looks great. Do you like bargain-hunting, then?
B: Oh no. I like clothes, but I hate shopping for them. I find it really stressful.
A: Me too. I always end up buying things that aren't right and have to take them back.

5
A: I'm supposed to have given up sweet things, but I can't stop eating this cake.
B: I know. It's delicious, isn't it?
A: Actually, it was my New Year's Resolution to stop eating things like this. But I haven't kept it. In fact, I don't think I've ever kept a New Year's Resolution. Have you?
B: No, I gave up making them years ago.

6
A: Whereabouts are you from?
B: I live in Lublin … in the east of Poland.
A: Really? I don't know Lublin.
B: No, I don't think many people have heard of it.
A: So, what's it like? Is it a good place to live?
B: Well, it depends. The suburbs aren't very interesting, but the old town is nice and because it's a university town, it gets quite lively at night.

8

1 Do you normally eat here?
2 What's it like living in New York?
3 What sort of apartment have you got?
4 How do you like the new building?
5 Do you fancy a coffee or something?

9

Hello, everyone. First of all, can I extend a warm welcome from me and all the staff. My name's Sarah Curtain, and I'm the Principal here at King's College. I'm very happy to see, once again, such a large and diverse range of nationalities at the college. This year we have over 60 different nationalities, speaking 33 different languages. It's that diversity and international perspective that makes King's College a unique place to study.

I'm afraid I have to mention a few administrative matters first, but then I'll give you some more general advice about how to make the most of your time here.

So, immediately after this session, there will be coffee in the Students' Union where you can meet and chat to staff and other students. That's from 11 to 12.30 p.m.

Course registration takes place on Monday morning. That is compulsory for everyone to attend and it'll be in the main university hall – this room – between 10 a.m. and 2 p.m. You must attend to officially register for the courses you are going to do this year.

96

Also during the next week, I'd ask those of you who haven't done so already, to bring copies of all your documents to the Admissions office – Room 301 – so that we can keep them on file. So that's all official documents – secondary education certificates, student visas, bank account details – to Room 301 by the end of next week. This applies to all overseas students, that is everyone except those from the UK and the European Union. Even if you don't think you have all of these, please come and see us anyway – that's very important.

Now, as for your orientation here at King's College, …

▶ 10

OK, everyone, I'd just like to say a few words about reading – something you're going to be doing a lot of here. At the end of this session, I'll give you your reading list for this particular course. Your other tutors will do the same. There'll be thirty or so books on each list, but please don't think that means you have to read every page of every book. There are three or four key books highlighted at the top of each list, which we do recommend that you read in full, but the others will mainly be for reference – that's to say, there'll be one or two chapters in them that are relevant to a particular essay or piece of work.

So, most importantly, when I give you the list, please don't go out to the nearest bookshop and buy them all. If you do that, you'll leave yourself no money for food or anything else. All these books are, in principle, available in the library – some may be out on loan of course when you want them. You'll probably want to buy some of the more important ones. My advice to you is first to look at one of the internet booksellers and see if you can pick up any second-hand or at least cheaper copies there. There's also a second-hand section in the main university bookshop, where you might find what you're looking for.

What about strategies for reading? As I said at the beginning, you'll have a big volume of reading to do, so it's important that you get faster at it. Is there a secret to that? Well, I'm afraid the answer is not really. What I would say though is that the more you read, the faster you will get. So don't worry too much if it seems like it's taking ages at first – everyone feels that …

Unit 2

▶ 11

The animal herders of western Mongolia have been called the last nomads. Their livelihood is the horses, goats and cattle that travel with them, from which they get their food, clothing and money to buy other goods.

Among these nomadic peoples are Kazakhs. Increasingly, many Kazakhs are trying to make a better living by seeking new jobs or trades in the city, but there are some who have maintained the traditional way of life, living in tents in the summer and in small houses during the cold winters. Among their customs, the most unusual, perhaps, is eagle hunting – an art practised since the days of Genghis Khan.

Wrapped in warm clothes and fur hats to keep off the cold, eagle hunters can still be seen riding their small ponies across the plains of western Mongolia, tracking foxes and other small animals. An eagle hunter spends ten years with each bird, training it – a task which requires great skill and patience – and forming an intimate working relationship with it. They even share with the eagle the meat of the animals it kills.

For many hunters these days, eagle hunting is less an occupation and more a sport, but nevertheless, it's still a tradition that they want to keep alive.

▶ 13

My grandfather was a forestry commissioner, which meant he was responsible for managing forests. I think he'd intended originally to be a biologist, but then he got a job looking after forests in Wales. He's retired now, but he's still fascinated by trees and plants. I guess his job was a way of life for him because it occupied all his time and he spent so much of his life living in or around forests. Over the years, I've often thought about working outdoors too, but I don't think I'll follow in his footsteps.

▶ 14

P = Presenter, K = Kerry, R = Reporter

P: We'd all like to jump into a fire, right? Er, I don't think so, but that was how smokejumper Kerry Franklin explained her career choice when she was interviewed by this programme. For those of you that don't know, smokejumpers are firefighters with parachutes who are dropped into inaccessible areas to tackle forest fires. Here's what Kerry said when she spoke to one of our reporters earlier.

K: Women firefighters are well suited to this kind of work. We weigh on average around 70–80 kilos, so we're the right weight for it. If you're much heavier than that, you descend too fast and you can get injured when you hit the ground. If you're a lot lighter and there's a strong wind, you might be carried a long way from your intended landing point.

R: You mean like towards the centre of the fire itself?

K: Yeah, that's been known to happen. But personal safety's not the first thing on your mind – in this kind of job you can't wrap people in cotton wool.

R: No, I guess not. So, having landed near the fire, what do you do then? 'Cos I imagine there's no fire engine or fire hydrant nearby, so you can't start putting out the fire in a conventional way.

K: No, that's right. We're like the first line of attack before other crews get there. We get dropped in with tools – chainsaws, axes, chemicals for fighting fires; we're given water pumps too, portable ones. But first the fire needs to be assessed to see how bad it is and how it's going to develop – this information has to be relayed back to base as quickly as possible. Of course, if it's a bad fire, we've got to look for a way to try and contain it. Usually that means finding a natural firebreak.

R: What's that?

K: Something like a road, or an area of rock, or perhaps some area of thinner vegetation that the fire has to cross before it continues on its path. When we've located one, then we do our best to make sure it's going to be effective by getting anything that could catch fire out of the way. Sometimes that means using controlled burning. So, we actually start another fire to make the firebreak wider.

R: I see. And can I ask: what's it like being a woman in what's traditionally a male profession?

K: That's not an issue. The job involves being trained to a certain standard and you either make the grade or you don't. Those who come through it successfully have a natural respect for each other. I met a few guys during my training who had a different attitude, but since then? No. A smokejumper's a smokejumper, regardless of gender.

▶ 17

C = Careers Advisor, K = Katy

C: OK, Katy, so can you tell me a bit about yourself?

K: Yes, of course. So, I'm 23 years old and I live in south London. I was brought up in France 'til I was twelve – my mum's French – so I speak fluent French. I studied history at Liverpool University – that was a really good experience – and I graduated from there last June. Since then I've been looking for a job in journalism. To be honest, the media is not an easy sector to break into unless you have the right contacts – and I don't particularly. So, I decided that the best thing to do was to get more work experience in the meantime and currently that's what I'm doing – bits and pieces of office work so that I can improve my general computer and admin skills while I look for something more permanent.

C: Yes, I think that's very sensible. Companies are always worried that university graduates lack those basic skills. What kind of organization would you like to work for, ideally?

K: Well, a news company, really – either online, TV or radio, or print. That's what I'm working towards. But I'd be perfectly happy to start at the bottom and then work my way up. You know, I really wouldn't mind doing a basic job to start with – just so I could get my foot in the door.

C: Well, I think that the fact that you did a history degree rather than one in media or journalism could be a positive thing. Employers are always looking for people with a slightly different background. Have you done any blogging or written anything that's been published?

K: Yeah, I wrote a regular blog about university life when I was in Liverpool. That was quite popular.

C: Mmm. Good. And what do you see as your strengths, Katy?

Audioscripts

K: Well, obviously, I think I write well – also I'm good at spotting a story. I wrote something on my blog last year about the problem of students getting into debt, which got picked up by a local newspaper. I guess I'm very focused and conscientious – once I start something, I follow it through. For example, in my current job I've spent the last two weeks helping to reorganize the office. I went in at the weekend because I wanted to finish the job before they took in a group of new interns.

C: OK. And what would you say are your weaknesses?

K: Um, well, I'm only 23, so I realize I've got an awful lot to learn still. For example, when it comes to gathering information, I don't have all the skills or resources of an older journalist. I have some experience of interviewing people – I know that the trick is to get them to tell *their* story, not the story that *you* want to hear – just not enough yet. In the past I had a tendency to get carried away with my own ideas sometimes.

Unit 3

▶ 18

Wherever I go, I always make a point of looking up and taking in my surroundings, particularly the architecture. I'd recommend anyone to do that; it's very informative. By looking a little more closely, you learn a lot about people and how they organize their lives. In Hong Kong you can't help looking up because almost all the buildings are at least twenty or thirty storeys high.

This photo was taken from the middle of an apartment complex and two things strike you immediately. The first is the density of population here – it's incredible! People live in tiny apartments, one on top of another, because the cost of renting is so high. Those air-conditioning units sticking out from the windows also tell a story, 'cos for most of the year, Hong Kong is a really hot and humid place. Then, the other thing that strikes you about the buildings is that they're such a mixture: old and new, smart and shabby. I think you get that in any city, but here it somehow seems more marked.

Actually, when you see people out in the streets you get a different impression – like everyone seems to be doing pretty well – and that's because appearances are incredibly important for most Hong Kongers: looking your best, wearing designer fashions, carrying the latest phone. You see, a lot of people come here to make money: bankers and real estate developers and so on. It's busy, it's crowded, it's competitive and frankly, it makes a lot of other big cities seem pretty sleepy. It's not for everyone, but I found it completely addictive.

▶ 21

P = Presenter, J = Jonas Wilfstrand

P: Hello and welcome to *Your Property*. Today we're going to look at something completely different: small homes – extremely small homes, in fact. The average house size these days is half the size that it was in the 1920s and there are good reasons for that, as we'll hear. So, I'm very pleased to welcome architect Jonas Wilfstrand, who specializes in the design of compact living spaces and who's going to talk us through this a bit. Jonas, I've been looking at compact homes on your website, and I must say some of them are really stunning. The timber and glass vacation house with a built-in sauna struck me particularly. But it did make me wonder: is this just a passing fashion or is there something more behind the trend for smaller homes?

J: Oh, no, there is definitely a trend for smaller homes – in Britain, but also in other Western countries. One reason is that in large cities we're incredibly short of space – it's a really big problem nowadays. The other thing is affordability. A house or flat half the size should in principle cost half the money – although it doesn't always work out that way. I know it seems completely wrong, but that's the way it is now. Unfortunately, for some people that can mean the difference between having somewhere to live or not.

P: And where did you get the inspiration for your compact homes? Were they based on something you'd seen?

J: Yes – probably a lot of things I'd seen, in fact. But one particular source of inspiration was a people called the Dolgan who live in northern Russia. It's absolutely freezing there – it can go as low as minus 40 degrees – so a small living space is very practical. The Dolgan houses are shaped a bit like a sugar cube and they're extremely basic – a single room with two or three beds, a table and a stove. They're constructed from wooden frames and reindeer skins, which is a great insulator, and they sit on sled runners, so that they can be pulled along by the reindeer. So, when the Dolgan need to move their reindeer to find new places for them to feed, they can literally move house at the same time. It's so simple. They've made the best of available resources and just kept it very functional. I must say, I liked that.

P: I guess small often means living more simply.

J: Yes, I've seen some cabins in California of ten square metres – that's about 25 times smaller than an average American home – where people had to reduce their possessions to only what was absolutely essential. But small doesn't always equal simple. The architect Gary Chang, who is another person I've been strongly influenced by, lives in an apartment block in Hong Kong that's only 32 square metres. He's rethought the concept of living space in a totally unique way using a clever series of sliding walls and moveable built-in units so that he can transform his small apartment into any room he wants – a living room, a kitchen, a library, a bedroom. It's quite amazing really – there are 24 different rooms he can make from just the one space.

▶ 24

A: Have you seen these pictures of the artwork that's being proposed for the main square in the city centre?

B: No. Er, what is it?

A: It's a sculpture in the shape of an open book, and quotes and jokes by various famous local people appear on the page electronically.

B: Oh, I see.

A: Yeah, the quotes change every few minutes. I think it's rather clever. What do you think?

B: Well, yeah, it looks quite fun, but I have to say, I didn't get the idea straightaway – not until you explained it. Personally, I'd rather have something a bit more artistic, if you know what I mean. I'm also not convinced that it'll stand the test of time. I imagine people will get bored of it pretty quickly.

A: Oh, no. I disagree. I reckon people – both locals and visitors, that is – will really like the fact that it tells you something about the city – in the sense that it features people that have been part of our history. I don't think you should underestimate the value of the educational aspect.

B: Yeah, I see that and I'm all in favour of something that's relevant, or rather that reflects our heritage, but I'm afraid it just seems a bit ugly to me.

A: Well, for me, it's very important that it's something interactive – not just a static artwork – because that's more likely to attract people to the square. It's fairly clear that's what the artist is hoping, anyway.

Unit 4

▶ 26

A woman who has been virtually blind for the last six years has spoken about her happiness at being able to see again after surgeons at Oxford's John Radcliffe Hospital inserted a tiny electronic chip into the back of her right eye. Within seconds of switching the device on, Rhian Lewis was able to see light and colour in a way that had been impossible before. It'll probably take months for Lewis to train her brain to see properly again but the early signs are extremely positive; she can already distinguish nearby objects like knives and forks on a table.

Bionic body parts are a fast-developing technology which don't have to be only for people with disabilities. New ear buds developed by a company in San Francisco promise to help anyone hear better by allowing the wearer to choose what sounds to ignore and what to focus on. For example, they can filter out the background noise in a busy restaurant or amplify surrounding sounds when you're riding a bicycle. All this raises the question of whether it is likely that one day in the not so distant future, bionic body parts will actually be more efficient than our own biological body parts.

Audioscripts

▶ 28

P = Presenter, M = Martha Kay

P: Life must have been very different before the invention of certain things, but it's not always so easy to imagine what it was like. For example, if you're in your teens or twenties, you might never have considered how people searched for information before the internet existed. The electric light is another thing that we all take for granted. But how do such inventions come about? Is it necessity that drives innovation? Or commercial profit? Or something else? Here to discuss these questions is business historian, Martha Kay. Martha, we have so many things around us that we needn't have acquired – I mean, we could clearly live without them – so the necessity argument is not the whole answer, is it?

M: Hello, Evan. No, of course it isn't. History's full of inventions that people thought they didn't need at the time. In 1878, a British Parliamentary committee, which had to comment on the usefulness of Alexander Graham Bell's telephone, said '… it is good enough for our transatlantic friends, but unworthy of the attention of practical men.'

P: Yes, well, they probably should have been more open-minded. But in 1878 people didn't need to have phones, did they? You could conduct your daily business perfectly well without one. But now it's become a necessity – a need has been created, if you like.

M: Well, I think people in the nineteenth century felt they had to find a way to communicate at a distance more effectively; they just hadn't envisaged the telephone. Of course, there are some inventions which fill an urgent need – vaccines against particular diseases, for instance. But most innovations aren't like that. Entrepreneurs often come up with ideas to make our lives a little more convenient or comfortable and then, over time, we come to rely on them. Television is a case in point. Remote shopping – like mail-order, or these days internet shopping – is another. *Time* magazine in the 1960s said it wouldn't catch on because, and I quote, 'women like to get out of the house and to be able to change their minds'.

P: I'm sure they did – like to get out of the house, that is, and away from the housework. It can't have been easy. That certainly was a different era.

M: Another form of innovation is to take something that's at first expensive to produce and therefore exclusive to rich people, and make it available to many. There are quite a few things that we now see as everyday necessities that have come to us in this way – where an entrepreneur has found a way to produce something more cheaply, like the mobile phone or the computer. Another example, in the 1890s, the motor car was thought to be a luxury for the wealthy. *Literary Digest* predicted that it would never come into common use.

P: I see, so in that sense, it's about wants rather than needs. But what about all those things that we really don't need. I'm thinking of things like …

▶ 31

First of all, say in a few words what your product or service does, without using jargon, so that anyone could understand it. Make clear what problem it solves and say why your solution is different from the competition. Lastly, you need to convince the other person that you are a good person to implement this idea, so explain your relevant background.

▶ 32

Our idea is a phone app that makes volunteering in the community easier. It's called *Volunteer Planner*. How does it work? Basically, it's an interactive diary that links people who want to volunteer to charities who are looking for help. Why is that necessary? Well, essentially the problem is that voluntary organizations always want people to commit to a regular time – like once a week – so they miss out on all the people who have time here and there and want to help, but can't commit to anything regular. So they never come forward. Of course, there are other apps that do meeting planning like Doodle and Timepal, but ours is unique to this sector because it lists each volunteer's qualifications and skills in a separate database that organizations can easily access.

We're a team of IT experts with experience of working with charities, so we understand this sector well. So, what are we asking for? Well, we've made a prototype and now we need some funding to bring it to market. Honestly, we think it will revolutionize the field of volunteering.

Unit 5

▶ 34

Three people visit the same place and each one leaves with a different story. One remembers a romantic evening in a cosy restaurant and a long walk through a beautifully lit city by night; another remembers an argument with an officious museum curator about the closing time of an art gallery; another remembers sitting and watching the world go by on a lazy, hot afternoon in an elegant park.

Our travel experiences are influenced by so many different factors: the circumstances and state of mind in which we arrive; the people we happen to meet – an affable fellow traveller or a wary local; the preconceptions that we bring to each place we visit. The gift of a good travel writer is to capture the essence of a place in a way that we can all identify with, so that it's instantly recognizable not just superficially – in its grand architecture or lively cafés – but in the way that a particular place feels and thinks. Because the best travel writers aren't really writing about travel, they're writing about how people have shaped places and how places have shaped people.

▶ 36

1 I do regret not stopping there.
2 She does travel a lot.
3 We do miss home sometimes.
4 I did spend a lot of time at the beach.

▶ 37

I = Interviewer, M = Maggie Richards

I: The idea of a mystery tour was made famous by the Beatles' 'Magical Mystery Tour' film in which the band head off westwards out of London in an old bus in search of adventure. Since then, the idea of taking a journey to an unknown destination has been taken up by coach tour operators who offer 'exciting' locations and 'top' hotels, usually to parties of more elderly holiday-makers. But a London-based company called *Secret Adventures* is targeting a younger age group by adding a twist to the concept of the mystery tour. They have developed a number of travel experiences designed, in their words, 'to generate a sense of exploration and wonder'. *Travel Book*'s own Maggie Richards went on one of the trips and talked to me afterwards about it. So, Maggie, a magical experience or not?

M: Absolutely. Definitely one I'd recommend.

I: How much did you know about the adventure before you left? How secret was it?

M: Basically, all we were told was that we'd meet in London and that we'd need a bicycle, a swimming costume and a dry bag – oh, and also that the trip would be over two days.

I: And did you know how far you'd have to swim?

M: Yeah, I did ask that – fifty metres. I thought about asking where we'd be swimming but then I decided not to.

I: No, I guess that would've spoiled the surprise. So can you explain what the trip consisted of?

M: OK, so we all met up in Hackney in north London – eight of us and our guide, Madoc. And then we set off down the track next to the River Lea. It was a beautiful afternoon and the path was flat so it was easy cycling. And that gave us the chance to chat and get to know each other. Occasionally, Madoc would give us a clue about the trip, like 'Only fifteen miles to go' or 'Is that our island? No, I don't think so.' It all added to the anticipation. Then, as the sun was setting, he told us to stop and put our bikes in the long grass and get ready to swim. We packed our stuff into dry bags and then got into the water. It wasn't warm and a few people were screaming and gasping – I know I was – but actually it felt really exhilarating to be heading off for the night with just your swimming things and a dry bag. Madoc had gone ahead and by the time we reached the island, a fire was burning. He cooked an amazing stew for supper and we shared stories around the fire.

Audioscripts

I: Did you have tents?
M: No, we didn't. We slept in the open, but it was fine – it wasn't cold. In the morning, we swam back and cycled to a café for breakfast. Then we caught a train back into London. It was very strange arriving back in the busy city. It made the whole thing seem as if it had been a magical dream – actually it had.
I: Are the trips expensive?
M: Not at all. Well, it depends which one. Some of the shorter ones are less than £40. You could travel a long way and spend a lot more to create that kind of magic, but what Secret Adventures taught me was that you really don't need to.

(Based on a real Secret Adventures trip. Madoc is a real character, but Maggie is a fictional character.)

▶ 38

1 A: You have to be careful not to get overcharged in the local markets.
   B: Yes, I know that.
2 A: Would you like to drive?
   B: No, I'd rather you did.
3 A: Did he take warm clothes with him?
   B: I hope so.
4 A: Do you mind travelling alone?
   B: No, I actually prefer it.
5 A: Are there many good guidebooks about this region?
   B: Yes, there are some excellent ones.
6 A: Did she enjoy visiting Russia?
   B: Yes, she loved it.

▶ 40

I think it's a well-known fact that a lot of exposure to strong sun is a dangerous thing, particularly if you're a person with fair skin. So these days people are generally more careful – they take precautions not to get sunburned. But I'm afraid it wasn't always like that.

I have my clinic in Patong. It's on the island of Phuket in Thailand – which you've heard about, I'm sure: it's famous for having beautiful beaches and consequently, we get a lot of tourists and sunseekers here.

A few years ago, I was in my clinic and a young man with red hair and very fair skin came in. His legs were the colour of his hair – like a lobster – and he was in great pain. I applied some cream to his legs and then I wrapped them both in bandages from the ankle to the thigh. I told him to stay out of the sun and to take it easy for a few days until the redness had disappeared. The following morning, I was walking to work along the street by the beach. By chance, I happened to glance down at the people on the beach who were arranging their sunbeds and parasols for a day of relaxing by the sea and there, to my amazement, was the same man! He was lying stretched out on his back, not in the shade, but in full sun with just his swimming costume and his bandages on! It was so crazy it was almost funny.

Unit 6

▶ 42

W = Woman, R = Rashmi
W: How do you advise people to stay fit and healthy, Rashmi?
R: You know, there's so much contradictory information out there about how to keep in shape: whether you should watch your weight by controlling what you eat or by exercising; what kind of exercise regime is best, and so on. I was reading a scientific journal just this morning saying that intensive exercise, like working out at the gym is actually less effective than gentle exercise, like going for a walk regularly in the park.
W: Really? Why did it say that?
R: I think the idea is that if you do really intensive exercise, then your body demands calorie compensation afterwards – in other words, you're more likely to reward yourself with a bigger snack at the end of the session. Whereas if you just stretch your legs often or take regular gentle exercise, it doesn't have the same effect.
W: So what do you do? You're in pretty good shape.
R: Well, mainly I try not to obsess too much about my weight. I don't go on diets and I don't weigh myself every day. I just do active things that I enjoy. I've never been a fan of the gym, I have to say, and I never go for a run – I find it boring. The kids keep me pretty active anyway. But recently I've got into road cycling. Every couple of weeks a few of us go out for a ride in the countryside – forty or fifty kilometres. We often go up in the woods and hills around the South Downs. The scenery's beautiful and it's a great way to enjoy nature and stay fit at the same time.

▶ 44

P = Presenter, B = Ben Newborn
P: … thanks for those comments, Lydia. I'd like to turn now to someone who should know more about sports injuries than most and that's ultrarunner Ben Newborn. Ben, before we get into the question of injuries, can you just explain for our listeners what ultrarunning is?
B: Sure, basically ultrarunning is running distances beyond a usual marathon distance. So, it could mean running 100 kilometres in a single day, or it could involve running several marathons on consecutive days.
P: And how did you get into it?
B: I was a runner anyway and I just wanted to take it to another level – to really test myself physically and mentally. So in 2008, I registered for the Ultra-Trail race in the Alps which requires runners to run 161 kilometres around Mont Blanc.
P: Didn't you worry about doing yourself real damage?
B: Actually, I wasn't so concerned about injuries. I was more worried about failure. And I knew that if I wanted to succeed in overcoming exhaustion and the things that can make you feel sick, I had to get my diet and nutrition right. That's ultimately what would let me run in relative comfort.
P: Comfort's not a word I'd normally associate with a 161-kilometre run, but anyway … What about injuries? This must put intense strain on your body.
B: I think the most important thing in any sport is to recognize when your body's in pain. A lot of sports people try to go through the pain. I'm not talking about when they're in a really bad way, but when they have a small muscle strain or pain in a joint – an ankle, for example – they tend to take some painkillers or put on some kind of support and just carry on exercising. Because they feel they can't afford to rest. But of course that's completely wrong. Pain is your body warning you to be careful – to stop, very often – because minor problems will inevitably develop into more severe injuries. So that's the first thing: to listen to your body.
P: Yes, but we all get aches and pains. Surely that shouldn't discourage us from doing exercise?
B: Well, no, but if you do the right kind of preparation, which I'd really urge people to do, you can avoid getting injuries in the first place. I follow a method developed by a sports physiologist, which is a series of stretches and gentle exercises that strengthen the key muscles and ligaments. It's definitely prevented me from getting ankle sprains and helped with some of the other things I used to suffer from: lower back pain, runner's knee and so on …

▶ 45

1 A: I heard Sarah came off her bicycle. Is she in a bad way?
   B: Luckily she didn't break anything; she was pretty shaken up though.
2 A: Is it true that Jack nearly cut his finger off?
   B: Yes, he practically passed out when he saw what he'd done. It was quite a deep cut, but he's on the mend now, I think.
3 A: You look a bit off colour. Are you feeling under the weather?
   B: No, I'm not ill. I'm just run down from working too much.

▶ 48

C = Chair, S = Sophia, T = Tariq
C: Hello, everyone. Welcome to this brainstorming session on promoting health and fitness among employees. David Grant, our CEO, is very keen that we, as a company, take some positive action on this – not only because there's also an obvious benefit in terms of productivity and days lost through sickness, but because he genuinely believes it'll make for a happier workplace. So, with that in mind, I'd like to hear any ideas you have. Who'd like to start? Yes, Sophia …
S: Thank you. Yeah, well, as I see it, there are probably two routes we could

100

go down. One possibility is just to encourage people to do simple things like walking to work or not spending such long periods at their computers, that kind of thing. Or the other alternative is to spend some serious money on the problem – so, something like installing a gym or a fitness centre on site that people can use in their breaks, or after work. Having said that, I realize there may not be a budget for that kind of thing.

C: OK, thanks for that and … Yes, Tariq …

T: Yeah, for me the key is getting people to enjoy exercise. If you offer activities that people think are fun, then I think you'll get much better participation.

C: Such as …?

T: Such as team sports – football, basketball, that kind of thing – you could even have competitions. Another idea could be dance classes. Admittedly, a lot of people may do these things anyway in their free time, but I bet there are a lot more who want to and never find the time.

C: Thanks, Tariq. I think those are interesting ideas. And what about the idea of group exercises in the mornings? The kind of collective warm-up routine you used to see in companies fifty years ago. It's not a particularly original idea, I'll grant you, but it might be fun – and it would definitely build team spirit.

S: Yeah, I think you have to be careful there. People might think that you're trying to force them into some sort of exercise regime. You know, I know that isn't the intention, but it might look that way. I think it'd be better to give people incentives to do things on their own, like a 'bike to work' scheme, where you offer to pay part of the cost of a new bicycle – I haven't thought the details through exactly, but I think that kind of individual incentive probably works much better.

C: Yeah, I like that. The only problem I see is that it wouldn't be so easy to monitor how much they used the bike, but I guess that's a risk you'd have to take.

SECOND EDITION

Life

WORKBOOK | ADVANCED

Contents Split A

Unit 1	Lessons for life	page 104
Unit 2	More than a job	page 112
Unit 3	Design for life	page 120
Unit 4	Innovation	page 128
Unit 5	The magic of travel	page 136
Unit 6	Body matters	page 144
Audioscripts		page 152
Answer key		page 161

NATIONAL GEOGRAPHIC LEARNING

PAUL DUMMETT

Australia • Brazil • Mexico • Singapore • United Kingdom • United States

Unit 1 Lessons for life

1a Things they never taught you

Listening eight rules for life

1 🎵 **1** Listen to a talk given to a group of college graduates and answer these questions.

1 What was the speaker going to talk about originally?
   ....
   ....

2 What does he actually talk about?
   ....
   ....

Glossary
entitled (adj) /ɪnˈteɪt(ə)ld/ believing you deserve to get what you want
flipping burgers (exp) /ˈflɪpɪŋ ˈbɜː(r)ɡ(ə)z/ a job that involves cooking hamburgers in a fast-food restaurant
nerd (n) *colloquial* /nɜː(r)d/ a person skilled at something technical but lacking in social skills

2 🎵 **1** Listen again and choose the correct options to complete the rules that the speaker mentions.

1 What you get in life is *just / unjust*.
2 You *must aim for / can't expect* great job conditions from the start.
3 Employers are generally *more strict / less strict* than teachers.
4 Flipping burgers is *a beginning / not a job you should do*.
5 Things will go wrong in your life and most probably it will be *your / someone else's* fault.
6 The boring chores in life *can be left to others / have to be done by everyone*.
7 In the real world, you will *often / seldom* get a second chance to get things right.
8 Don't underestimate people with good *technical expertise / social skills*.

Grammar time phrases

3 🔊 **1** Complete the sentences with these time phrases. Then listen to the talk again and check your answers.

> about fifteen years ago   at the time   before that
> currently   many years ago   next year
> over the last twenty years   rarely   sooner or later

1 _____, I'm writing a book about scientific inventions.
2 I'm going to give you some rules of life that I read _____ in a book.
3 _____, I had believed myself to be – as you probably do now – one entitled individual.
4 You will not make eighty thousand dollars _____.
5 _____, your grandparents had a different word for burger flipping.
6 But they were like that because _____ they were paying your bills.
7 _____, schools have abolished the idea of winners and losers.
8 That _____ happens in real life.
9 _____, you'll end up working for one.

4 Look at the time phrases in these sentences spoken by a student who is about to graduate. Complete the sentences with the correct form of the verbs in brackets.

1 At the moment, I _____ (take) a break from my studies.
2 Last week, I _____ (attend) a lecture on a career in the diplomatic service.
3 Before that, I _____ (never / be) to a careers advice talk.
4 Nowadays, most graduates _____ (seem) to think that the world owes them a living.
5 I _____ (wonder) for some time what I'm going to do with my life.
6 But I _____ (have) to make a decision in the coming weeks whether to continue studying or apply for a job.

Vocabulary life lessons

5 Complete these sentences. You have been given the first letter of the missing words.

1 My father told me: 'Be kind to people and, as much as possible, forgive them when they do wrong. Because in the end anger and bitterness will just eat you up.' He was right, but it's easier s_____ than d_____.
2 I think the most v_____ lesson anyone has ever taught me was my English teacher, who said: 'Keep an open mind and you will learn a lot.'
3 'Do things that take you out of your comfort zone' is a g_____ principle in my life. Because no one has ever managed to progress by playing safe.
4 I always make a p_____ of listening to what older people have to say – not just dismissing them as out of touch.
5 I try to learn f_____ my m_____ in life. One thing I've learned is that it's much better to travel light than take loads of stuff with you that you'll never use, which is what I always used to do.
6 I think to remain humble and to try to live as simple a life as possible is a good rule of t_____.

6 Dictation the problem with advice

🔊 **2** Listen to someone describing how advice and wisdom can be misinterpreted. Complete the paragraph.

One _____
_____.
An example _____
_____.
One of his main ideas was _____
_____,
they will _____.
He called _____.
People _____
_____,
but _____
_____.
Unfortunately, _____
_____
_____,
which _____.

105

1b What's in a name?

Reading the importance of names

1 Read the article. Which of these statements (a, b or c) best represents the author's view?

a Our names should help describe our character.

b Names are useful in giving a person a sense of identity.

c Native American names are useful because they identify social status.

2 Read the article again. Are the sentences true (T) or false (F)?

1 Native American Indians share a belief in the significance of names.

2 It is common for Native Americans to name people after things in the natural world.

3 Native American names can evolve as people go through life.

4 Names usually reflect something the parents saw at the time of the child's birth.

5 Many cultures still use names to indicate the place people were born in.

6 In the West, nicknames are always used to identify someone's social status.

What's in a name?

Do you feel that your name is an essential part of who you are? What factors did your parents consider when they named you? Had they already been thinking about the name before you were born? Have you changed your name at any time in your life because you thought it did not suit you?

For some, names mean little. For others, such as Native American Indians, who have been following the same naming traditions for generations, it is a critical part of one's identity. Although traditions differ from one Native American tribe to another, all tribes attach great importance to the name or names that each individual is given.

You are probably familiar with Native American names taken from nature, such as Laughing Water, Rolling Thunder, White Feather, etc. (NB the belief that such names derive from what their parents were looking at when the child was born is false.) You are probably less aware that their names can also describe certain attributes, such as character (e.g. Independent) or physical appearance (e.g. Broad Shoulders) or social status (e.g. Wife). Among some tribes, these names are continually changing according to people's achievements or life experiences. In some cases, a person will change names three or four times during their life.

Names in Native American Indian culture are descriptive, reminding the bearer of their place in nature or of their reputation in society. In other cultures, surnames often denoted where a person came from or what their family profession was: 'Julie London', 'James Carpenter' are examples in English. But even if such names still exist, they are no longer an indication of a person's identity.

Perhaps the most similar thing to the Native American tradition in modern western society is the nickname. My given name is Sarah, but my parents and childhood friends know me as 'Sally', a derivative name which has no particular meaning. The people I met at university nicknamed me 'Starah' (i.e. 'starer') because I have a bad habit of staring at people. Since I have been with my husband, my name has returned to Sarah. Such nicknames may not have the descriptive power of Native American names, but they do serve as important markers of the stages in our lives. Who knows what name people will be calling me in another ten years?

Unit 1 Lessons for life

Grammar the continuous aspect

3 Find and name five different continuous tenses used in the article.

4 Look at these pairs of sentences with simple and continuous verb forms. What is the difference in meaning – if any – in the pairs of sentences?

1. a The name Lucas **is** very popular.
   b The name Lucas **is getting** very popular.
2. a People always **pronounce** my name wrong.
   b People **are** always **pronouncing** my name wrong.
3. a They**'ve made** a list of names for their baby, who is due in May.
   b They**'ve been making** a list of names for their baby, who is due in May.
4. a At one time they **had thought** of giving all their children names beginning with 'M'.
   b At one time they **had been thinking** of giving all their children names beginning with 'M'.
5. a When I **got** married, I decided to change my surname to 'Romano'.
   b When I **was getting** married, I decided to change my surname to 'Romano'.
6. a They've had five boys, so they **hope** the next baby is a girl.
   b They've had five boys, so they**'ll be hoping** the next baby is a girl.

5 Complete these sentences with the correct tense. Use six continuous forms and two simple forms.

1. Sorry I was late picking you up. _____ (you / wait) there long?
2. I can smell cigarettes. _____ (someone / smoke) in here?
3. I heard a scream and ran towards the river. A boy _____ (play) too close to the bank and (fall) _____ in.
4. Sorry I can't meet you later. I'm afraid I _____ (work) late tonight.
5. We _____ (live) in one room for the last three months because builders _____ (repair) our roof.
6. I _____ (hear) a lot of strange stories in my time, but that is probably the strangest.

Vocabulary personality and identity

6 Match the personality types (1–6) with the descriptions (a–f).

1. a control freak
2. a driven person
3. a family person
4. a free spirit
5. a larger-than-life character
6. the life and soul of the party

a. is very lively and sociable
b. is independent and does not follow conventions
c. wants to manage every aspect of a situation
d. has a strong and forceful presence
e. puts home life before other things
f. is motivated and ambitious

Wordbuilding binomial pairs

7 Choose the correct options to complete the sentences.

1. Can I have some *quiet and peace / peace and quiet*, please? I'm trying to concentrate.
2. I do exercise *as and when / when and as* I can, which is not often enough!
3. As far as business trips go, it was great – *sweet and short / short and sweet*.
4. That was my first marathon. I've got a few *pains and aches / aches and pains* now, but no injuries.
5. *Then and now / Now and then*, I wonder if I should have gone to college.
6. The event is not all *fun and games / games and fun*. There is a serious side to it too.
7. *First and foremost / Foremost and first*, we choose a name that we hope is not too common.
8. *Large and by / By and large*, it's a pretty good place to live.

8 Pronunciation linking in word pairs

a 🔊 **3** Listen to how these binomial words pairs are linked with *and* as a weak form.

1. I hear you **loud and clear**.
2. He'll be **up and about** in no time.
3. It's a game of **cat and mouse**.
4. She's **sick and tired** of people asking what she's going to do with her life.
5. The job has been a bit **up and down** lately.
6. It's **part and parcel** of being a parent.

b Practise saying the sentences in Exercise 8a in the same way.

9 Match the binomial word pairs (1–6) from Exercise 8a with the correct definitions (a–f).

a. changeable
b. out of one's sick bed
c. an integral element
d. clearly
e. fed up (with)
f. one trying to catch the other

107

1c The English we speak

Listening the evolution of English

1 🔊 4 Look at these statements about the English language. Do you think the statements are true (T) or false (F)? Then listen to a lecture on the evolution of English and check your answers.

1 Throughout its history, the English language has been subject to outside influences.
2 English is principally a Germanic language.
3 The language of Shakespeare is very different from modern English.
4 People living in the colonies tried to preserve the integrity of British English.
5 Many people around the world speak a very simplified, functional form of English.
6 The constant adaptation of English has been a negative thing.

2 🔊 4 Listen again and choose the correct option (a or b) according to the speaker. Pause the CD each time before moving onto the next question.

1 The English language has:
  a influenced other cultures.
  b both influenced and been influenced by other cultures.
2 The fact that Anglo-Saxon, not Latin, was the dominant influence on English is:
  a unlike other countries in Western Europe.
  b because the Romans were hated in Britain.
3 The language stopped changing so fast after the 16th century because:
  a books became more common.
  b no one invaded Britain after that date.
4 The speaker implies that compared to British English, the language used by Americans is:
  a more open.
  b more refined.
5 The author suggests that English is now a global language because:
  a it is such an adaptable language.
  b it became the language of international trade.
6 Non-native speakers who want to speak English:
  a must choose for themselves what kind of English they want to speak.
  b must be careful not to learn the wrong version of English.

3 Choose the correct definition (a or b) for the words in bold from the lecture.

1 The **legacy** of the Romans is evident in the Romance languages.
  a great achievement
  b gift to future generations
2 Instead of replacing English, French was **assimilated** into it.
  a incorporated   b transformed
3 The language continued to remain quite **organic**.
  a basic   b in a state of evolution
4 From this point in history, British colonialism **thrived**.
  a did well   b began to diminish
5 English was successful in its global reach because it was a **versatile** language.
  a simple to use   b easy to adapt

Word focus *life*

4 Complete the sentences with *life* using these words.

| brings | fact | larger | lifelike |
| saver | story | time | walks |

1 Jenny is a _____-than-life character; you know when she's in the room!
2 Thanks for covering my shift yesterday. It was a real **life-**_____.
3 Teaching is a profession that attracts people from **all** _____ **of life**.
4 The way he reads the stories really _____ **them to life**.
5 It's **a** _____ **of life** that you won't get anywhere without effort.
6 Making the wrong career move has been **the** _____ **of my life**.
7 That statue of a cat in your garden is incredibly _____.
8 My daughter loves university. She's **having the** _____ **of her life**.

1d How did you get into that?

Real life getting to know people

1 🔊 5 Listen to the conversations. Note down where each conversation takes place and what details you learn about each person.

Conversation 1
Place: _____
Teresa: _____
Ana: _____
Conversation 2
Place: _____
Jeff: _____
Khalid: _____

2 🔊 5 Complete these questions and statements using ONE word in each space. Then listen to the conversations again and check your answers.

Conversation 1
1 What did you _____ the talk?
2 Sorry, I _____ _____ introduced myself. I'm Teresa.
3 _____ in Spain is it?
4 Do you _____ joining me?

Conversation 2
1 Where are you _____ ?
2 I'm Jeff, _____ the _____ .
3 What are you _____ to be _____ ?
4 Wow, that sounds _____ .

3 What do you think the speakers meant (a or b) when they used the phrases in bold?
1 a lot of **food for thought**
   a things that need serious consideration
   b unanswered questions
2 it's **not a million miles from** there
   a not so far from
   b not so different from
3 let me just **get rid of** all these papers
   a throw away
   b find somewhere to put
4 your **best bet** would be …
   a best chance
   b best route
5 **way above my head**, I'm afraid
   a too stressful for me
   b too difficult for me

4 Pronunciation merged words in everyday phrases

a 🔊 6 Listen to the sentences with merged words. Complete the sentences.
1 _____ the exhibition?
2 _____ going out for some fresh air?
3 _____ company is it, exactly?
4 _____ being the only boy in a family of girls?
5 Sorry, _____ that before.
6 _____ the course?
7 _____ coffee or something?
8 So, _____ before?

b Listen again and repeat each sentence.

5 Listen and respond meeting a stranger

🔊 7 You have been invited to dinner by an old friend, Nicola, in a foreign town you are visiting. Someone at the dinner who you don't know comes up to speak to you. Respond with your own words. Then compare your response with the model answer that follows.

> Hi there, I don't think we've met. I'm Antony.

> Hi, Antony. Good to meet you. I'm José.

109

1e Holiday policy

Writing taking notes

1 🔊 8 Look at these notes that an employee made during a short talk about leave (i.e. time off work) and sabbaticals (i.e. a long period of leave given every few years in some jobs, e.g. universities). Listen and complete the notes.

Sabbaticals and unpaid leave

- formal document in 2 wks

- sabbaticals, i.e. paid leave: 3 mths for every 6 yrs worked if on [1] _____ or above; only for full-time staff; part-time staff arrangements tbc

- unpaid leave: [2] _____ decides on each case, e.g. sick parents; no unpaid leave for people who have worked for less than [3] _____

---

2 **Writing skill** using abbreviations

🔊 8 What do you think these abbreviations from the notes mean? Write the words in full. Then listen again and check the words the speaker actually uses.

1 wks _____
2 i.e. _____
3 mths _____
4 yrs _____
5 tbc _____
6 e.g. _____

3 Write abbreviations for these words.

1 approximately _____
2 with reference to _____
3 including _____
4 and so on _____
5 ten in the morning _____
6 hours _____
7 please note _____
8 per cent _____
9 second _____
10 per week _____

4 Write this message in full sentences.

> Jeff rang 11 a.m. Wants you to go to London to discuss contract details, i.e. commission, quantities, etc. Time of mtg tbc. NB not in office til Thurs.

5 🔊 9 You are going to take notes on a talk to company employees about holiday policy. First look at the guidelines for taking notes. Then listen and complete the notes.

1 Only include important information.
2 Reduce the number of words by omitting articles, auxiliary verbs, unnecessary pronouns.
3 Use abbreviations.

New policy
_____
_____
_____
_____

Reasons for policy
_____
_____
_____
_____

Employee responsibilities
_____
_____
_____
_____

Details
_____
_____
_____
_____

110

Unit 1 Lessons for life

Wordbuilding binomial pairs

1 Underline the correct word to complete each binomial pair.

1 more *and / or* less
2 take it *and / or* leave it
3 cut *and / but* dried
4 out *and / or* about
5 slowly *and / but* surely
6 live *and / but* learn
7 wear *and / to* tear
8 sink *and / or* swim
9 give *and / but* take
10 back *and / to* front

2 Complete these sentences using the pairs in Exercise 1.

1 I think you've got your jumper on _____ .
2 There's _____ in any relationship. You can't have everything your own way.
3 The sofa looks almost new. There's a little bit of _____ on the cushion covers, but that's all.
4 My grandmother's 89 now and _____ stuck at home. She doesn't get _____ as she used to.
5 In my first job, no-one showed me what I had to do at all – it was just _____ .
6 The negotiation is pretty _____ , as I see it. I've said what I want and, frankly, they can _____ .
7 We're making progress _____ . It hasn't been an enjoyable experience, but you _____ , I suppose.

Learning skills using idioms

3 Try to answer these questions about idioms. Then compare your answers with those on page 162.

1 What are the benefits of using idioms in your English?
2 What is the effect on the listener if you get the idiom wrong?
3 Are these statements true (T) or false (F)?
   a Choosing whether to use an idiom or not depends on the context (your audience, whether you're writing or speaking, etc.).
   b Even if you don't speak the language well, including a few idioms can give a better impression.
   c Idioms change more quickly than other aspects of the language.
   d Only use idioms that are new and current.
   e Idioms and slang are pretty much the same thing.

4 Look at the options in these sentences. Do you think it is appropriate to use the idiom or not in each case?

1 A job interview

A: So tell me a little about yourself, Mr Barton.
B: Well, I'm 34 years old and *a real go-getter / very ambitious*.

2 A letter advising a friend about investing money in shares

A good *rule of thumb / principle* is always to spread your investments between different sectors.

5 Try some of the idioms that you learned in Unit 1 in context. Ask your teacher if your use of them is correct and appropriate.

Check!

6 Do the quiz. All the answers are in Student's Book Unit 1.

1 Complete these quotes.
   a 'Better to walk without knowing where than to _____ doing nothing.' (Tuareg proverb)
   b 'If you want to make peace with your enemy, you have to _____ with your enemy.' (Nelson Mandela)
   c 'Learn from the mistakes of others. You can't live long enough to make them all _____ .' (Eleanor Roosevelt)
   d 'But love is _____ , and lovers cannot see.' (Shakespeare)

2 What are the opposites of these types of people? You have been given the first letter.
   a a realist ≠ a d_____
   b a serious person ≠ a j_____
   c a shy type ≠ an o_____ type

3 Rearrange the letters to make time phrases.
   a present simple
      n a y d o w a s _____
      l e g a r e n l y _____
   b present perfect
      o s   f r a _____
      c l e r e n t y _____
   c future
      r o o n e s   r o   t e l a r _____
   d past perfect
      r o r i p   o t   t a h t _____

111

Unit 2 More than a job

2a Golden worm diggers

Listening *yartsa gunbu*

1 🔊 10 Look at the photo and then listen to a news report. Answer the questions.

 1 Where are these people?

 2 What are the people looking for, and why?

 3 What would they normally be doing for a living?

2 🔊 10 Read this summary. Then listen again and complete the summary using one word in each space.

In May and June, on the Tibetan Plateau, you can see people ¹ _____ the grass for a small ² _____ called *yartsa gunbu*. *Yartsa gunbu* is highly valued for its ³ _____ properties. It grows inside the body of a ⁴ _____ and then sends a small ⁵ _____ above the ground. The Chinese believe it improves your life ⁶ _____ and so demand for it has ⁷ _____ in recent years. The local people, who in the past made a living by herding ⁸ _____ and sheep, now make much more money from *yartsa gunbu*. But ecologists are worried about the ⁹ _____ of *yartsa gunbu* and think it may die out.

Wordbuilding phrasal verb *get*

3 Choose the correct option.

 1 I'm the only one in the family earning at the moment, but we *get by / get through*.

 2 I'm really not in the mood for a party, but I can't *get away with / get out of* it. I promised Sheree I'd go.

 3 Well, thanks for all your advice. I'll *get back / get through* to you if I need anything else.

 4 I think Jake will go a long way. He's very positive. If he has a disappointment, he *gets over / gets round* it very quickly.

 5 I wish she had said what was on her mind. I couldn't understand what she was *getting at / getting to*.

 6 I'm sorry I haven't fixed the catch on the window yet. I'll try to *get round to / get away with* it later today.

Grammar perfect forms

4 🔊 **10** Look at these sentences from the report. Which verb did the speaker use? Listen to the report again and check your answers.

1 It's as if someone *had dropped / had been dropping* a valuable ring and then asked their friends to help search for it.
2 What they *have looked for / are looking for* is a small fungus called *yartsa gunbu*.
3 It's so prized in China that half a kilo *has been known / was known* to sell for up to $50,000.
4 One couple I talked to *had searched / had been searching* all day and *has found / found* only thirty specimens.
5 For centuries, herbal doctors *have prescribed / had prescribed yartsa gunbu* for all sorts of medical problems.
6 Zhaxicaiji *has started / started* her own *yartsa* company in 1998.
7 Since then, the business *has grown / grew* year on year.
8 These communities *thrive / are thriving* on *yartsa gunbu*'s rarity.
9 The cycle will stop, because the fungus that infects the larvae *will be disappearing / will have disappeared*.
10 Perhaps the next generation of golden worm diggers *will be searching / will have searched* harder than ever.

5 Complete these sentences by putting the verbs in the correct tense. Use simple or perfect forms.

Does *yartsa gunbu* actually work? Recent research ¹_____ (show) that it helps the blood absorb more oxygen, which in turn, ²_____ (help) the user to feel more energetic.

People in the West ³_____ (criticize) the use of herbs in Chinese medicine for being unscientific, but in fact, it is a practice which ⁴_____ (be based) on thousands of years of practice. Moreover, many of the ingredients are the same as those in western medicines. An American study in 2002 ⁵_____ (show) that in nearly fifty per cent of the new drugs produced in the previous twenty years, scientists ⁶_____ (use) natural plants as a starting point.

So far, western medicine ⁷_____ (not / exploit) Chinese knowledge of herbs. One drug, however, that ⁸_____ (be) very successful in treating malaria, comes from the plant artemisinin. But there is no sign that more drugs like this ⁹_____ (be developed) any time soon. This is a shame as, without a doubt, there ¹⁰_____ (be) a lot that the West can learn from Chinese medicine.

Vocabulary work and life

6 Complete these sentences. You have been given the first letter of the missing words.

1 The animals are our l_____. Without them we couldn't survive.
2 When we interview new applicants, we always give them a simple t_____ to perform.
3 Some students go on to university, but many opt to learn a t_____ like interior decorating or plumbing or building.
4 Medicine is more than just a job; it's a v_____.
5 It's difficult to make a decent l_____ as an artist, unless you become very well known.

7 Pronunciation extra /ɪ/, /iː/ or /aɪ/

🔊 **11** Look at the underlined syllables in these words and put the words into categories according to the vowel sound each contains: /ɪ/ as in *bit*, /iː/ as in *beat* or /aɪ/ as in *bite*. Then listen and check your answers.

medi<u>ci</u>nal	sur<u>vi</u>ve	spe<u>ci</u>fic	<u>ti</u>ny	<u>fi</u>nancial
<u>pri</u>vate	<u>pre</u>vious	pre<u>sc</u>ribe	re<u>vi</u>talize	<u>vi</u>sa
un<u>sci</u>entific	spe<u>ci</u>men	cater<u>pi</u>llar	<u>ki</u>lo	art<u>i</u>st

8 Dictation interview with a journalist

🔊 **12** Listen to an interview with the journalist who reported the story of the golden worm diggers and complete his answers.

I: So, John, how did you come across this story?
J: ¹ I _____.

I: And what was it that interested you this time?
J: ² Well, _____.

I: And what was that in this case?
J: ³ I _____.

⁴ So I _____.

113

2b Deep-sea line fishers

Reading a game of cat and mouse

1 Read the article about an expedition to catch a bluefin tuna and answer the questions.

1 What is difficult about catching these fish?

2 What method do the people in the article use?

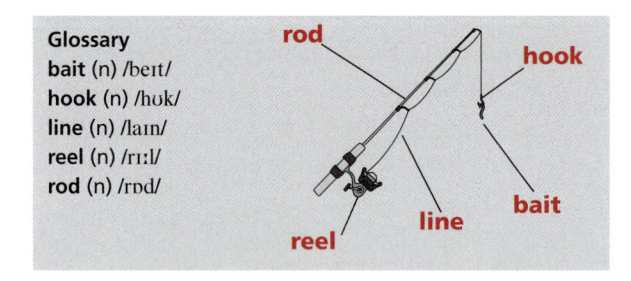

Glossary
bait (n) /beɪt/
hook (n) /hʊk/
line (n) /laɪn/
reel (n) /riːl/
rod (n) /rɒd/

2 Read the article again. Are these sentences true (T) or false (F)? Or is there not enough information (N) to say if the sentences are true or false?

1 The narrator is new to sea fishing.
2 If the fish weren't so heavy, they'd be easy to catch.
3 Numbers of bluefin tuna have declined because of the high number of line fishers.
4 Bluefin tuna generally feed on other smaller fish.
5 Troy used his instinct to know where the fish were.
6 It's necessary to leave the line a little loose to make the fish think you are not interested.

Deep-sea line fishers

Some people have compared catching a bluefin tuna to trying to catch a car going at eighty kilometres per hour. So, not having done any line fishing at sea before, I was pretty apprehensive – but also excited – about the trip that my friend, a professional line fisher called Troy had organized.

At the same time, my hopes were not high. 95 per cent of the time, bluefin tuna line fishers come back empty-handed and a few hundred dollars worse off in the attempt. Just finding the fish is difficult enough, but once you've found them, you are then faced with the task of landing a fish that can weigh in excess of 300 kilos.

Of course, tracking them down has become more difficult in recent years because of overfishing. Because demand for tuna is so high, fishing companies employ an intensive form of fishing called 'purse seine,' where they use big circular nets to trap the tuna. This has devastated the Atlantic tuna population, reducing it by over eighty per cent in the last thirty years.

Three days before we were due to set off, Troy got a call from a friend who informed him of a secret fishing spot about forty miles off the coast. Since we had nothing else to do, we headed there that evening, and the following morning, just as he had said, thousands of bluefin tuna showed up.

In order to keep our prey interested, we dropped chunks of fish into the water and then baited our lines and let them out. Tuna feed at depths of fifty to a hundred metres, so you need a lot of line. For about two hours, we sat there waiting for something to happen, and then suddenly Troy's rod bent dramatically and the reel started spinning furiously, casting line out at an incredible rate.

Knowing the fish like to swim towards the boat to make you think they are off the line, Troy jumped on the rod so that he could keep the line tight. Then we followed the fish, steering the boat in the same direction, while Troy slowly reeled it in. After about an hour of this, the fish started to get tired of us chasing it and it came closer to the surface, where we could see it. 'Grab the harpoon gun,' Troy shouted and I knew that my moment had come.

Idioms safety

3 Match the two parts to make idioms connected with safety.

1	second	a	side
2	cut	b	the book
3	be on the safe	c	side of caution
4	follow	d	nature
5	do things by	e	cotton wool
6	better to be safe	f	corners
7	wrap someone in	g	than sorry
8	err on the	h	the correct procedure

4 Complete these sentences using idioms from Exercise 3.

1 I always wear a bicycle helmet, even if I am riding a short distance – just to _____ .

2 You can't _____ your children _____ all the time. You have to allow them to take some risks.

3 Safety is actually _____ to me because I used to have a job repairing electricity lines.

4 It's very tempting to _____ when you think you can do something more quickly by not observing all the safety rules.

5 If you _____ rather than thinking you know better, you will be fine.

Grammar passive forms

5 Rewrite the sentences transforming one verb in each sentence to make a passive construction.

1 My friend, Troy, had organized the trip.

2 Once you've found the fish, that's only the beginning of your task.

3 In 'purse seine' fishing, people use big circular nets to trap the tuna.

4 'Purse seine' fishing has devastated the Atlantic tuna population in the last thirty years.

5 Troy jumped on the rod so that he could keep the line tight.

6 The fish started to get tired of us chasing it.

6 Complete these sentences with passive constructions using the verbs in brackets. Use *be* or *get* to form each passive verb as you think appropriate.

1 Did you hear about poor Esty? She _____ (call) in to work at the weekend on her birthday!

2 I wish they would just let me get on with the job. I'm tired of _____ (tell) what to do.

3 Please be careful using that axe. You _____ (injure).

4 I don't mind driving, but it's more relaxing _____ (drive) – depending on who the driver is, of course!

5 I submit my photos to the newspaper, but if they don't like them, I _____ (not / pay).

6 _____ (you / invite) to the opening of the exhibition? It's next Friday.

7 Read the passage and underline the best options (active or passive) to complete the text. Where you think either could work, underline both.

> If you had to say what the most dangerous professions in the world were, probably ¹*you would not include fishing / fishing would not be included* on your list. Yet, statistically, deep-sea fishing is the world's riskiest job. In the UK, fishermen have a one in twenty chance of ²*fishing killing them / being killed* during their working lives. When you consider the conditions that ³*fishing forces them / they are forced* to work in, it is not surprising: rough seas, freezing temperatures, long hours and lots of heavy, moving equipment. Another industry that has a similarly high injury rate is logging (cutting down trees for wood). ⁴*Loggers also work long hours / Long hours are also worked by loggers* and they, too, use heavy, dangerous equipment. They are also at risk of injury from heavy tree trunks slipping or falling. One job that might have been on your list is mining. Although ⁵*they employ fewer people / fewer people are employed* in mines these days, it remains a dangerous professions. This is not just because of the obvious risks of mines collapsing but also because of the long-term effects of ⁶*breathing in poor air / poor air being breathed in*.

2c Guerrilla geographer

Listening Daniel Raven-Ellison

1 🔊 **13** Listen to part of a radio programme about Daniel Raven-Ellison's new approach to geography. Which of these statements (a, b or c) best summarizes this new approach?

a   a critical approach that challenges people to question traditional geography teaching

b   an inclusive approach that encourages communities to redesign their neighbourhoods

c   a practical and fun approach that promotes social and environmental awareness

2 🔊 **13** Listen again and complete these sentences and questions.

1   What does one of Daniel Raven-Ellison's challenges ask participants to find?

2   What was Raven-Ellison's job before?

3   For Raven-Ellison geography is more than just _____ .

4   What kind of exploration does he want to promote among children?

5   Guerrilla geography is all about having _____ .

6   He says most city guides are selective in what they show, but his films show the _____ .

7   What is the best way to appreciate your neighbourhood properly?

8   The fun nature of *Mission: Explore*'s tasks disguise the fact that you need to _____ .

9   What is one children's survey of the community designed to measure?

10 For Raven-Ellison, education should encourage people to be _____ .

3 Look at the words in bold from the programme. Choose the correct synonym (a or b).

1   Outdoor exploration **spurs** innovative problem solving …
    a encourages   b involves

2   Walking gives you a different, more **tangible** perspective …
    a enjoyable   b real

3   It's a **hands-on** format that's very accessible.
    a lively   b practical

4   … moments that will be **crucial** to tackling issues like climate change …
    a essential   b helpful

Word focus *foot/feet*

4 Match the idioms (1–4) with their definitions (a–d).

1   I **got off on the wrong foot** with my boss when I told him I didn't like using computers.

2   He offered to give the talk with me, but then at the last minute he **got cold feet**.

3   The company **shot itself in the foot** by not investing in new technology when it had the chance.

4   Don't worry if it all seems strange at first. You'll soon **find your feet**.

a   have a bad start

b   start to feel more confident in a new situation

c   withdraw from doing something because you feel anxious

d   do something that damages your own situation or prospects

5 The idioms in bold are in the wrong sentences. Replace the idioms with the correct ones.

1   She **found her feet**, but relations with her colleagues are much better now.

2   I hope I didn't **have two left feet** when I told her how like her sister she was.

3   I've never been good at dancing – I **get off on the wrong foot**.

4   She really **followed in her father's footsteps** by not taking the promotion when she was offered it.

5   People often ask me why I didn't **get my foot in the door** and become a doctor like him.

6   Hannah **got cold feet** very quickly at university and made some good friends.

7   I'm now working for Google. I was very lucky to **put my foot in it** because so many people want to work there.

8   She was going to jump from the ten-metre board but she **shot herself in the foot**.

116

2d Tell me a bit about yourself

Vocabulary personal qualities

1 Look at the statements and write the adjective that sums up this quality. You have been given the first letter.

My strengths? Well, …

1 I care about doing a good job.   c............
2 I will always get the job done.   r............
3 I love my work.   e............
4 I want to do well.   m............
5 I don't get distracted from my work.   f............
6 I'm willing to do anything I'm asked to do.   f............
7 I keep things in order so as to be efficient.   w............-o............
8 If I don't have the tools to do something, I'll find another way.   r............

Real life presenting yourself

2 🎧 14 Listen to a man, Hiroki, presenting himself at an interview for a graduate training programme. Answer the questions.

1 What kind of work does the company do?
2 What relevant experience does Hiroki have?

3 🎧 14 Listen again. Write the five qualities from the list in Exercise 1 that you think Hiroki possesses. Give reasons for your answers.

1 c............
Reason: ....
2 w............-o............
Reason: ....
3 r............
Reason: ....
4 e............ and m............
Reason: ....

4 Pronunciation word stress

a 🎧 15 Look at these words used in the interview and underline the stressed syllable(s) in each word. Then listen and check.

1 experience
2 commendation
3 infrastructure
4 authorities
5 suitability
6 particular
7 relevant
8 important
9 enthusiastic

b 🎧 15 Listen again and practise saying each word with the same stress.

5 Listen and respond a suitable candidate

🎧 16 You are at an interview for a job working as a trainee hotel manager at a top London hotel. The interviewer asks you some questions. Respond with your own words. Then compare your response with the model answer that follows.

1
So can you tell me a little about yourself and what attracted you to this job?

Yes, my name is Eduardo Torres and I'm a graduate in Hotel Management. I have been working for the last year at a country hotel and I would like to get a job with a bigger chain of hotels.

2e A letter of application

Writing a covering letter or email

1 Writing skill fixed expressions

a Complete these phrases from a covering letter. You have been given the first letter of the missing words.

a The job a_____ me because I know of your company's reputation for …

b I am a_____ for interview any time.

c I am writing in r_____ to your advertisement for …

d C_____, I am working for …

e A_____ someone who has worked in this field previously, I think I am a s_____ candidate.

f Please find a_____ my CV.

g Thank you for t_____ the time to c_____ this application.

h Regarding the specific r_____ you mention, I also have: …

b Look at the key elements of a covering letter and match 1–8 with the phrases (a–h) from Exercise 1a.

1 State the job applied for and where and when it was advertised.
2 Refer to your CV.
3 Mention your present situation.
4 Explain why you are suited to the job.
5 Show that you know something about their organization.
6 Respond to any key qualifications that you have that are needed for this job.
7 Thank them for their time.
8 Explain where and when you can be contacted.
9 Give the letter a personal touch.

2 Read the covering letter. Which of the key elements (1–9) from Exercise 1b are missing?

> Dear Ms Newman
>
> I am writing in response to your advertisement on the Jobsonline website for a fundraiser at Harmon Adult College. I enclose my CV, which details my qualifications and relevant experience.
>
> The job attracted me because I know several people who have studied at Harmon College and I am aware of the good work that you do in helping the long-term unemployed get retrained to enter the world of work again.
>
> Regarding the specific requirements that you mention:
>
> • I have a Master's degree in Economics.
> • I am a resident in the London area.
> • I have my own car.
>
> I am available for interview at any time, given reasonable notice. Many thanks for considering this application.
>
> I look forward to hearing from you.
>
> Yours sincerely
>
> Jane Knowles
>
> Jane Knowles

3 Write extra text for each missing element. Use your own or invented information. Mark on the letter in Exercise 2 where the extra text should go.

Wordbuilding *get*

1 The verb *get* has multiple meanings (when used alone as well as in phrasal verbs). Try to guess what *get* means in these sentences. (Note that the last two are phrasal verbs.)

1. Sorry, I just don't *get* what you're trying to say.
2. Don't *get* too excited about it. It's not certain yet that we'll move to Canada.
3. I'm going to try to *get* some time off work next week so that I can revise for my exams.
4. You go and have your shower and I'll *get* us some supper.
5. Put your wallet away. I'll *get* this.
6. I'll try to *get* her to change her mind, but I'm not optimistic.
7. Can you *get* me a glass of water if you're going to the kitchen?
8. Don't worry about giving me a lift. I can easily *get* the bus.
9. It really *gets to* me that he can make jokes about other people, but he can't take a joke himself.
10. To *get on* in this profession, you have to keep constantly up-to-date with new technology.

2 Match the meanings (a-j) with the verb *get* in 1–10 in Exercise 1.

a fetch	f obtain or be given
b pay for	g annoy
c progress	h make or persuade
d go (on/in)	i prepare
e understand	j become

Learning skills listening: top-down strategies

3 Before listening to an extract in English, try to use the same strategies that help you understand content when listening in your own language. Ask yourself these questions.

1. What is the context for this listening (an everyday conversation, a lecture, a scientific report, an interview, etc.)?
2. What is the probable attitude of the speaker (e.g. are they trying to persuade/inform/complain, etc.)?
3. Am I listening just for gist or for some specific information (dates, times, names, etc.)?
4. What do I know already about this subject/situation and what questions would I like to have answered by what I am about to hear?

4 Look at these contexts (1–3). Ask yourself questions 2–4 from Exercise 3. Decide a) the probable attitude of the speaker; b) whether you are listening for gist or specific information; and c) what questions you want answered.

1. a news report about a new electric car
   a _____
   b _____
   c _____
2. an interview with a sociologist about her new book on attitudes to childhood
   a _____
   b _____
   c _____
3. a discussion between three friends about a recently released film
   a _____
   b _____
   c _____

Check!

5 Do this quiz. All the answers are in Student's Book Unit 2.

1 Complete the descriptions of these people from Unit 2.

a Kazakh _____
b M_____ people
c s_____

2 Look at the attributes (a–c) of each person in Exercise 1 and say what each enables them to do.
   a great patience
   b extraordinary vision
   c being the right weight

3 Complete these grammar explanations.
   a Perfect forms are used to look _____ at an event that has an impact on a _____ time.
   b We sometimes use _____ + past participle, rather than *be* + past participle, to form the passive.

4 Complete the sentences. Then rearrange the first letters of each word to make the name of a character in this unit.
   a Please do _____ hesitate to _____ me if you have any questions.
   b Oh dear! I hope I didn't put _____ foot _____ it.
   c _____ look forward to _____ from _____ soon.
   d Female smokejumpers do the same _____ as _____ smokejumpers.

   Name: J_____ C_____

Unit 3 Design for life

3a My town

Listening my town

1 🔊 **17** You will hear two people talking about towns they live or have lived in. Listen and complete the table. If no information is given, write NM (not mentioned).

	Glastonbury	Ghent
Location		
Size of town		
Type of town		
Reasons for liking		

2 🔊 **17** Listen again and choose the correct option (a, b or c) to complete each statement.

1. Glastonbury Festival takes place:
   a in the town of Glastonbury.
   b in some fields near Glastonbury.
   c at a world heritage site.

2. Glastonbury town changed when:
   a some festival-goers began to settle there.
   b the first festival was held in 1970.
   c people realized what a magical place it was.

3. Now the town has an unusual mixture of:
   a ethnic groups.
   b people with different lifestyles.
   c commercial activities.

4. The speaker suggests that not many people visit Ghent because:
   a it's a long way from Brussels and Bruges.
   b they don't know how attractive it is.
   c they think it's just a small provincial town.

5. Ghent is home to a lot of:
   a traditional industries.
   b shipping industries.
   c large industries.

6. The variety of activities in Ghent means that people are:
   a quite tolerant.
   b quite educated.
   c quite socially active.

3 Look at these expressions used by the speakers. Match the words in bold in 1–8 with their definitions (a–h).

1. pleasant **period** houses
2. a **transformative** experience
3. an **alternative** lifestyle
4. it's all a bit **wacky**
5. my **adopted** town for a while
6. part of its **charm**
7. around the old **docks**
8. The other **drawback**

a life-changing
b attraction
c disadvantage
d unconventional
e area where ships are loaded
f strange and funny
g belonging to a past time
h that you have chosen to live in

120

Vocabulary describing towns

4 Complete the definitions. You have been given the first two letters of the missing words.

1. A town which is deserted is a gh_____ town.
2. A town which is pleasantly old-fashioned is qu_____.
3. An area of very poor housing on the edge of a city is called a sh_____ town.
4. A part of a city that grows without any planning we call a sp_____ suburb.
5. Another word for *untidy* is sc_____.
6. Buildings which are boring and unimaginatively designed are ch_____.
7. A village where very little ever happens we call a sl_____ village.
8. Another word for a holiday town by the sea is a seaside re_____.
9. An area which has not been looked after or renovated is r_____-d_____.

Grammar qualifiers

5 🔊 **17** Look at these sentences from the descriptions you heard. Underline the most appropriate form. Then listen again and check your answers.

1. Glastonbury is *fairly / rather* well-known around the world for its music festival.
2. All in all, it was *a bit sleepy / quite a sleepy*, traditional kind of English town.
3. Well, now the town is a *quite / rather* odd mix of older, more conservative residents and younger people.
4. … shops selling healing crystals … it's all *a bit / quite* wacky, really.
5. But actually I *like it quite / quite like it*!
6. Actually, it might be *cheating slightly / rather cheating* to call it a town.
7. One of the benefits of having that kind of mix is that people tend to be *a little / quite* open-minded.
8. There's also masses to do but going out isn't *particularly / rather* cheap.
9. The other drawback is the weather, which is *a bit / pretty* terrible most of the time – grey and rainy.
10. I'm from Italy and, I have to say, it got me down *a bit / fairly* at times.

6 Complete this conversation using an appropriate qualifier in each space.

A: Where were you brought up?
B: Not ¹_____ far from here, actually. In Bourneville.
A: Where's that? I'm not ²_____ familiar with this area.
B: It's ³_____ near the centre of Birmingham. I suppose you'd call it a suburb.
A: So what was that like? I imagine it was still ⁴_____ an urban area, wasn't it?
B: Well, no, actually. Bourneville is a very pleasant, leafy kind of suburb. It's got a ⁵_____ interesting history, in fact.
A: In what way?
B: Well, it was specially designed as a model village for workers at the chocolate factory to live in. You know, to keep them happy and productive. And it really is ⁶_____ a special place to live.

7 Pronunciation *quite*, *fairly* and *pretty*

🔊 **18** Listen to the conversations. For which items does speaker B mean '… but probably not enough'.

1. A: Are you warm?
   B: Mmm. I'm quite warm.
2. A: Are you feeling optimistic?
   B: Hmm … pretty hopeful.
3. A: How was the film?
   B: I quite liked it.
4. A: Is he interested in the job?
   B: Mmm. He's pretty keen, I think.
5. A: Are we late?
   B: We're in quite good time.
6. A: Is it safe?
   B: It's fairly safe.

8 Dictation talking about places

🔊 **19** Listen to a conversation about a visit to Russia. Complete the answers.

A: How was your trip to Russia?
B: Great, thanks. We _____, but _____.
We started _____ Red Square. _____ the metro. Each _____. The _____.
A: And how did it compare to St Petersburg?
B: Very different. St Petersburg _____. Actually, it _____, _____ Moscow _____. But _____. You _____ there.

121

3b Sky caves of Nepal

Reading mysterious dwellings

1 Look at the photo of some unusual caves. Then read the extract from an article about the caves and answer the questions.

1 What do you learn about the geography and climate of this area?

2 How many caves are there like the ones in the photo?

3 Why was this place important historically?

4 What was found in the caves?

5 What was the function of the earliest caves?

6 Why did people choose to live in them?

Sky caves of Nepal

Mustang, a former kingdom in north-central Nepal, is home to one of the world's great archaeological finds. In this [1] incredibly inhospitable, wind-savaged place, hidden within the Himalayas, there are an extraordinary number of human-built caves.

Some sit [2] completely by themselves, a single open mouth on a vast face of weathered rock. Others are in groups, occasionally stacked eight or nine storeys high, making a sort of a vertical neighbourhood. Some were dug into the cliff side, others were tunnelled from above. Many are thousands of years old. The total number of caves in Mustang, conservatively estimated, is 10,000. Why anyone would choose to build rooms which are [3] extremely difficult and dangerous to access has remained a mystery and the evidence that might supply an answer has been almost [4] totally erased.

We know that 700 years ago, Mustang was a bustling place: a centre of scholarship and art, and a key place on the salt trade route from Tibet to India. Salt was then an [5] extremely valuable commodity. Later, when cheaper salt became available in India, an economic decline set in. Soon the region was all but forgotten, lost beyond the great mountains.

Pete Athans first noticed the caves of Mustang while trekking in 1981. Many appear impossible to reach unless you are a bird and Athans, a [6] very accomplished mountaineer, was stirred by the challenge they presented.

Over a twelve-year period, Athans made several visits. Most of the caves he looked into were empty, though they showed signs of domestic habitation. But in others the treasures he and his team found were [7] quite stunning. In one cave they discovered a 26-foot-long mural, in another 8,000 calligraphed manuscripts. Many caves seemed to be elaborate tombs full of [8] absolutely amazing riches.

Evidence now shows that the caves divide into three general periods. 3,000 years ago, they were used as burial chambers. Around 1,000 years ago, they became primarily living quarters. Because the territory was frequently fought over, people took refuge in them, placing safety over convenience. After AD 1400, when most people had moved to traditional villages, the caves continued to be used – as meditation chambers, military lookouts or storage units. Some remained as homes, and even today a few families live in them.

Grammar intensifying adverbs

2 Look at the intensifying adverbs in the article. Then cross out the adverb(s) that could NOT replace each adverb in the article.

1. absolutely / extremely
2. entirely / extremely
3. completely / incredibly
4. absolutely / completely
5. absolutely / very
6. extremely / utterly
7. absolutely / very
8. incredibly / quite

3 Complete the exchanges about the sky caves story with these intensifying adverbs. There is sometimes more than one possibility.

| absolutely | completely | incredibly |
| quite | really | totally | very |

A: You must have to be a(n) [1] .... skilled climber to get into these caves.

B: Yes, you have to be [2] .... fearless.

C: I find it [3] .... incredible that people could have lived in these caves.

D: I know. It must have been [4] .... difficult to get provisions like food and water up to them.

E: I would [5] .... love to be involved in this kind of work.

F: Yes. It must be [6] .... exciting to discover what's inside the caves.

G: The entrances to some of the burial caves were [7] .... sealed with large boulders.

H: Yes, that's right. The climbers had to [8] .... literally risk their lives to open them up.

4 Pronunciation stress in intensifying adverbs

a 🔊 20 Listen to these sentences with intensifiers and underline the stressed syllables.

1. I'm utterly exhausted.
2. I'd really appreciate that.
3. It's so hot today.
4. It's OK. I quite understand.
5. You're absolutely right.
6. It's very difficult to say.

b Practise saying the sentences with the same stress.

Vocabulary adverb and adjective collocations

5 Match the adverbs (1–10) with the adjectives (a–j) to make collocations.

1. deadly   a. amused
2. ideally   b. familiar
3. hopelessly   c. obvious
4. mildly   d. optimistic
5. painfully   e. reasonable
6. patently   f. serious
7. perfectly   g. slow
8. closely   h. in love
9. vaguely   i. suited
10. wildly   j. associated with

6 Complete the sentences with collocations from Exercise 5.

1. I think your estimate that ninety per cent of the people will say 'yes' is .... It'll be more like forty per cent.
2. His name sounds .... to me. I think perhaps I met him at a party about three years ago.
3. I don't know why you're even asking me that question. The answer is ....
4. Even if you bought the suitcase three years ago, it's .... to ask for a refund if it has a five-year guarantee.
5. I thought she was joking when she said she was going to run the London marathon, but she was ....
6. I wish he would get to the point sooner. I find his explanations ....

Vocabulary features in a home

7 Look at these features in a home. Which are for:

a. storage?
b. health and fitness?
c. enjoying the sun?
d. leisure?
e. convenience?

a conservatory	en suite bathrooms
a games room	a garage/workshop	a gym
a home cinema	a state-of-the-art kitchen
a library	a roof garden	a sauna
a walk-in wardrobe

3c Biomimetic architecture

Listening the influence of nature

1 🔊 21 Look at the photos and captions. Then listen to an interview with an architectural historian about 'biomimetics'. Answer the questions.

1 What does 'biomimetics' mean?

2 How do the three structures in the photos relate to biomimetics?

2 🔊 21 Listen again and choose the correct option (a, b or c). Pause the CD each time before moving onto the next question.

1 According to the historian, the term biomimetics:
   a is relatively recent.
   b is an old science.
   c can be applied to anything that copies nature.

2 The examples of new materials she gives are materials that copy:
   a water-based animals.
   b animals in general.
   c animals and plants.

3 When designing the Sagrada Familia, Gaudi took inspiration from:
   a models he had made.
   b nature's forms.
   c the human body.

4 The design of the Sagrada Familia:
   a confused the public.
   b divided public opinion.
   c brought Gaudi great fame.

5 There are a lot of biomimetic buildings now that are:
   a named after animals.
   b known by the name of something in the natural world.
   c given nicknames by their creators.

6 The Eastgate Centre in Harare uses biomimetics to avoid:
   a becoming too cold.
   b looking like a conventional office and shopping complex.
   c having to be cooled artificially.

Sagrada Familia, Barcelona

Swiss Re Tower, London

A termite mound, Africa

3 Match these words in bold from the interview with the correct definition (a or b).

1 … the term biomimetics, which was **coined** in the 1950s …
   a first created   b made popular

2 … hi-tech swimsuits that **replicate** shark skin.
   a use   b imitate

3 … he created a very **organic**-looking building …
   a simple   b natural

4 … one of the most **hideous** buildings in the world.
   a beautiful   b ugly

5 … to imitate the heating and cooling system in a termite **mound**.
   a small hill   b body

Word focus *ground*

4 Complete these sentences to make idioms with *ground*.

1 He's only sixteen and enjoying enormous success, but it's very important that he .... his .... **on the ground**.

2 You shouldn't give in to pressure just because it comes from people who have more experience. .... **your ground**.

3 She refused to comment on the situation **on the** .... **that** it was a private matter.

4 Using the latest laser technology, they are **breaking** .... **ground** .... medical surgery.

5 He has some great ideas, but that's all they are: ideas. Because none of them ever .... **the ground**.

6 Thanks – that was really productive. I'm amazed that we .... **so much ground** in just an hour.

Unit 3 Design for life

3d A lot to recommend it

Real life expressing opinions

1 🎧 **22** Listen to part of a discussion about a proposal to put a new coffee lounge into a large open-plan office, which is on the 14th floor of an office block. Write down two of the arguments mentioned in favour of the proposal and one against it.

For

....

....

....

Against

....

....

2 🎧 **22** Complete the phrases used by the speakers to express their opinions. Then listen again and check your answers.

1 First of ...., I should say that I think it's .... a good idea.
2 It's got a lot of things to .... it.
3 But I .... say there's a risk in that.
4 I kind of .... that. The thing about an open-plan office is …
5 The informal chats are something we .... the importance of.
6 What I .... is, if we assume that people relaxing and having coffee at work …
7 So I'm very .... in .... of this proposal, particularly .... that we are all working in …
8 Oh, and .... the ...., including a screen with industry news on it in the room is a clever ....

3 Pronunciation linking vowel sounds (intrusion)

a 🎧 **23** Listen to these phrases and write the sound or letter that links *and* to the word before it.

1 food and water ....
2 tea and biscuits ....
3 vanilla and chocolate ....
4 wait and see ....
5 go and ask ....
6 you and me ....

b 🎧 **24** Look at these phrases and mark the words which are linked. If an extra sound (/w/, /j/ or /r/) is needed, write this too. Then listen and check your answers.

0 every so_w_often
1 first of all
2 with a bit of luck
3 as a matter of fact
4 as far as I'm aware
5 between you and me
6 let's be honest
7 at the end of the day
8 I've no idea, I'm afraid

c Practise saying the phrases in the same way.

4 Listen and respond giving your opinion

🎧 **25** Someone is going to ask your opinions on where we choose to live and the importance of our surroundings and also give their opinions. Respond with your own words. Then compare what you say with the model answer that follows.

1
Would you prefer to have a large living space or somewhere that's small and cosy?

Personally, I'd like to have a lot of space, but maybe that seems a bit selfish.

3e High-rise living

Writing an opinion essay

1 Look at the elements of an opinion essay (1–4). Then read the two paragraphs (a and b) from an opinion essay about whether it is good for people to live in high-rise buildings. Which elements do the paragraphs represent?

1. analyse the question and set out your starting point
2. give your opinion and present the arguments supporting it
3. deal with opposing arguments
4. make your conclusion

a So, as with so many things, in the end we must balance the advantages and disadvantages and then make a choice. For me, even though there are great benefits of high-rise buildings, these benefits are outweighed by the cost to human interaction. After all, what use is a pleasant environment if most of the time you are isolated from other people in a small flat seventy metres from the ground?

b The pressure for space in our cities has demanded that we build upwards, with taller and taller buildings, rather than build outwards. It is true that it is not particularly desirable to keep expanding our cities outwards into green, undeveloped land outside the city limits, but there are other solutions to providing more homes, such as the creation of compact living spaces. Some high-rise buildings could still be retained for non-residential activity, for example, as offices.

2 Do you think the writer is for or against high-rise living? What arguments does he/she concede to the other side?

3 **Writing skill** discourse markers

Match the two halves of each comment about city life.

1. Living in an apartment building in the centre is a bit noisy.
2. Even though we live twenty storeys up,
3. It feels very nice to live in an old house.
4. Our building is not the tallest in the neighbourhood.
5. Most of the flats are rented by companies for their employees.
6. We wanted to be somewhere with a sense of community,

a. After all, very few indivifuals could afford to rent privately.
b. Having said that, it is extremely convenient.
c. that is to say, a place where people enjoy interacting.
d. Admittedly, the maintenance costs are higher.
e. our view of the city is blocked by other tall buildings.
f. Indeed, there are some buildings over sixty storeys high.

4 Write your own answer to the question: *Is it good for people to live in high-rise buildings?* Follow the structure suggested in Exercise 1. You can use ideas from those two paragraphs if you wish.

Unit 3 Design for life

Vocabulary renting a flat

1 Use these words to complete the conversation between a student looking for a flat and a letting agent.

> advance   bills   budget   charges
> commission   deposit   furnished   landlord
> lets   move   properties   references   rent
> share   studio   tenant

S: Hi, I'm looking to ¹_____ a small apartment, like a ²_____ apartment, for three months. Do you do short ³_____?

LA: Yes, but only for ⁴_____ flats. Is it just for you or are you planning to ⁵_____? And when is this from?

S: Just me and I'm hoping to ⁶_____ in as soon as possible.

LA: OK. And what's your ⁷_____?

S: Well, including the ⁸_____ and ⁹_____, no more than $900 a month.

LA: OK. I think we have a few ¹⁰_____ that will interest you. You just need to know that we don't take any ¹¹_____ from you, the ¹²_____, just from the ¹³_____, who has to pay us a small fee. But you will need to pay a ¹⁴_____ of one month's rent and one month's rent in ¹⁵_____. And you'll also need to provide some ¹⁶_____, including one from your employer.

Learning skills listening: bottom-up strategies

2 When you listen to fast native speech, you will often be faced with the difficulty of decoding the sounds you hear. Look at this list of key things to recognize in native speech.

1 being able to recognize a word from its stressed syllable
2 understanding the place of weak forms (auxiliary verbs, prepositions, articles) in a sentence
3 understanding linking so that you can separate the words that have been linked
4 picking out the key word in a sentence (the one that carries the main meaning)

3 🔊 26 Look at the stressed syllables in the words in this sentence. Then listen to the sentence.

The de<u>vel</u>opment of <u>en</u>ergy-efficient <u>homes</u> has <u>changed</u> the way <u>hous</u>es are <u>built</u>.

4 🔊 27 Underline the stressed syllables in the words in these sentences. Then listen to the sentences.

1 There are only two interesting buildings in the area around Newport.
2 The green belt should definitely be protected from developers.

5 Underline the stressed syllables in sentences from the listening extracts in this unit. Use the audioscript at the back of your book. Then listen and check.

Check!

6 Do the crossword. All of the words are in Student's Book Unit 3.

Across

5 poor (8)
8 past, present or future (4)
9 opposite of 5 across (4)
10 small and neat (7)
11 attached to the bedroom (2, 5)

Down

1 new, current (6)
2 slightly (1, 3)
3 appear (4)
4 with a lot of room (8)
6 lively (7)
7 discussion (7)

Unit 4 Innovation

4a The Boring Company

Listening future transport

1 ◎ 28 Why do you think someone would name their company 'The Boring Company'? What does this have to do with future transport? Listen to a radio feature and check your answers.

2 ◎ 28 Listen again and answer the questions. According to the speaker:
1 what are the three possibilities for overcoming an obstacle?
2 what can building new roads be compared to and why?
3 what is the problem with building 'roads in the air'?
4 what is the problem with building roads underground?
5 how would cars travel in Elon Musk's proposed underground system?
6 how would he make the tunnelling process cheaper?
7 how would he avoid congestion in the tunnels?
8 what technology might the Hyperloop tunnel use in the future?
9 how fast can pods travel in this system?

3 ◎ 28 Complete these sentences and phrases used by the speaker. You have been given the first letter and a definition of the missing words. Listen again and check your answers.
1 We've already tried going round it by building **r**_____ **roads** around our cities …
   = roads which take you around the edge of a city
2 … have an impact on those below when **d**_____ falls from a height.
   = pieces of broken material, e.g. rock
3 And given his amazing record … he could **p**_____ this **off**.
   = make something a success
4 His latest **v**_____, The Boring Company, proposes building a network of tunnels …
   = a business enterprise or project involving risk
5 … so that there would be nothing to block them or **h**_____ them **up**.
   = delay
6 … Hyperloop project, has already been **t**_____ **and tested** …
   = experimented with and shown to work

Glossary
sled (n) /sled/ a small vehicle that slides over the ground
vacuum (n) /ˈvækjʊəm/ a space that has had all the air removed from it

Grammar future probability

4 🔊 28 Complete the statements made by the speaker with these words. Then listen again and check your answers.

could good chance likely might possibly should

1 … such solutions are never _____ to work because …
2 … rather than removing the problem, you _____ just be moving it somewhere else.
3 … collisions or accidents in the air _____ also have an impact on those below …
4 And given his amazing record …, there's a _____ that he could pull this off.
5 Musk's idea is that … his techniques _____ reduce the cost enormously.
6 In his mind, also, is the idea that in future, the tunnels will _____ use vacuum technology …

5 Rewrite the sentences from Exercise 4 so that they have the same meaning. Use the words in bold.

probably
1 _____
chances
2 _____
possible
3 _____
may well
4 _____
likely
5 _____
could
6 _____

6 Complete the answers to these questions about future transport using the correct form of the words in brackets.

Do you think that there's any chance this idea of Elon Musk's will become a reality?

It ¹_____ (may well). I think he ²_____ (almost certainly / come up with) a working model. He always does. Then it will be a question of whether city authorities are willing to support it. I think that some more forward-looking ones ³_____ (probably / be) supportive of it.

And, just leaving aside that possibility, what do you think our city streets will look like thirty years from now?

I think most of us ⁴_____ (likely / drive) electric vehicles. We're already moving in that direction. So we ⁵_____ (should / have) cleaner air in our cities. But there ⁶_____ (probably / be) some petrol cars on the streets too.

Why do you say that?

Because the oil companies are incredibly powerful. And that ⁷_____ (be / unlikely / change). Also, replacing petrol will need a whole new infrastructure in place of petrol stations and I think ⁸_____ (likelihood / that / happen) within thirty years ⁹_____ (be) very small.

Wordbuilding -able

7 Form the correct (positive or negative) adjective from the verb in brackets to complete these sentences. The negative adjectives can begin *un-*, *in-*, *ir-* or *non-*.

1 I think it's _____ (do). The question is: is it _____ (desire)?
2 I'm afraid the price is _____ (negotiate).
3 They're an advertising agency and they have this terrible slogan: 'Imagine the _____ (imagine)'!
4 I felt so bad about breaking her china plate. She said it was very rare and virtually _____ (replace).
5 There are problems with the plan, but I don't think they are _____ (surmount).
6 I couldn't go through another dental procedure like that again. The pain was _____ (tolerate).

8 Complete these sentences with a suitable adjective ending in *-able*.

1 If you don't like the shirt, I'm sure you can take it back to the shop. Things are usually _____ within two weeks of buying them.
2 These new glasses are supposed to be _____ , but I sat on them and they snapped in half!
3 The tap water is _____ in the sense that it's safe. But I'm afraid it doesn't taste very nice.
4 How far is the station from here? Is it _____ or should I get a bus or taxi?
5 The label on this tablecloth says '_____', but actually I put it in the washing machine and it's come out fine.
6 I'm afraid I won't be _____ for the next few days; the place I'm staying in has no phone signal.

129

4b DIY innovators

Reading future transport

1 Read the article about DIY innovators and match the headings (a–d) with the four paragraphs (1–4).

a   What drives innovation
b   An unidentified need
c   Making do with bits and pieces
d   There's an inventor in all of us

2 Read the article again and complete these sentences using one word in each space.

1   The mistake we make about technology is that we think it is something only .... can be involved with.
2   Thomas Jefferson's clock was unusual for its time because it could tell you the ....
3   The invention of eyeglasses for chickens solved something most people didn't think was a ....
4   Most DIY inventors are not really motivated by ....
5   In the Great Depression, some people created homemade versions of gadgets that they couldn't ....
6   Robert Goddard is an example of a scientist who did .... using old household objects.

Glossary
DIY (abbrev) /ˌdiː aɪ ˈwaɪ/ do it yourself
hose (n) /həʊz/ a flexible water pipe
peck (v) /pek/ (of a bird) strike quickly with the mouth
piston rings (n) /ˈpɪstən rɪŋz/ metal rings that go around the cylinder of an internal combustion engine
scaffold (n) /ˈskæfəʊld/ a supporting structure used when repairing a building

DIY innovators

1 In today's electronic convenience age, many of us imagine that technology is something that brainy scientists in state-of-the-art laboratories create for us. But that isn't really a true reflection of how technology comes about – now or in the past. The strict definition of technology is designing a device to perform a particular task. Seen like that, we are all innovators, because we have all, at one time or another, improvised our own solutions to specific problems. It's just that some of us take it further than others. America's third president, Thomas Jefferson, filled his home with DIY gadgets. In his living room, for example, he had a homemade clock which, using a pair of cannonballs on ropes, told him both the hour of the day and the day of the week. He made himself a swivelling seat – an early version of the type of office chair many of us sit on today – and built an automatic signing machine so that he **didn't need to hand-sign** his letters.

2 DIY inventions rarely catch on, because often the inventor is providing a solution to something that is not generally perceived to be a problem. What was the inventor of glasses for chickens thinking? Obviously he thought there needed to be some way to prevent chickens pecking at each other's eyes. But he **should have realized** that they were never going to become a best-seller. Similarly, the self-tipping hat, which used parts of a clock to tip a man's hat when a lady passed him in the street, **must have seemed** to fill a need that was obvious to the inventor.

3 While a few DIY innovators in the past **might have been motivated** by money and the dream of making their fortune, others have been motivated by necessity. World War II servicemen in North Africa who **needed to wash** took empty oil drums and hoses, mounted them on scaffolds built from scrap wood and created improvised showers. Others have been motivated by economic hardship. During the Great Depression of the 1930s, some people **had to build** their own devices and equipment, because they couldn't afford new items in the shops. Cecil Burrell, when he wanted tables for his patio, made them from old piston rings from industrial engines.

4 But DIY can extend to professional scientists too. Dr Robert Goddard, who pioneered modern rocketry in the 1920s and 1930s, built much of his test equipment and rockets from bits and pieces he found lying around: clock parts, tobacco tins, etc.

Unit 4 Innovation

3 Look at the words in bold from the article. Choose the correct definition (a or b).
1 a **swivelling** seat
   a turning   b with arms
2 rarely **catch on**
   a work   b become popular
3 to **tip** a man's hat
   a take off   b raise
4 **mounted** them **on** scaffolds
   a hang … from   b put … on top of
5 **scrap** wood
   a old but re-usable   b old and useless
6 who **pioneered** modern rocketry
   a was ignorant of   b led the way in

Grammar past modals

4 Match the past modal verbs (1–6) from the article with the functions (a–f).
1 didn't need to hand-sign
2 should have realized
3 must have seemed
4 might have been motivated
5 needed to wash
6 had to build

a expresses what was expected
b describes an obligation
c talks about a necessity
d talks about a lack of necessity
e speculates about what was possibly the case
f speculates about what was probably the case

5 Read the story in the next column about someone who got a bicycle puncture. Rewrite the underlined phrases with past modal verbs.
1 _____
2 _____
3 _____
4 _____
5 _____
6 _____
7 _____
8 _____

So there I was on a country road in the middle of nowhere with a flat bicycle tyre. ¹ Almost certainly I had ridden over a nail or something. ² The advisable thing would have been to take a puncture repair kit with me, but because the roads are very new around there I had imagined ³ it wasn't necessary. ⁴ One possibility was to wheel my bike back to the nearest town six kilometres away, but that would have taken ages. Besides, ⁵ I had an obligation to be home for supper, as a friend was coming to dinner. So I decided ⁶ it was my duty to find a way to fix the puncture. (In fact, ⁷ there was no need to worry because the friend had cancelled, but I didn't know that at the time.) All I had with me was a bicycle pump. What I needed was a patch for the puncture. I looked around on the road. ⁸ Perhaps someone had dropped something I could use. After some searching, I found some old chewing gum stuck to the road. It was very hard and I realized that there was only one thing to do …

6 **Pronunciation** weak forms in past modals

a 29 Listen to these sentences. Circle the weak forms.
1 I needn't have bothered.
2 She may have got lost.
3 It can't have been much fun.
4 You didn't need to wait for me.
5 It might not have been his fault.
6 She had to leave early.

b Practise saying the expressions in Exercise 6a in the same way.

Vocabulary phrasal verb *come*

7 Complete the text using prepositions to make phrasal verbs with *come*.

We've all eaten popcorn in the cinema, but few stop to think how the success of this all-American snack came ¹ _____ . I came ² _____ an article about its origins the other day when browsing the internet. It has an interesting history. The Guatemalans discovered popcorn thousands of years ago, presumably when someone had the bright idea of putting a corn kernel in a hot pan. But popcorn didn't really take off in the United States until the invention of the popcorn machine in the 1890s. Manufacturers spotted the growing trend, and came ³ _____ with the idea of adding caramel and marketing it as a sweet snack. In the Depression of the 1930s, popcorn filled an important need because it was cheap. Since then, even though popcorn has come ⁴ _____ against some opponents who say that it is unhealthy, it remains very popular and is even marketed today as a health food. Its success probably comes ⁵ _____ to the fact that it is so cheap and easy to make.

4c The new philanthropists

Listening supporting good causes

1 🔊 30 You are going to listen to a conversation about philanthropists. Read the definition. Then listen and make notes.

> **philanthropist** (n) /fɪˈlænθrəpɪst/ a person who cares about their fellow human beings; especially one who donates money to people less fortunate than themselves

1 two ways these new philanthropists made their money

2 two ways their approach to giving differs from philanthropists in the past

2 🔊 30 Listen again. Are the sentences true (T) or false (F)?

1 The speaker implies that philanthropists in the past didn't have to work for their money.
2 The new philanthropists' attitude to their money is that they want to use it now.
3 The new philanthropists don't want the projects they invest in to be run by business people.
4 The Daniela Papi story shows how a social enterprise project can evolve and spread.
5 John Caudwell believes that success in life is just a question of hard work.
6 The speaker suggests that the new philanthropists ultimately care only about their business reputation.

3 🔊 30 Complete these phrases from the conversation. Then listen again and check your answers.

| bring about | counterparts | ethos | return |
| seed money | self-confessed | self-made |
| no strings |

1 … so many more of these do-gooders are _____ businessmen and women …
2 … these philanthropists and their 19th–century _____?
3 … business terms like 'getting a good _____ on capital' …
4 The money they put into philanthropic projects is like _____ …
5 … helping to _____ positive change in areas where social problems exist.
6 … none of the old-fashioned '_____ attached' kind of giving …
7 He's a _____ capitalist who believes in people helping themselves …
8 I'd say that was very typical of the _____ of the new philanthropists.

4 Write the words from Exercise 3 next to the correct definition.

1 set of beliefs and values _____
2 early investment in a new company _____
3 profit _____
4 make happen _____
5 succeeding without help _____
6 someone who does the same job in a different time or place _____
7 admitting to being _____
8 without special conditions _____

Word focus give

5 Complete the expressions with *give*.

1 I **gave it my** _____, but I didn't win – he was a much better player.
2 It's not a decision you can take lightly. You need to **give it some serious** _____.
3 **Give her a** _____. She's only 12. I didn't know what I wanted to do until I was 20!
4 I've never tried to steer a boat before, but I'll **give it a** _____.
5 The council have finally **given them the go-**_____ to build a new factory on the site.
6 Don't rush it. You broke your leg. You need to **give it some** _____ to heal properly.

4d An elevator pitch

Real life making a short pitch

1 ⊙ **31** Listen to a short pitch for a product called the 'Solidarity Bag'. Listen and answer the questions.

1 Who is the product aimed at?

2 What is unique about this idea?

3 What problem does it solve?

4 What features does the bag have?

2 Speaking skill using rhetorical questions

⊙ **31** Listen again and complete these rhetorical questions.

1 What's _____ _____ about that, you _____ ?
2 Why _____ children _____ to do _____ , when they have a desk at school and a table at home?
3 But _____ will _____ in poorer countries _____ to afford the bag?

3 Write the answers to the questions in Exercise 2.
1 _____
2 _____
3 _____

4 Complete these other rhetorical questions you might ask when pitching a new product or service.

1 Operation
So how _____ ?
2 Cost
Isn't _____ , you ask?
3 Need
So why _____ ?
4 Ambition/Goal
So, what _____ ?

5 Pronunciation word stress

⊙ **32** Look at the words in bold in these sentences and underline where you think the stress falls in each word. Then listen and check.

1 **Clearly**, we want to help others.
2 **Financially**, we are in a good position.
3 **Essentially**, it's a school rucksack.
4 **Practically**, it has many advantages.
5 **Of course**, this is not the finished design.
6 **Honestly**, I don't know the answer to that.
7 **Obviously**, not all kids need a bag that functions as a desk.
8 **To be honest**, I think people will pay extra.
9 **Basically**, we'd like to help kids learn.

6 Listen and respond defending your idea

⊙ **33** Imagine you have just presented this Solidarity Bag to a potential investor. Listen to their questions. Respond with your own words. Then compare what you say with the model answer that follows.

1 *Can you just explain to me what your ambition is for this product?*

Yes. We would like it to have successful sales in Europe and on the basis of that to be able to provide many of these bags to children in developing countries.

Unit 4 Innovation

133

4e Problem or solution?

Writing a proposal

1 Read the proposal and answer the questions.

1 Does the company currently recognize the importance of innovation and if so, how?

2 What specific, concrete suggestions does the proposal make?

3 What recommendations does it make without giving specific examples?

2 Answer these questions about the structure of the proposal.

1 What is the purpose of the introduction?

2 In what two ways does the author make a list of points?

3 What phrase does she use to signal the conclusion?

3 Writing skill making recommendations

Choose the correct options to complete the recommendations.

1 We suggest employees *are / to be* given a structure in which to innovate.
2 We recommend the company *could / should* reward employees for their ideas.
3 We strongly recommend *to give / giving* innovation a more formal position.
4 We recommend that employees *have / having* scheduled discussion opportunities.
5 We also suggest that they *are to visit / should visit* other organizations to get ideas.

Introduction
This proposal suggests a new way to encourage innovation and creativity among staff.

Current situation
Our company needs innovation to be successful. At the moment, although we say that 'we encourage creativity and innovation', in fact we receive very few ideas from employees about how to improve our products and processes. Innovation is important because it can:

- help to make the company more efficient
- create new products and services for our customers
- motivate staff
- help to secure the company's future

So how can we achieve more creativity and innovation in practice, not just in words?

Possible solutions
First of all, we suggest that employees should be given a structure in which to innovate. This could take the form of a scheduled discussion between groups of colleagues every two to four weeks. Or it could involve giving employees the opportunity to visit other organizations to see how they work. Secondly, we recommend rewarding employees for good ideas. This does not have to be a financial reward, but it must involve recognition of their effort. Lastly, we believe that creating a more relaxed relationship between employees and management would also help the flow of ideas.

Recommendations
In summary, we strongly recommend that innovation and creativity are given a more formal position in the company's working practices. Until that happens, we are unlikely to see much innovation from staff.

4 Use these notes to write a proposal for a way to make students more aware of ways we waste energy.

Problem: Students are conscious of dangers of pollution, but not of their own waste of energy (leaving on lights, phone chargers, etc.)
Possible solutions: awareness-raising campaign, fines for wasting energy, offer free 'green' charging devices

Vocabulary partitives

1 Complete the partitive expressions using these words.

| bit | bit | bite | drop | gust | hint | plot | shred |
| stroke | word |

1 I'm really thirsty. I haven't had a _____ of water all day.
2 It was a _____ of luck getting those tickets. They were the last two.
3 I'm sorry. I didn't mean to offend you. It was just a _____ of fun.
4 We had a _____ of trouble finding the bus stop, but otherwise everything went smoothly.
5 A sudden _____ of wind blew my hat off and it landed in a puddle.
6 He tried to be positive but I think there was a _____ of disappointment in his voice.
7 They bought a _____ of land near the sea and they intend to build a house there.
8 Can I give you a _____ of advice before you start out on this venture?
9 There's not a _____ of evidence to suggest that there is life on other planets.
10 We'll get a _____ to eat* when we get there.

* used with a verb (*to eat*) rather than a noun (*of food*)

2 Which three expressions in Exercise 1 emphasize a small amount?

a _____
b _____
c _____

Learning skills vocabulary extension (1)

3 You can use your dictionary to extend your vocabulary. If you see a word that you think you know but the meaning does not seem to fit, check the other meanings of this word in the dictionary. Look at this example.

1 You see this sentence but don't know this meaning of *capital*.

'Running a railway network is a very capital-intensive activity.'

2 You find these entries for *capital* in the dictionary (see the next column). Which meaning does it have in this sentence?

capital /ˈkæpɪt(ə)l/ noun
1 the administrative centre of a country or region
2 money or assets that are or can be invested

capital /ˈkæpɪt(ə)l/ adjective
3 (of a letter of the alphabet) large
4 (of punishment or crime) punishable by death

3 Note any new meanings in your notebook and write an example sentence for each one.

4 Look at these words with more than one meaning. What meanings do you know for each?

| crane | fair | fine | sole |

5 Read the sentences. Do you know the meanings of the words in bold in these sentences? Check other meanings in the dictionary. Write example sentences for the meanings that are new to you.

1 In Japan, the most popular origami shape is a paper **crane**.
2 I went to the Frankfurt book **fair** last week.
3 There's a **fine** line between confidence and arrogance.
4 It's not a company: he is a **sole** trader.

Check!

6 Answer these questions. All the answers are in Student's Book Unit 4.

1 What is the 'mother of invention'?
_____
2 What adjective describes gadgets you can fold? '_____ technology'
3 What type of eye did you see on the opening page of this unit? _____
4 What is the name for a short presentation where we have a limited time to convince someone of our idea? _____
5 What do we call someone who wants to make money but help people at the same time? _____

7 Complete the sentences. The first letters of each word spell the name of Blake Mykoskie's company.

1 I'll certainly give your idea some _____.
2 It's a very risky venture. I'll be surprised if it comes _____.
3 It's unlike John to be late. He _____ have had a problem.
4 To make something smaller you can _____ it, bend it or fold it.

Name of company: _____

Unit 4 Innovation

135

Unit 5 The magic of travel

5a In defence of the guided tour

Listening a traveller's view

1 **34** Look at these features of organized tour holidays. Think about which features appeal to you and which don't. Then listen to someone talking about the benefits of such tours and tick the items he mentions.

1 Being with knowledgeable guides ☐
2 Comfort and safety ☐
3 Meeting fellow travellers ☐
4 Having a fixed itinerary/schedule ☐
5 No planning – everything is arranged for you ☐
6 Known costs – no financial surprises ☐
7 Optional free time ☐

2 **34** Read the statements. Then listen again and choose the best answer (a, b or c) to complete each statement.

1 The speaker says that in the past he didn't consider organized tour holidays an option because:
   a he couldn't relate to the type of people who went on them.
   b he thought they were too controlled and restricting.
   c the destinations were not places he wanted to visit.

2 The speaker says that he joined the guided tour at the Metropolitan Museum of Art because:
   a he thought it would at least be a new experience.
   b it was still raining outside.
   c it was highly recommended by the museum staff.

3 The difference between the museum tour and one of his normal visits to a museum was that:
   a he learned a lot about a lot of things.
   b he learned a little about a lot of things.
   c he learned a lot about a few things.

4 Most of the guides on the Italy trip:
   a had also been guests on the trips before.
   b had done months of research before the trip.
   c had academic qualifications.

5 The speaker says the fact that everything is organized beforehand saves a lot of:
   a money.   b stress.   c time.

6 The speaker says many organized tour operators these days give their guests:
   a the option of more free time.
   b a choice of excursions to go on.
   c mini guided tours with local people.

3 Try to complete these expression used by the speaker. Use one word per space.

1 to be herded around like a _____
2 Never in a _____ years!
3 Don't get me _____ – I like museums.
4 It'll be an experience, if _____ else.
5 Not holding _____ much hope, I joined it.
6 Transport, hotels, food: it's all taken care _____.

Vocabulary repeated word pairs

4 Complete these repeated word pairs with the correct word.

1 She only had her operation a week ago, but she's getting better day _____ day.
2 The film went on _____ on. I thought it was never going to end.
3 Yes, we met face _____ face for the first time last week.
4 People ask me if I prefer writing the music or the lyrics, but actually the two things go hand _____ hand.
5 Their new business is going strength _____ strength.
6 We don't see eye _____ eye on a lot of issues, but we're still good friends.

Grammar emphatic structures

5 🎧 34 Use the words in brackets to rewrite the sentences with emphatic structures you heard in Exercise 1. Then listen again and check your answers.

1 I want a bit of independence and freedom from travel. (what)

2 A guided tour I took changed my mind. (thing)

3 I like visiting museums. (do)

4 It made me reassess my whole attitude to organized tours. (did)

5 How knowledgeable and interesting some of the other travellers were surprised me. (what)

6 … particularly if you're visiting a more remote or not-so-safe place. (it)

6 Read this account of family holidays. Rewrite the underlined sentences below as emphatic structures, using the words in brackets.

¹ I remember best about my childhood how amazing family holidays were. Every few years we took a camper van and set off somewhere new. We didn't have a strict itinerary. ² A rough idea of where we were going was enough. We just took things day by day, without any planned stops or timetable. ³ We stopped when we saw things that interested us. We went wild swimming. We cooked on our camp stove usually. ⁴ Money wasn't the issue. If we saw a restaurant or cafe menu that looked good, we'd stop and eat there. We packed as little as possible and stopped at laundrettes when we needed to wash clothes. ⁵ I loved the lack of any kind of routine. Sometimes we'd wake up early, sometimes late. We'd often take a nap in the afternoon at some scenic spot. ⁶ I like sleeping in the afternoon. The whole thing was magical. ⁷ When I have children, I'm going to recreate a similar experience for them.

1 .... (thing)
2 .... (it)
3 .... (did)
4 .... (it)
5 .... (what)
6 .... (do)
7 .... (what)

7 Pronunciation *do*, *does* and *did*

🎧 35 Listen to these sentences and write in the missing emphatic auxiliaries. Note how the auxiliary verbs are stressed.

1 I .... wish I had been able to spend more time there.
2 He .... say that he'd help us.
3 We .... prefer to take holidays close to home.
4 She .... get very sunburnt.

Vocabulary describing people and places

8 Complete the crossword using the clues below.

Across
1 warm and comfortable (4)
4 not fast (4)
7 evoking feelings of love (8)

Down
2 using authority in a self-important way (9)
3 stylish and graceful (7)
5 cautious or suspicious (4)
6 large and impressive (5)

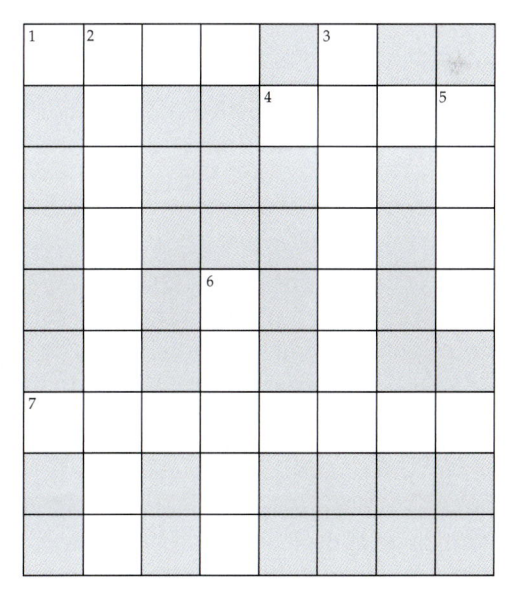

5b Pilgrimages

Reading their Africa

1 Read the article about the Pilgrimages project and answer the questions.

1 What is the aim of the Pilgrimages project?

2 What inspired the project?

3 How are the books different from the usual travel books we read?

4 What are the writers trying to avoid?

2 Read the article again and find words with these meanings.

a randomly (para 1)
b take hold of firmly (para 1)
c easily noticed (para 2)
d troubled (para 3)
e a picture (para 3)
f unoriginal (para 4)
g announce an order (para 4)

Pilgrimages

'For one month, nearly a billion eyes will follow the wayward movement of one small ball, bouncing about haphazardly on a lawn – controlled by the feet of 22 men speaking a language billions understand very well.' These are the opening words on the Pilgrimages website, a project set up by the Chinua Achebe Centre for African Writers and Artists, to seize the opportunity presented by the football World Cup in South Africa in 2010 to educate the rest of the world about Africa. The way the **association** did this was to ask thirteen African writers to write about their experiences of thirteen cities spread across Africa. Each **author** had two years, and help from a local guide, to produce a book of approximately 30,000 words on each city.

The result is travel writing of a very different kind. Rather than experiencing a place through the eyes of an outsider, Pilgrimages aims to reveal **it** as seen by Africans themselves. The advantage for each writer is that although they are visiting cities previously not well-known to them, many things are already familiar to them. **This** means that they can concentrate on observing the details and while **doing so**, not be as conspicuous as a non-African visitor **would**. Ugandan author Doreen Baingana, whose subject is the Somalian city of Hargeisa, says: 'Goats in a city, for example, do not surprise me in the way they would if I were from the UK.'

Among the **other thirteen** is Yvonne Owuor of Kenya, who has written about Kinshasa, the capital of Congo. The city is a great mix of different African cultures and languages with a turbulent history of colonization and struggle for independence. Like other Pilgrimages writers, Owuor is cautious about painting her portrait of Kinshasa with too broad a brush, fearful that what will emerge is a one-dimensional, stereotyped view of Africa.

This promises to be a refreshing series of travel books: not **ones** that throw out clichéd images and stereotyped views of other worlds. As Owuor says, when writers decree that a given place is like this or like that, then the reality disappears from view.

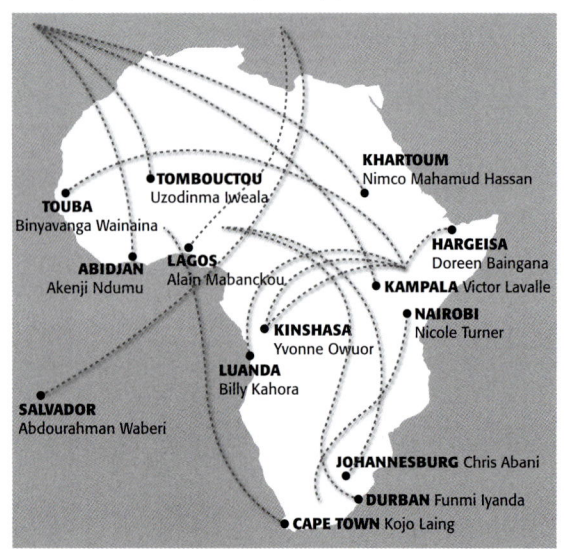

TOUBA Binyavanga Wainaina
TOMBOUCTOU Uzodinma Iweala
KHARTOUM Nimco Mahamud Hassan
ABIDJAN Akenji Ndumu
LAGOS Alain Mabanckou
HARGEISA Doreen Baingana
KAMPALA Victor Lavalle
KINSHASA Yvonne Owuor
NAIROBI Nicole Turner
LUANDA Billy Kahora
SALVADOR Abdourahman Waberi
JOHANNESBURG Chris Abani
DURBAN Funmi Iyanda
CAPE TOWN Kojo Laing

Grammar avoiding repetition

3 Look at the words in bold in the article and answer the questions.

1 What words have these words replaced to avoid repetition?
   a association (para 1)
   b author (para 1)
2 What clauses do these words refer to?
   a This (para 2)
   b doing so (para 2)
3 What nouns do these words refer to?
   a it (para 2, line 3)
   b This (para 4, line 1)
   c ones (para 4)
4 What words have been omitted after these words?
   a would (para 2)
   b other thirteen (para 3)

4 Replace the underlined words with other words or omit the underlined words to avoid repetition.

1 I was going to buy a new umbrella, but then I found my old umbrella.

2 I didn't want to go, but he persuaded me to go.

3 I want to phone her to find out what's going on, but if I phone her, she might think I'm being pushy.

4 I downloaded all the Bob Marley songs, but I didn't bother with the other songs.

5 The temperature is expected to drop to zero degrees tonight. The temperature dropping to zero degrees means there will be a frost.

6 It's a brilliant company. You couldn't find a better company to work for.

7 I'd love you to give me a hand moving this table, if you can bear to give me a hand.

8 It's not a cheap solution, but I understand why you might think it is a cheap solution.

5 Pronunciaton stress in short responses

a 🔊 36 Look at these exchanges. Mark the two (or three) words that you think are most stressed in each response.

1 A: Would you like to come to dinner one evening?
   B: Yes, I'd love to.
2 A: Do you need to borrow a pen?
   B: No, I've got one, thanks.
3 A: Are you coming?
   B: No, I'm afraid not.
4 A: I didn't get the assistant manager job.
   B: Oh, I'm sorry to hear that.
5 A: Are you going away this summer?
   B: I hope so.
6 A: Do you like detective stories?
   B: Oh, yes. I love a good thriller.
7 A: What are you doing here so early?
   B: Catching up on emails.

b 🔊 37 Listen to Student A's part of the exchanges. Respond using the correct stress.

6 Dictation a mystery tour

🔊 38 Listen to someone describing a mystery tour. Complete the paragraph.

I've been _____ ,
but _____ in Prague
_____ .
And _____
_____ .
If you _____ ,
_____ .
I'm _____
because _____
_____ .
What _____
_____ .
If _____
_____ .

5c Heart of Darkness

Listening a voyage into the unknown

1 🔊 **39** You are going to listen to an extract from the book *Heart of Darkness* by Joseph Conrad. The setting is the Congo around 1880. The extract describes the beginning of the journey that Marlow, a ship's captain, makes to this area. Listen and answer the questions.

1 What did Marlow dream about as a boy?

2 What had happened to the place he had been most fascinated by?

3 How did his dream become a reality?

2 🔊 **39** Listen again and complete these details of the description.

1 What did you find on maps of the world at that time?

2 In contrast, what had the map of this place (Congo) become filled with?

3 What does he compare the river on the map to?

4 What was the strategic importance of the river?

5 What had happened to the captain that Marlow was replacing?

6 What was his impression of the African coast as the boat sailed along it?

3 Look at these sentences from the extract and answer the questions about the descriptive words in bold.

1 I would look for hours at South America, or Africa, or Australia, and **lose myself in** all the glories of exploration.

   Do you think *lose myself in something* has a positive or a negative connotation?

2 But there was one [place] yet – the biggest, the most blank – that **I had a hankering after**.

   Have people who hanker after something experienced it yet or not?

3 … a mighty big river, that you could see on the map, resembling an immense snake **uncoiled**.

   What is a snake usually doing when it is coiled?

4 I went on along Fleet Street, but could not **shake off** the idea.

   Which of these things would you not try to shake off?

   a a cold   b a new skill   c a bad reputation

5 Watching a coast as it slips by the ship is like thinking about **an enigma**.

   Do you think *an enigma* is:

   a a mystery?   b a new idea?

6 … and always **mute** with an air of whispering …

   If *blind* means 'cannot see' and *deaf* means 'cannot hear', what does *mute* mean?

Word focus *matter*

4 Choose the correct options to complete these phrases with *matter*.

1 Getting stuck in a lift underground might seem amusing, but believe me, at the time, **it was no** *joking / funny / laughing* **matter**.

2 They say that you can control pain; it's just a question of **brain** / **mind** / **will over matter**.

3 You should always use a safety belt, **as a matter of** *course / process / mode*.

4 I'm sorry – I'm vegetarian. I don't eat meat **as a matter of** *belief / principle / morals*.

5 **No matter which** *angle / point / way* **you look at it**, being a teenager isn't easy.

6 Thankfully, it's not my concern; or yours **for** *that / any / what* **matter**.

140

Unit 5 The magic of travel

5d To my amazement

Real life telling an anecdote

1 🔊 **40** Listen to an anecdote about hitchhiking and answer the questions.

1 Where were the two men hitchhiking to and why?
2 What piece of good luck did they have?
3 What happened to change their mood for the worse and how did the story end?

2 🔊 **40** Listen again and complete these phrases that link or introduce the events in the story. Use one or two words per space.

1 Very few people still hitchhike, _____ .
2 _____ it can be dangerous.
3 _____ , a group of us from university had a competition …
4 _____ , within about ten minutes … we got a lift …
5 We couldn't _____ our luck.
6 … a resting point, which, _____ , _____ to have an area for pitching tents.
7 _____ , we woke up early …
8 … but, to _____ , it had gone.
9 _____ , we started to pack up our tent.
10 But _____ , we heard a loud horn sounding.

3 Speaking skill linking events

Substitute these phrases for a similar phrase from Exercise 2.

a As luck would have it, …
b Just then, …
c Despondently, …
d Nowadays, …
e To our great surprise, …
f Last summer …
g The next day, …
h To our horror, …

4 Pronunciation long vowel sounds

a Look at the underlined vowel sounds in these words and put them in the correct place in the table below.

| amazement   annoyance   astonishment   delight |
| dismay   embarrassment   frustration   horror |
| regret   relief   shock   surprise |

Long vowel sound	Short vowel sound

b 🔊 **41** Listen and check your answers. Say each word after you hear it.

5 Listen and respond telling an anecdote

🔊 **42** You are going to tell a story about falling asleep on a train and ending up in the wrong place. A friend will ask you some questions. Respond with your own words. Then compare what you say with the model answer that follows.

1 *So, tell me what happened?*

Well, a couple of weeks ago, I got the train to go and visit my aunt. She lives in Newville.

141

5e Book of the month

Writing a review

1 Read this book review of *The Siege of Krishnapur* by J.G. Farrell and mark the parts of the review that do the following.

   1 describe the theme of the book
   2 give the reader's opinion of the book
   3 describe the setting and the plot
   4 describe the style of writing

Early morning at Victoria Memorial, West Bengal

It is 1857 and the British Empire in India is facing severe unrest from the indigenous population. For the ruling British class in the northern town of Krishnapur, life is calm and polite until the sepoys at a nearby military fort rise in mutiny and the British are forced to retreat into the British Residency. Food and other supplies become short, disease sets in and the inhabitants' resources are tested to the limit.

This is the first part of J.G. Farrell's empire trilogy, an examination of the British Empire in its decline. *The Siege of Krishnapur* serves as a metaphor for this decline as each character is forced to examine their own view of the world.

Although the situation is desperate, Farrell describes it with great elegance and humour, conveying the ridiculousness of the British position. Some would argue that in not describing the hardship and injustice suffered by the local Indian population, Farrell has done them a great injustice. But I do not think that was his aim. What he has done is to write both a gripping story and a thought-provoking study of colonial life.

2 Which of these techniques (a–e) has the writer used to begin this review?

   a giving an opinion about the book directly
   b talking about the writer's background
   c describing the opening of the story
   d giving a short summary of the whole story
   e discussing the topic or theme of the book

3 **Writing skill** descriptive words

Complete the definitions of words describing books and writing with these words.

| convincing | fetched | going | poorly |
| provoking | uneventful | uninspiring |
| wrenching |

1 A book that makes you think is a thought-_____ book.
2 A book that is difficult to read is said to be heavy-_____.
3 A story in which nothing much happens is _____.
4 A plot which is very difficult to believe is far-_____.
5 A fictional character who you believe could really exist is _____.
6 An ending which is extremely sad is heart-_____.
7 A book which is a bit dull and flat is _____.
8 The opposite of *well-written* is _____ written.

4 Think of a novel you have read and write two short alternative opening paragraphs. For the first, give a short summary of the whole story. For the second, discuss the topic or theme of the book.

1 _____

2 _____

Wordbuilding synonyms

1 Complete these sentences using a synonym for the underlined word. You have been given the first two letters of the missing words.

1 It's a very picturesque <u>place</u> and a great sp_____ for a picnic.
2 I didn't <u>succeed in</u> finding cooking chocolate, but I ma_____ to get some ordinary chocolate.
3 It didn't <u>spoil</u> my enjoyment of the book generally, but it ru_____ the ending.
4 It's the most <u>durable</u> suitcase I've ever had. It's made of a very to_____ kind of plastic.
5 He <u>dealt with</u> the audience very skilfully and co_____ with every tricky question.
6 She showed enormous <u>bravery</u>, I thought. It takes co_____ to stand up to such criticism.
7 We had <u>hopes</u> that the film would do well, but it has surpassed all our ex_____ .
8 Can you <u>recognize</u> that figure on the left of the picture? I can't ma_____ it ou_____ .
9 We <u>started out</u> at 9 a.m. and the others se_____ of_____ an hour later.
10 The climb was <u>exhilarating</u> and reaching the top was even more th_____ .

Learning skills vocabulary extension (2)

2 You can use pictures to extend your vocabulary. Follow these steps.

1 Find a picture that interests you and look at the objects in it. The picture could also include people's expressions, feelings or actions that are happening.
2 See how many items you can name in English and then write the other words in your own language.
3 Look up the English equivalents of these words in a bilingual dictionary. Check the example sentences to see that the meaning is the same and check the pronunciation.
4 Now label five new items in the picture with words you have just learned.
5 Look at the picture thirty minutes later and test yourself. Can you remember the new words?

3 Look at the photo and follow the steps in Exercise 2. You will find a larger version of the photo on the Unit 5 Opener of your Student's Book (page 57).

Check!

4 Complete these sentences about characters and events with the correct form of the words given. All the answers are in Student's Book Unit 5.

1 The travel writer in the Opener referred to a bad experience with an _____ museum curator in Paris. (official)
2 In 5a, the writer says his trip to Chile, where he stayed at a _____ lodge on a nature reserve, fulfilled his _____ . (sustain, expect)
3 In 5b, the speaker describes going on a _____ mystery tour to an _____ destination. (magic, know)
4 In 5c, the writer describes Hergé's *Tintin* books as _____ novels. (graph)
5 In 5c, we learn that Hergé was not just a great _____ but also a great storyteller. (cartoon)
6 In 5d, we looked at adverbial linking phrases like 'to my _____ ,' and '_____ '. (relieve, worry)
7 In 5e, the writer describes the *Bridge of San Luis Rey* as a _____ -_____ book. (think, provoke)
8 In 5f, the writer describes a _____ experience that he had while walking in Spain. (transform)

Unit 6 Body matters

6a Here comes the sun

Listening a healing regime

1 🔊 43 Listen to a man describing his search for an exercise regime to help him recover from an injury. Answer the questions.

1 Where did he travel to? ....

2 What was he hoping to heal? ....

3 Was the exercise regime successful? ....

2 🔊 43 Listen again. What is significant about each of these numbers in the story?

1 1968: the date when ....
2 40: the number of ....
3 hundreds of thousands: the number of ....
4 200: the number of ....
5 6.50: the time when ....
6 20 centimetres: the height of ....
7 two weeks: the length of ....
8 30 minutes: the length of time that ....

3 Choose the correct synonym (a or b) for the words in bold from the extract.

1 … at least **put off** the day when I would have to face back surgery.
   a postpone   b cancel

2 … it supports around 200 disadvantaged boys – some **orphaned** …
   a without homes   b without parents

3 There were no other distractions – no New Age tunes playing, no yoga **outfits** …
   a equipment   b special clothing

4 The yoga carried on in a **serene** way for two weeks, never causing me even to break sweat.
   a calm   b intense

5 The **persistent** pain hasn't entirely gone away, but it has subsided.
   a constant   b irritating

6 I can now **put up with** it because I've given up worrying about it.
   a tolerate   b forget

Grammar phrasal verbs

4 🔊 43 Look at these phrasal verbs that the speaker uses. Then listen again and write the object of the transitive verbs. If there is no object, write *intransitive*.

1 turn up ....
2 end up ....
3 get over ....
4 put off ....
5 look for ....
6 pull in ....
7 put up ....
8 work on ....
9 carry on ....
10 put up with ....
11 give up ....

5 Answer these questions about the transitive phrasal verbs in Exercise 4.

1 Which of the verbs is clearly a separable verb?

2 Which of the verbs is clearly inseparable?

3 Of the rest, which do you think are separable and which inseparable?

6 Add the pronouns to these sentences.

1. The pain is quite bad, but I've learned to put up with. (it)
2. I got the injury playing football and it took me a long time to get over. (it)
3. If you think going to yoga classes will help, then there's no point putting off. (it)
4. I used to ski a lot, but I gave up. (it)
5. Reducing the cost of the course for students really pulled in. (them)
6. Can you put up for the night on Tuesday when I'm in town? (me)
7. I'm not as supple as I used to be, but I put down to my age. (that)
8. I can't touch my toes yet, but I'm working on. (it)

Vocabulary phrasal verbs

7 Choose the correct phrasal verb to complete the definitions.

1. To *come across / come out of* something means 'to find it unexpectedly'.
2. To *set apart / set aside* money or time means 'to reserve it'.
3. To *pick up / take up* a new hobby or sport means 'to begin practising it'.
4. To *put someone off / turn someone off* something means 'to discourage them from doing it'.
5. To *go up for / go in for* an activity means 'to like doing it'.
6. If something *takes off / lifts off*, it becomes successful.
7. To *get away from / get out of* a difficult task means 'to avoid having to do it'.
8. To *carry out / carry off* a task means 'to perform it'.
9. If something *comes about / comes up*, it happens or comes into existence.
10. To *fall back on / go back on* something means 'to use it as a reserve or back-up'.

Vocabulary exercise and health

8 Complete this conversation using one word in each space.

A: How do you ¹_____ so fit, Bella? Do you ²_____ loads of exercise or something?

B: Not so much these days. I used to work ³_____ at the gym twice a week, doing weights and working on the running machine.

A: So what's the secret? How do you keep in such good ⁴_____?

B: I think I'm just lucky really. I've never been ⁵_____ any kind of diet and I find that if I ⁶_____ reasonably active, I don't really have to ⁷_____ my weight.

A: I think that's my problem. I just never seem to find time to exercise.

B: What about going ⁸_____ a run with me one evening after work?

A: Yes, that would be good – as long as it's not too far.

9 Dictation fitness crazes

🔊 **44** Listen to this conversation between two people about fitness classes. Complete the conversation.

A: The other day _____.

B: Did you _____?

A: Not really. I didn't _____.

B: You mean like Zumba?

A: Yes. I knew Zumba _____,
_____.

B: And do you? _____

A: Yes, I do. _____.

6b Cross-training

Reading advice for athletes

1 Read the article and underline the three sentences that tell you the following.

1. the definition of cross-training
2. its most significant benefit
3. what cross-training teaches us

2 Read the article again and choose the correct option (a, b or c).

1. The main benefit of swimming to a cyclist is to help them:
   a relax. b build muscle. c have more stamina.
2. Marathon running is given as an example of a sport which is:
   a anti-social. b boring. c lonely.
3. Cross-training helps athletes to avoid injuries by adding:
   a variety. b gentler exercise.
   c breaks from exercise.
4. The writer implies that an athlete's career is relatively:
   a dangerous. b short. c easy.
5. The word *diet* in paragraph 3 could be replaced by:
   a routine. b menu. c day.
6. The result of taking up a new form of exercise is that your body:
   a becomes stressed. b feels happy.
   c gets stronger.

Cross-training

In recent years, there has been an increased focus among practitioners of all types of sports on cross-training. It has become in fact a critical part of most top athletes' regular routines. Simply put, cross-training **means practising** other sports or forms of exercise to improve, indirectly, your abilities in your main or target sport. An example of this would be a cyclist going swimming a couple of times a week. Swimming **requires you to control** your breathing and so it can also **help more generally to increase** a cyclist's endurance. It also **lets you build** strength in a more relaxed way because the support of the water puts less strain on joints and muscles.

There are several benefits to cross-training. First, it **tends to be** more interesting for the athlete to be engaged in different activities. If their sport is a solitary one, like marathon running, playing a team sport like football could provide a social aspect to their training. Secondly, it can strengthen and improve joints and muscles that are vital if they are to **succeed in performing** their sport at the highest level. Finally, and most importantly, it **prevents athletes from getting** the kind of repetitive strain injuries that they often suffer if they only practise the same activities day in, day out. It can not only improve performance, but also extend an athlete's life. In recent years, several footballers have used yoga to **enable them to continue playing** into their late thirties and even in some cases, their early forties.

Cross-training is not just useful for the elite sportsperson either. It has benefits for all of us. To stay injury free, I **recommend everyone incorporate** the following elements into their exercise diet:

- two parts cardio-vascular exercise (e.g. running, swimming, cycling, skipping, tennis)
- one part strength building (weight training)
- one part stretching (e.g. yoga, dance, aerobics)
- one part balance training (e.g. yoga, surfing, gymnastics)

The lesson of cross-training is that the body reacts well to new experiences. Each time you embark on a new form of exercise, whether it be weight-lifting or cycling, the body must **learn to deal with** new stresses and new demands. And in doing that, it will naturally strengthen.

Grammar verb patterns

3 Look at these verb patterns (1–6). Complete the table with examples of the verb patterns from the article.

1 Verb + *to* + infinitive	
2 Verb + object + *to* + infinitive	
3 Verb + object + infinitive	
4 Verb + *-ing*	
5 Verb + preposition + *-ing*	
6 Verb + object + preposition + *-ing*	

4 Complete the sentences using the correct form of the verbs. You sometimes also need to use a preposition.

1. Many people forget _____ properly before taking exercise. (warm up)
2. Sports therapists encourage athletes _____ cross-training as a way to extend their careers. (do)
3. I don't recommend _____ more than one hour of intensive exercise a day. (do)
4. You can't make people _____, but you can help them _____ the benefits. (exercise, see)
5. I miss _____ football, but at my age it's just not worth the risk of injury. (play)
6. If I worried _____ injured all the time, I would never try anything new. (get)
7. I thank my teacher _____ me interested in rowing. (get)
8. The best exercise routines seem _____ the ones which incorporate different elements of exercise. (be)
9. I started _____ tennis when I was ten, but then I switched to basketball. (play)
10. I love _____ sports, but I dislike _____. (play, train)

Vocabulary injuries

5 Complete the sentences with the correct form of these verbs to make collocations.

> bruise   bump   chip   graze
> lose   pull   sprain   stub

1. He fell over in the playground and _____ **his knee**.
2. I got up in the night and _____ **my toe** on the bed leg.
3. I didn't notice how low the doorway was and I _____ **my head**.
4. I bit on a nutshell in my cereal and _____ **my tooth**.
5. The doctor said nothing was broken – I've just _____ **my ribs**, apparently.
6. Sorry, I've _____ **my voice**. I was talking all day yesterday to a group of schoolchildren.
7. I trod in a hole in the pavement and _____ **my ankle**.
8. I can't play tennis this weekend. I _____ **a muscle** in my shoulder the last time I played.

6 Complete these idioms with prepositions. Then replace the underlined expressions in the sentences with the idioms.

> to be _____ a bad way   to pass _____
> to be _____ colour   to be _____ the mend
> to be shaken _____   to be run _____

1. It was so hot in the room. I practically <u>fainted</u>.
2. I'm glad Pete's <u>getting better</u> now; he seems to have been ill for ages.
3. I've been working solidly for months and I'm very <u>lacking in energy</u>.
4. I think she felt very <u>distressed</u> by the incident, even though no one got hurt.
5. You look a bit <u>pale</u>. Are you feeling OK?
6. So sorry to hear about Jim falling off the stepladder. Is he <u>seriously hurt</u>?

7 Pronunciation stress in two-syllable verbs

a 🔊 45 Circle the verbs that have stress on the second syllable. Which two do not? Then listen and check your answers.

> admire   avoid   convince   delay   expect
> insist   involve   postpone   practise
> prevent   rely   require   succeed   welcome

b What is the difference between the two verbs that have stress on the first syllable and the others?

Unit 6 Body matters

147

6c The beauty industry

Listening globalizing beauty

1 🎧 46 Listen to an interview with an expert on the fashion and beauty industry. Which of these statements (a, b or c) best summarizes her views?

a Globalization has made us all aspire to the same ideal of beauty.
b Companies have come to realize that local traditions are important.
c Companies try to convince us to want the same things because it's cheaper for them.

2 🎧 46 Listen again and complete the examples that the speaker gives to illustrate the following points. Pause the CD each time before moving onto the next question.

1 General economic growth has affected our view of beauty.
   a The global cosmetics industry _____ .
   b Americans _____ .

2 New markets keep being found.
   _____ brings in over $30 billion.

3 In the early 20th century, cosmetics companies were peddling a western and 'white' ideal of beauty.
   Some promised that _____ .

4 The more recent era of globalization is one in which companies definitely have to be more conscious of local traditions and values.
   A company like _____ .

5 Multinational companies adapt their products to include local and traditional ingredients.
   a _____ for skin cleansing
   b the Huito fruit _____

3 Replace the words in bold from the interview with one-word synonyms.

1 Has a globalized world made our ideal of beauty more **homogenized**?
2 If you go back to the early 20th century … cosmetics companies were **peddling** a Western ideal of beauty.
3 … if people everywhere could aspire to the same **notion** of beauty …
4 … McDonald's **alters** its menu to suit the tastes of each local market …
5 … a clear skin, healthy-looking hair, a youthful **glow** …

Word focus face

4 Complete this conversation using one word in each space.

A: Why the ¹_____ face? Are you depressed about something?
B: Yes, I'm going to a school reunion and all my clothes make me look too old. The last time I saw all those people I was 26!
A: Well, be careful. If you wear something that makes you look like you're obviously trying to look younger, no one will be able to **keep a** ²_____ face.
B: I know. I think I should just go as I am and **put a** ³_____ **face on it**.
A: Well, **let's face** ⁴_____ , none of them are going to be looking any younger either.
B: I wouldn't bet on it. Sue Williamson always used to spend loads on her appearance. She looked fantastic the last time I saw her.
A: Well, I don't see what the big deal is. If she thinks she's going to ⁵_____ **face** by looking old, that's her problem, not yours …
B: No, you're right. It's all very superficial. I'll just choose something smart and go and **face the** ⁶_____ . If they want to make judgements, let them.

6d It'll do them good

Real life discussing proposals

1 🔊 **47** Listen to four speakers each discussing a different proposal for the workplace. Write the number of the speaker (1–4) next to the proposal they discuss (a–f). Note that there are two extra proposals.

　　　　a a way to help people feel less stressed
　　　　b a way to help people get more exercise
　　　　c a way to reduce car use
　　　　d a way to have a healthier atmosphere
　　　　e a way to help people eat more healthily
　　　　f a way to build team spirit

2 What was the specific proposal in each case?

1 do without a _____
2 do without _____
3 provide a _____
4 provide opportunities for _____

3 🔊 **47** Listen again and note down the possible problem with each proposal.

1 _____
2 _____
3 _____
4 _____

4 Speaking skill proposing and conceding a point

🔊 **47** Complete the phrases the speakers used to propose and concede points. Then listen again and check your answers.

1 A better _____ would _____ to have just one which can be a service lift.
2 I _____ that sometimes people who have heavy things to move … will sometimes want to use the lift, but we can _____ work _____ that.
3 It _____ be _____ better just to have straightforward fresh air sucked in from outside.
4 _____, it wouldn't always be cool air, _____ it would be a lot healthier – and cheaper.
5 I haven't really thought _____ who should be responsible for making the list, but I do think it's important to make one.
6 I _____ not _____ will want to join in in that way, but for a lot of people the social element will really be a big attraction.

5 Pronunciation toning down negative statements

a 🔊 **48** Listen and underline the words which have most stress in these sentences.

1 I'm not very much in favour of the proposal.
2 It's not exactly what I had in mind.
3 It's not a particularly cheap option.
4 It hasn't proved to be so successful.
5 I'm not entirely convinced.

b Practise saying each sentence in Exercise 5a in the same way.

6 Listen and respond giving your opinion

🔊 **49** Imagine you are at a meeting to discuss a proposal to install a gym in your workplace to help staff keep fit. Your colleagues ask you questions. Respond with your own words. Then compare what you say with the model answer that follows.

1 *What do you think of the proposal?*

I think it's a great idea. It would really help staff to keep in shape and get exercise during their lunch hour or after work.

Unit 6 Body matters

149

6e A balanced diet

Writing a formal report

1 Read the report and answer the questions.

1 What prompted the report to be written?

2 What was the main finding?

3 What action is proposed?

Background and aims

There is concern that children at the school are not eating healthily enough, and this is affecting both their general health and their academic performance. In view of this, a short study was commissioned to look into children's diets and make recommendations. The aim of this report is to present those findings and make recommendations.

Findings

Most children are not getting a balanced diet. In the 14–16 age group, only 55 per cent of children have school meals. Overall, the lunches provided are a good balance of meat or fish, vegetables and carbohydrates (bread, potatoes, etc.). However, it is a self-service system and there is no obligation for pupils to choose a good variety of foods. Accordingly, children tend to choose mainly the carbohydrates, especially items like chips and sweet puddings rather than healthier items.

The remaining 45 per cent of pupils bring in a packed lunch. The content of these lunches varies greatly – from crisps and sweets to sandwiches and fruit, and apparently, the school makes no specific recommendations on what packed lunches should include.

Recommendations

Although pupils at the school are given options as to what they can have for lunch, most are making choices that are not balanced; specifically, this means they are eating too many sweets and not enough protein. We recommend that school meals should be compulsory for all pupils. We also suggest that they are given the choice of different meals, but not a choice of different elements within each meal, i.e. they must have a balance of vegetables, protein and carbohydrates.

2 Find words and phrases in the report with the following meanings, but expressed more formally.

1 Because of this
2 In general
3 But
4 So
5 people say
6 in particular

3 Writing skill avoiding repetition

a Find these words (1–6) in the report. Then find different ways of expressing the same idea later in the report.

1 children in the school
2 meals
3 balanced diet
4 The content of these lunches
5 options
6 We recommend

b Express these ideas in other words.

1 The canteen staff …
   Those
2 Most children …
   The
3 Hot meals would be good for children
   Hot meals would

4 Write a report encouraging school children to do more sport using the notes below. Write three paragraphs.

Background and aims
Local school wants to encourage everyone to do sport, not just in school teams.

Main findings
Pupils sit around at break times; no equipment; not enough PE lessons.

Recommendations
Organized group early morning exercise; semi-organized sports at break times.

Glossary
PE (n) /ˌpiː ˈiː/ physical education: a school subject where students do exercise and play sport

Wordbuilding compound words

1 Choose the correct options to complete these sentences.
1. The film is about Jim when he's an old man, but it contains a lot of *cutbacks / flashbacks* to his earlier life.
2. The *turnout / turn-up* for the election was over 70% this time, because many more young people registered to vote.
3. This is probably the most important *break-in / breakthrough* in medical science for thirty years.
4. I sent her a *follow-on / follow-up* letter stressing how interested we are, but I still haven't heard.
5. Sorry, I can't really stop now, but I'd love to meet soon for a proper *catch-up / round-up*.
6. There's been a complete *breakdown / clampdown* in relations between the two sides – they're not even talking anymore.
7. You should try and get a gig at the Beat Café. They're always on the *lookalike / lookout* for new musical talent.
8. She had a kind of *faraway / getaway* look in her eyes.
9. We reported the *break-in / break-up* to the police, even though nothing valuable was stolen.
10. The final will be a *showdown / show-off* between the two best teams in the division.

2 Underline the compound word to complete each definition.
1. A *break-up / getaway* is a quick escape.
2. A *cutback / clampdown* is a reduction in spending.
3. A *turn-up / clampdown* is a severe restriction on activity.
4. A *lookalike / show-off* is a person who is always drawing attention to their achievements.
5. A *turn-up / follow-on* is an unexpected (positive) event or result.
6. A *break-in / break-up* is a separation or disintegration.

Learning skills using phrasal verbs correctly

3 Read the notes below about using phrasal verbs.
1. Often in dictionaries you will find one-word synonyms given for phrasal verbs. These can be misleading. For example: *make up = invent*.
2. Most phrasal verbs are limited in the contexts in which they can be used. You can *make up a story* or *make up an excuse*, for example, but you can't *make up a new product*.
3. So a full definition would be: *make up = invent an account of something*.
4. When you learn a new phrasal verb, you must also learn its limitations before you start to use it.

4 Look at these phrasal verbs and their full definitions, and tick (✓) the words that collocate with the phrasal verbs.
1. *call off* = cancel (a scheduled event)
   I called off:
   a the meeting.
   b the hotel booking.
   c the football match.
   d the wedding.
2. *put across* = communicate (one's ideas or feelings)
   She put across:
   a her proposal.
   b her views.
   c her decision.
   d the news by email.
3. *set up* = establish (a new organization or connection)
   We set up:
   a a good relationship.
   b our own company.
   c a video link.
   d a daily routine.
4. *find out* = discover (an answer by consulting or by experience)
   I found out:
   a an old map in his attic.
   b a new car.
   c why she left.
   d the meaning of the word.

Check!

5 Complete these sentences about exercise and beauty. All the answers are in Student's Book Unit 6.
1. Swogging is a mixture of _____ and _____.
2. Radio Taiso is a callisthenic exercise routine in _____.
3. Yoga originated in _____.
4. Ultrarunning means running _____ distances.
5. Women of the Paaung tribe in Myanmar put copper coils around their _____ to make them longer.
6. People say that beauty is _____ deep (but 'ugly' goes clean to the bone)!
7. In Washington State, USA, restaurants have to say how many _____ are in each dish.
8. In 6e, the writer reported on a proposal to make smokers pay more for their _____.

Audioscripts

Unit 1

1

Hello, everyone. My name's Herb Sokolowski and I'm a college graduate, just like you. You might have heard of me, because I used to present a TV programme called *Weird Science*. Currently, I'm writing a book about scientific inventions, and when I was asked to come and speak to you, I thought I'd talk about that. But then I thought: 'What's the use of that? It'll probably only interest a few of them.' So instead, I'm going to give you some rules of life that I read about fifteen years ago in a book by a guy called Charles Sykes. I believe the book was called *Dumbing down our kids*. Before that, I had believed myself to be – as you probably do now – one entitled individual. But it changed my attitude and, who knows, perhaps it'll change yours. I've reduced the number of rules a bit and put them in my own words. So, are you ready? Here we go.

RULE 1: Life's not fair; get used to it.

RULE 2: You will not make eighty thousand dollars next year. You won't be a vice president with a car phone, not until you've earned the right.

RULE 3: If you think your teacher is tough, wait till you get a boss.

RULE 4: Flipping burgers is not beneath your dignity. Many years ago, your grandparents had a different word for burger flipping; they called it opportunity.

RULE 5: If you mess up, it's probably your own fault. So don't whine about your mistakes: learn from them.

RULE 6: You probably thought growing up that your parents were pretty boring. But they were like that because at the time they were paying your bills, cleaning your clothes and listening to you talk about how cool you are. So before you go off and save the world, clean up your own room.

RULE 7: Over the last 20 years, schools have abolished the idea of winners and losers – but life hasn't. In school, they give you as much time as you want to get the right answer. That rarely happens in real life.

RULE 8: Be nice to nerds. Sooner or later, you'll end up working for one.

2

One of the problems with advice is that people tend to interpret it to suit their own purposes. An example of this is the wisdom of the 18th-century economist, Adam Smith. One of his main ideas was that if you allow people to seek wealth for themselves, they will naturally create jobs and wealth for others. He called this 'the invisible hand'. People trying to improve their own situation also help their neighbour to improve theirs, but without meaning to, as if with an invisible hand. Unfortunately, a lot of people took Smith to mean that it was all right to be greedy and selfish and not to help others directly, which is not at all what he meant.

4

Like many islands, Great Britain and its language, English, have been subject to many influences over the centuries. What developed as a result is a language with a very rich and large vocabulary. Later in British history, the influenced would become an influencer, an exporter of its language and culture, to a point where its language again became subject to changes made by others who use it to communicate with each other in the worlds of business or academia.

The first influence is that of the Romans and their language, Latin. The legacy of the Romans is evident in the Latin-based or Romance languages that still survive in many Western European countries. However, after the fall of the Roman Empire in the fifth century, Britain was invaded by various Germanic peoples and it was their languages, notably Anglo-Saxon, or what is now known as Old English, that became the dominant force.

When William I of Normandy conquered Britain in 1066, he established French as the official language, but instead of replacing English, French was assimilated into it and Middle English, a close relation to the language, is still spoken in Britain today. This is a language made up of German vocabulary and simplified German grammar mixed with French-derived – often Latin-based – words. The language continued to remain quite organic until the invention of the printing press and the wider publication of the written word, when it started to become standardized. You can see this very clearly if you compare the writing of the poet Chaucer in the 14th century, which is difficult to understand without reference to a glossary, with Shakespeare's writing two centuries later. Shakespeare is not easy, but in fact it is relatively similar to the English of today.

From this point in history – the 17th century through to the end of the 19th century – British colonialism thrived. This had two implications for the English language: the first was the importation into the language of yet more words – *pyjama* and *bungalow*, for example, from India; the second was the spread of English around the globe – to India, America, East Africa and so on. With its spread came adaptation. Each country stamped its own mark on the language used, making it something different from the English spoken in Britain. The writer George Bernard Shaw famously spoke of Britain and America as 'two nations divided by a common language'. The new English-speaking settlers in America were keen to set their language and their country apart from Britain, and so brought in new words and new spellings, as well as a new, more direct style of speaking.

People have argued that English was successful in its global reach because it was a versatile and flexible language. But in fact its spread had far more to do with economic factors. People needed a language to do business and English was in the right place at the right time.

Which brings us to the present day and to a situation where many versions of English now exist. The writer Robert McCrum has identified two types in particular: English as spoken by native speakers in different countries around the world and Globish, a simplified form of the language used by non-native speakers to communicate on matters of business or work. According to McCrum, this is a utilitarian kind of English where you learn a limited vocabulary – maybe 1,500 words at most – and grammar, enough to enable you to do your job at the call centre, for example.

Although this characterization is too simplistic – there are many shades and versions of English between Globish and the language of Shakespeare – it does make an important point: that English, like any language, is a tool that people adapt and exploit to suit their needs. No one version is right or wrong; the question, rather, is which version you aspire to speak.

Audioscripts

5
Conversation 1
T: What did you think of the talk?
A: Yeah, I thought it was really interesting: a lot of food for thought.
T: Sorry, I should have introduced myself. I'm Teresa. I'm one of the conference organizers.
A: Good to meet you, Teresa. I'm Ana Muñoz, from Deusto University in Spain.
T: Oh, yes, I've heard of that. Whereabouts in Spain is it?
A: In San Sebastián, in the north.
T: Oh yes, where the Guggenheim museum is. Fabulous building.
A: No, I think you're thinking of Bilbao. We're not a million miles from there, but it's a different branch of the university. Are you an academic too, Teresa?
T: Yes, I lecture in Social Sciences at Toronto University.
A: Really? That's my field as well. Look, I'm going to get a coffee before the next session. Do you fancy joining me?
T: Yeah, that'd be great. Um ... let me just get rid of all these papers and I'll come over to the coffee area.

Conversation 2
K: Is this the right place for the bus into the city centre?
J: Yes, it is. We've just missed one, I'm afraid. But they come every twenty minutes. Where are you heading?
K: I've just flown in from Amman in Jordan and now I'm going to my university accommodation.
J: OK. So, you have the address.
K: Yes.
J: Is it near the centre?
K: Yes, I think so. It's in Princes Street.
J: OK. That's very central – and near the bus station. But you've got a big bag, so I think your best bet would be to get a taxi when we get off. What are you going to be studying … um, sorry, I didn't ask your name?
K: My name is Khalid. It's nice to meet you.
J: Hi, Khalid. Yeah, good to meet you too. I'm Jeff, by the way. So, what are going to be studying, Khalid?
K: I'm doing an M.Sc. in Quantum Physics.
J: Wow, that sounds impressive. Way above my head, I'm afraid .... I'm just a primary school teacher ... Hey, I think this is our bus now ...

6
1 What did you think of the exhibition?
2 Do you fancy going out for some fresh air?
3 What kind of company is it, exactly?
4 What's it like being the only boy in a family of girls?
5 Sorry, I should have mentioned that before.
6 How are you finding the course?
7 Shall we go and get a coffee or something?
8 So, have you been here before?

7
A= Antony, MA =Model answer
A: Hi there, I don't think we've met. I'm Antony.
MA: Hi, Antony. Good to meet you. I'm José.
A: So, how do you know Nicola?
MA: We're old friends. We were at school together, actually. And you?
A: Oh. I work with Nicola's husband ... at an electronics firm. So, are you from around here?
MA: No, I live in Spain. I'm just visiting.
A: Oh, I see. And what do you think of the city? Is it your first time here?
MA: Yes, it is. I'm really enjoying it, actually; though I have to say, I find it a bit expensive.
A: And what have you done while you've been here? Have you been to any of the museums or anything?
MA: Not yet. I only got here two days ago. I've walked around the centre a bit and I've done a bit of sightseeing.
A: I'm supposed to take my kids on a sightseeing boat at the weekend. They've never been on one. Have you?
MA: Yes, I've been on one in Paris. But it was raining the whole time so the views weren't fantastic. Still, the kids will love it, I'm sure.

8
So, everyone. There have been various rumours about what paid and unpaid time off staff are entitled to, and so the management would like to clarify the company's position so that everyone is clear on the situation. A short document will be sent to everyone's work email address to formalize these arrangements in a couple of weeks, but as I said, I just wanted to set the record straight now by talking to you. So, first off – sabbaticals, that's to say paid leave from work. The policy is that everyone on pay grade six or above is entitled to three months' sabbatical every six years worked. This applies only to full-time employees and not to part-time employees. Arrangements for part-time employees are being discussed, but these arrangements are to be confirmed.

Secondly, unpaid leave. This is purely at the discretion of your line manager. He or she will decide each case on the circumstances of the employee. For example, if they have a difficult situation at home, such as sick or elderly parents. Having said that, normally no unpaid leave will be allowed for any employee who's worked in the company for less than eighteen months.

9
Now I've called everyone here today because we're about to test out a radical new idea, which is to set no limits on how much or how little holiday each member of staff can take. That's right – no limits. Initially the company is going to try this new policy out for a limited period, that's to say six months. That's because we're not entirely sure if it's going to work or not, but we're pretty confident.

What are the reasons for this policy? Well, we think that it's much better to be adult and responsible about this. We all have busy working lives with meetings to go to and targets to reach. And we all also have busy lives outside work, with families to look after and interests to pursue. If we're given a little freedom, we can organize our own time better.

So what are your responsibilities in this new scheme? Note that this is not an excuse to take as much time off work as possible. Nor is it something you can organize completely independently: you'll still have to negotiate with colleagues in case the timing of your holiday disrupts business in some way. You'll also still have your work targets to reach.

And finally the details. The exact start date is to be confirmed, but it will begin in the second half of this year. The policy applies to every employee including part-time staff. It will be reviewed after approximately four months. And that's it. Any questions?

Unit 2

10
Take a walk on the mountain slopes of the Tibetan Plateau in May or June, and you are likely to come across groups of people on their hands and knees, intently searching the grass for something they cannot find. It's as if someone had dropped a valuable ring, and then asked their friends and relatives to come and help them search for it.

Actually, what they're looking for is a small fungus called *yartsa gunbu* which is so prized in China for its medicinal properties that half a kilo has been known to sell for up to $50,000. Not surprising, perhaps, when you realize how difficult it is to find. One couple I talked to had been searching all day and found only thirty specimens.

Yartsa gunbu occurs in very specific conditions. Only found on the Tibetan plateau and the Himalayas, the mushroom is formed when the larva of a particular type of moth hatches underground and becomes infected with the fungus. As the larva grows into a caterpillar, the fungus eats it from the inside. In late spring, the fungus sends a brown stalk up through the dead caterpillar's head and out of the ground. It is this tiny stalk that the worm diggers are searching for.

For centuries, herbal doctors have prescribed *yartsa gunbu* for all sorts of medical problems: back pain, fatigue, asthma, poor eyesight. The Chinese are convinced it revitalizes a person's 'chi' or 'life energy'. Legend says that yaks that eat it grow ten times stronger. Now, with China's growing wealth, demand for *yartsa gunbu* has soared and so has the income of the locals who farm it. Thousands of poor Tibetan yak herders now own motorcycles and iPhones and flat-screen TVs. Some are even more successful. Zhaxicaiji, a former yak herder, started her own *yartsa* company in 1998 and, since then, the business has grown year on year. It now has twenty stores and a turnover of $60 million.

These communities are thriving on *yartsa gunbu's* rarity. But that very rarity may also be their downfall. The harvest is currently roughly 400 million specimens, and ecologists say that if this overpicking does not stop and some stalks are not left in the ground, the cycle will stop, because the fungus that infects the larvae will have disappeared. Perhaps the next generation of golden worm diggers will be searching harder than ever.

🎧 11

/ɪ/	/iː/	/aɪ/
medicinal	previous	private
specimen	kilo	unscientific
specific	visa	survive
caterpillar		prescribe
artist		tiny
		revitalize
		financial

🎧 12

I = Interviewer, J = John
- I: So, John, how did you come across this story?
- J: I've been travelling in this region for many years and I'd seen this phenomenon before but never paid it much attention.
- I: And what was it that interested you this time?
- J: Well, often you'll visit a place with a particular story in mind. Then, while you're researching it, you find something else catches your interest.
- I: And what was that in this case?
- J: I was very struck by how well off people in the village seemed compared to when I'd last visited. So I decided to investigate and got this amazing story of the golden worm.

🎧 13

P = Presenter, RE = Daniel Raven-Ellison
- P: Could you cross a forest without touching the ground? What would you see if you walked through your entire city taking a photo every eight steps? How would it feel to locate a missing cat and return it to its owner? How far could you walk sucking on the same mint? This is geography Daniel Raven-Ellison style. A former geography teacher, Raven-Ellison uses films, books, websites and walks to take geography beyond memorizing dots on a map, challenging children and adults to experience every aspect of the world around them in a more meaningful, surprising way. Here is Daniel Raven-Ellison.
- RE: The internet makes us feel the world is becoming smaller and more available, but at the same time, many real, lived experiences are shrinking. For children, outdoor exploration improves mental and physical health, expands learning through risk taking, spurs innovative problem solving, and encourages empathy by meeting different people; yet too few children are allowed to play outdoors nowadays. As adults, although we share our cities with millions of other people, many of us are more disconnected than ever before, moving from the island of our home to the island of our car to the island of our office without meaningfully engaging with each other, nature or the places in between. But for our ancestors, going on adventures was normal. Adventure has now become something we only watch on TV though. But in fact, there are amazing adventures to be had right outside our doorsteps.
- P: For Raven-Ellison, this road to adventure is 'guerrilla geography': asking people to challenge their preconceptions about places, engage in social and environmental justice, and form deeper community connections. His *Urban Earth* films demonstrate guerrilla geography in action. He created them by walking across Mumbai, Mexico City, London, and ten other UK and US cities from one extreme edge to the other, while photographing whatever lay directly in front of him every eight steps. All photos, edited together, become a film portrait of each city. Raven-Ellison again.
- RE: Travel shows and guidebooks select what they want you to see. They twist things. My films give you an unaltered look at the reality of a city as a whole. When you're not protected by the speed or armour of a car, you see what's actually happening neighbourhood by neighbourhood.
- P: With more than half of the world's people living in urban areas, Raven-Ellison hopes the films will break down boundaries that isolate communities. He says that we need to engage with each other to reduce conflict, instead of being afraid to explore certain neighbourhoods.
  Raven-Ellison's films have inspired innovative walks for groups. He starts by handing the map to someone else. In one walk, he launched ten teams of people from different points outside London, all headed towards the city centre, converging at a pub where they compared experiences and shared ideas about how to improve Britain's neighbourhoods.
- RE: The act of actually walking and experiencing that space gives you a different, more tangible perspective of our environmental impacts.
- P: The educational project *Mission: Explore* has guerrilla geography incorporated into its children's programmes. They've developed a website and series of books with hundreds of challenges that show geography's fun side, including mini field trips, neighbourhood explorations and creative science experiments. It's a hands-on format that's very accessible to children. Many of the tasks seem fun and simple but actually require quite high-level thinking. One challenge suggests children conduct a survey to see how friendly their community is, write to their local politicians with the findings, and offer ways the community could be improved for children. Another proposes you blindfold yourself and get a friend to help you explore by using your other senses. I'll leave you with a last word from Raven-Ellison.
- RE: Memorizing things for quizzes isn't enough. Children need to have skills for interpretation, analysis and understanding. Education can't be based just on how much you know, but must also be measured by how creative and innovative you can be. Giving children time and space to explore outdoors allows moments to happen that will be crucial for tackling issues like climate change, water shortages and other big problems.

… Audioscripts

14
I = Interviewer, H = Hiroki Katagawa
I: So, can you tell me a little about yourself, Hiroki, and what attracted you to this graduate training programme?
H: So. Er … yes, thank you. My name is Hiroki Katagawa. I'm 24 years old and I'm master … I have a master's degree in Business Administration. So, my first degree was in Town Planning, um … Urban Planning. I spent one year in Japan working on a metro and transport hub in the city of Osaka – it's a major city on Honshu island. It was for work experience and I received a commendation when I left the project. So this is what attracted me to your company … because you are involved in such infrastructure projects.
I: And why do you think you are suited to this particular programme?
H: I have good planning and organization, and up-to-date IT skills. Perhaps you would like me to give you an example. In Osaka, I helped design the programme for planning work schedules for the staff working …
I: Sorry, you designed the programme or you were using bespoke software?
H: I'm sorry, what?
I: Was that software you adapted or created?
H: Oh no, it was a well-known programme used in Japan, but I had to adapt it, yes … So, as I was saying, it was for planning schedules for staff working on tramlines in the city. This work had to be arranged with the consent of the local authorities, the transport office of Osaka.
I: OK. Well, that is very relevant to what we do here …
H: And you also asked me about my suitability for this programme. I am very keen to join an international company. I am very open to different cultures, very interested in different cultures. I like travel very much and have made many friends and contacts in different countries. This is important for me – to work and live together with people from other cultures. I love to learn different approaches to life … in fact, in general I am very enthusiastic to learn.
I: OK. Thank you, Hiroki. A little earlier we gave you a form …

16
I = Interviewer, MA = Model answer
1
I: So can you tell me a little about yourself and what attracted you to this job?
MA: Yes, my name is Eduardo Torres and I'm a graduate in Hotel Management. I have been working for the last year at a country hotel and I would like to get a job with a bigger chain of hotels.
2
I: And what would you say your strongest qualities are?
MA: I'm well organized and I'm good at solving problems. In fact, I love the challenge of dealing with clients' problems and trying to find the best solution.
3
I: I see. And why do you think you would be suited to this particular hotel?
MA: I know this is a prestigious international hotel, so I imagine the challenge to maintain good standards is very high.

Unit 3

17
Speaker 1
You've probably heard of Glastonbury. It's in the west of England. It's fairly well-known around the world for its music festival, which is massive – over 170,000 people go each year. It takes place in the month of July on some agricultural land near the town, which is owned by a local farmer. Well, I live in the town of Glastonbury, which is not the same thing. I actually remember when it was just a small market town like others in the area: gentle countryside around it, pleasant period houses, a beautiful church, a few tea houses and quaint shops. All in all, it was quite a sleepy, traditional kind of English town. Well, that was before Glastonbury festival got big in the seventies and the hippies began to move in – I guess people had had such a transformative experience at the festival that they thought they'd stay to keep the magic alive somehow. Well, now the town is a rather odd mix of older, more conservative residents – I don't want to put myself in that category, mind you – and younger people who want an alternative lifestyle. So these days the High Street is full of vegetarian restaurants, second-hand music shops, bookshops that specialize in magic and ancient mysteries, shops selling healing crystals … it's all a bit wacky, really, but actually I quite like it!

Speaker 2
Ghent isn't my hometown but it was my adopted town for a while. Actually, it might be cheating slightly to call it a town. It's got around 250,000 inhabitants, which makes it more like a city, but it doesn't feel like a city, because it's quite compact. They say Ghent is Belgium's best-kept secret, because it's such an attractive place and yet remains relatively unknown. It doesn't get the number of visitors that Bruges or Brussels gets, which is also a bit odd because it's exactly halfway between the two. I guess part of its charm is that it's so many things rolled into one: it's a university town, a historic town, a port, an industrial town. So on one hand it feels a little like a working town, because of the industry around the old docks: there's a huge steel mill, a truck assembly plant, Europe's biggest fruit juice terminal … they say. But on the other hand, if you don't see that part, it seems like a well-preserved historic town. I was a student there and I had an amazing time. It was really lively and friendly. One of the benefits of having that kind of mix – I mean, old and new, academic and industrial – is that people tend to be quite open-minded and accepting. There's also masses to do – a good music scene, interesting museums and galleries, beautiful architecture, nice parks – but going out isn't particularly cheap. The other drawback is the weather, which is pretty terrible most of the time – grey and rainy. I'm from Italy and, I have to say, it got me down a bit at times.

19
A: How was your trip to Russia?
B: Great, thanks. We had quite a packed schedule, but it was very interesting. We started in Moscow and saw the sights around Red Square. Strangely, the thing I loved most was the metro. Each station is like a work of art in itself. The service is pretty efficient too.
A: And how did it compare to St Petersburg?
B: Very different. St Petersburg is a very grand and gracious city. Actually, it feels a bit closer in atmosphere to other cities in central Europe, whereas Moscow doesn't feel particularly European. But that's the thing about Russia. You don't realize what an enormous and diverse country it is until you travel there.

21
J = Jim, K = Kirsten Sommer
J: So I'm here with architectural historian Kirsten Sommer to talk about the subject of biomimetics and why it's relevant to architecture today. Kirsten, biomimetics – which I should explain to any listeners who are not familiar with the term – is the idea of

155

copying good design from nature and applying it to things that are man-made. It's something I associate more with material science and robotics, and things like that. But I think you've found strong evidence of it in the history of architecture too.

K: Yes, hello Jim, that's right. But first of all, I think we should be careful perhaps about how we label these things. We need to separate the term biomimetics, which was coined in the 1950s, from the practice of simply taking inspiration from nature's forms, which is obviously a much older phenomenon. The term Biomimetics is now used for the development of new technologies – like man-made fibres that can imitate the properties of duck feathers, or hi-tech swimsuits that replicate shark skin. A classic example of it is Velcro, which imitates barbs on the head of a thistle plant. But for a long time – and still very much today – architects have taken inspiration from the forms and shapes of nature.

J: Can you give us an example?

K: Yes, um … probably the best known building of this kind is Gaudi's Sagrada Familia in Barcelona …

J: That's not even finished yet, is it?

K: No. Its history is complicated, but before his death in 1926 Gaudi left very clear instructions – in the form of three-dimensional models – as to how he'd like it finished. The date for completion is now 2026. But anyway, Gaudi loved nature and understood that the natural world is full of curved forms, not straight lines. So with organic models in mind and the materials that nature uses to create its structures: wood, muscle, tendon, etc., he created a very organic-looking building in the Sagrada Familia, an architectural form that borrowed from nature in a way that no one had seen before.

J: It is, or certainly was, a controversial building, wasn't it?

K: Oh, absolutely. It's one of those buildings that people either love or hate. George Orwell called it 'one of the most hideous buildings in the world'. Others, like the surrealists, loved its originality and took Gaudi to their hearts. Gaudi's own explanation for its originality was that it had 'returned to the origin', in other words it was original in the sense that it had gone back to nature.

J: And who is using biomimetics these days in architecture?

K: Oh, my goodness, there are so many examples. You only have to look at the names of buildings to tell you that: The Swiss Re Tower in London is known as 'the Gherkin'; the Olympic stadium in Beijing, which people called the 'Bird's Nest'; Frank Gehry's 'Fish' in Barcelona. But it's about more than just the external shape and appearance of buildings. Architects are using biomimetics to create more environmentally friendly buildings.

J: Yes, I read about the Eastgate Centre in Harare being innovative in that way.

K: Yes, that's a very good example. It's not only unusual to look at – modern office and shopping complexes are typically all steel and glass these days. What's more interesting is the use of chimneys to imitate the heating and cooling system in a termite mound. It's called passive cooling, and it's very energy efficient and does away with the need for a modern air conditioning system. It works by storing heat that is generated inside the building in the walls and then letting this heat escape through the chimneys at night, so the building is nice and cool the following morning.

🔊 22

A: Well, first of all, I should say that I think it's basically a good idea – it's got a lot of things to recommend it: principally, that people won't have to waste time going down to the canteen to get their coffee. Also it'll encourage employee interaction, which of course is a good thing. But I have to say there's a risk in that, because if you make an area that's too comfortable or convivial, they might spend just as much time there as they did going down to the canteen – in other words, away from productive work.

B: I kind of disagree with that. The thing about an open-plan office is that it feels rather large and impersonal, and so the idea of putting in some area that feels more intimate and homely really appeals to me. I think you have to be careful about terms like 'productive work'. You said yourself that employee interaction was something to be encouraged and I think that can take different forms – from formal meetings to informal chats. The informal chats are something we shouldn't underestimate the importance of. What I mean is, if we assume that people relaxing and having coffee at work are wasting the company's time, then for me that is a sad state of affairs. So I'm very much in favour of this proposal, particularly given that we are all working in a rather impersonal environment, as I said before. Oh, and by the way, including a screen with industry news on it in the room is a clever touch.

🔊 25

C = Colleague, MA = Model answer

1
C: Would you prefer to have a large living space or somewhere that's small and cosy?
MA: Personally, I'd like to have a lot of space, but maybe that seems a bit selfish. After all, it's not a choice everyone can make.

2
C: Do you think that the architecture around you affects how you are feeling?
MA: Yes, I think it probably does. Not consciously maybe, but I don't think you should underestimate its impact.

3
C: I've heard it said that 80% of people end up living no more than 30 kilometres from where they were born. I think that's a rather surprising statistic.
MA: Do you? I disagree. I think most people like to stay near their family and friends. And also it's pretty clear that the bond that we form with our surroundings as we grow up is very strong.

4
C: I don't think there's enough new and radical design in architecture. There is for a few people who are prepared to pay for it, but most new buildings are just boring.
MA: I agree completely. A lot of new buildings either copy existing designs or go for the cheapest design. I'm in favour of people trying out new things and I don't think new always means more expensive.

Unit 4

🔊 28

There are three things you can do when you meet a physical obstacle – go round it, go over it or go under it. Now, imagine that physical obstacle is the traffic in our cities. We've already tried going round it by building ring roads around our cities, but, actually, such solutions are never likely to work because just as new channels around a sandcastle on the beach fill with water, so new roads fill with cars as soon as you build them.

That leaves two options: to build new traffic systems in the air or underground. But either way, rather than removing the problem, you might just be moving it somewhere else. The problem with the former is that collisions or accidents in the air could also have an impact on those below when debris falls from a height. The problem with the latter has always been the expense.

Until now that is. Because American entrepreneur Elon Musk thinks he has an answer. And given his amazing record of not only finding, but also implementing innovative solutions, there's a good chance that he could pull this off.

His latest venture, The Boring Company, proposes building a network of tunnels under cities that transports vehicles on high-speed electric sleds. The key to making this happen will be by speeding up the tunnelling process and making it a lot cheaper. Musk's idea is that by using smaller single-lane tunnels and more efficient boring or tunnelling machines, his techniques should reduce the cost enormously. Vehicles would then travel down each tunnel at high speeds and only in one direction, so that there would be nothing to block them or hold them up. In his mind, also, is the idea that in future, the tunnels will possibly use vacuum technology, in which pods carrying cars can travel at speeds of up to 900 kilometres per hour. This technology, part of Musk's so-called Hyperloop project, has already been tried and tested in an over-ground transport tube system in California.

🔊 30
P = Presenter, F = Freya Wint
P: Philanthropy is back in fashion – some say in America it never went out of fashion. Now a new generation of internet and mobile communications billionaires are supporting good causes like never before. The difference is that so many more of these do-gooders are self-made businessmen and women, whereas in the past they were individuals who relied on inherited wealth. Are there other differences between these philanthropists and their 19th-century counterparts? I put this question to social historian Freya Wint.
F: Very definitely. The philanthropists of the 19th-century tended to set up long-term foundations and scholarships so that their legacies would benefit future generations. What you have now is a number of people – Bill Gates being the most famous – who have made money relatively quickly in their lifetime and are now actively involved in doing good with it … and enjoying themselves. 'Giving while living' is the slogan.
P: And is there a difference in the way they give?
F: Oh, certainly. Because they are more hands-on, they are also more concerned to see the short-term benefits of what they are doing. In many cases, they treat their giving in much the same way as they treat their other business investments; they even describe their programmes in business terms like 'getting a good return on capital', 'making stakeholders accountable', and 'setting agreed and measurable targets'. The money they put into philanthropic projects is like seed money – they want to see the projects grow and prosper by themselves, become self-sustaining eventually.
P: Have you got any concrete examples of that?
F: Yes, a good example is Jeff Skoll, the Canadian founder of eBay, which is the world's largest online marketplace. He set up something called the Skoll Foundation which supports and promotes social entrepreneurship. The foundation aims to identify people and ideas that are already helping to bring about positive change in areas where social problems exist. I was particularly struck reading about one of the entrepreneurs he backed, a woman called Daniela Papi. She used to run voluntourism projects in Cambodia, where volunteers paid to come and help build schools there. But she soon realized that a more long-term and sustainable approach would be to promote teacher training and curriculum development in the schools. Then she realized that in these volunteers that came on her programme there was great potential … for them to go to other places and bring about positive change there. So now she focuses on that aspect too. I just thought that was a great example of how a little money behind the right person can develop into a much wider benefit and I think that's what today's philanthropists are all about.
P: So is there none of the old-fashioned 'no strings attached' kind of giving anymore?
F: Oh no … there are still a lot of donations – rather than investments – made to people who are in a bad situation and can't help themselves – medicines for HIV sufferers, water and food supplies for those who have been hit by drought or famine. John Caudwell, the man who made his fortune in the mobile phone business, gives most of his money to disabled children. He's a self-confessed capitalist who believes in people helping themselves, but he recognizes that there are some people that aren't born lucky like him. Essentially, by providing them with wheelchairs or walking aids, he's giving them greater independence and opportunity. I'd say that was very typical of the ethos of the new philanthropists. There's more emphasis on self-help than with former philanthropists.
P: It must make them feel good too.
F: Oh, absolutely. No one wants to be remembered only as the person who made a billion selling phones or laptops – they want to be remembered for the contribution they made to making the world a better place.

🔊 31
We have designed a school bag for children. What's so original about that, you ask? Well, this is a bag that also functions as a desk. So you can fold it out and work at it, anytime and anywhere you like. Why would children want to do that, when they have a desk at school and a table at home? Well, simply because not all children do have a desk at school or even a table at home. I'd like you to stop and just think about that for a minute. Our ambition for this school bag is that it will not only be used by children in Europe but also in developing countries. Because that is where it will really come into its own. It has numerous compartments for notebooks, pens and a water holder. Hydration, as you know, is very important for concentration. But how will people in poorer countries be able to afford the bag? Well, that's why we call it the Solidarity Bag. Because we're setting the price a little higher here in Europe to help lower the cost of a bag for a family in a developing country. So when you pay 35 euros for the bag here, you are helping to bring the price down to an affordable level elsewhere, showing solidarity with families less fortunate than you.

🔊 33
I = Investor, MA = Model answer
1
I: Can you just explain to me what your ambition is for this product?

MA: Yes. We would like it to have successful sales in Europe and on the basis of that to be able to provide many of these bags to children in developing countries.

2
I: And do you think that customers will support this ambition?
MA: Yes, I think that it's very important for people nowadays to feel they can do some good when they buy things. People want ethical products.

3
I: But the price of the bag is quite high for European customers.
MA: It is quite high, but it is a good-quality bag and I think people are prepared to pay a little extra for an ethical product.

4
I: And do you think the fact that it can function also as a desk is useful for children in Europe?
MA: It's not as useful as it is for children in some developing countries. But I think it is a feature that they will enjoy and it might encourage them to work in places where they didn't before.

5
I: And if we invest, what will you use the money for?
MA: The most important thing for us is to make people aware of the Solidarity Bag. So we will invest in an advertising and publicity campaign.

Unit 5

34

Maybe like me, you're one of those people who used to look at organized tours and think – never in a million years! Why would I want to be herded around like a sheep with a group of people I've never met before, tied to a strict schedule and taken to all the obvious tourist places rather than the more undiscovered ones? What I want from travel is a bit of independence and freedom.

Well, that's what I *used* to think. And the thing that changed my mind was a guided tour I took at the Metropolitan Museum of Art in New York. I was in New York on holiday and it was raining hard, so I dived into the museum to escape the rain. Don't get me wrong – I do like visiting museums; this just happened to be an unplanned visit. So I wandered over to the information desk and asked what was on and they said that, among other things, there was a tour of the museum's early Christian art collection and it was going to begin in a few minutes. OK, I thought to myself, it'll be an experience, if nothing else ... so, not holding out much hope, I joined it. Well, it *was* an experience – a really *good* one. Because rather than wander round the museum looking at 200 objects and not really taking in any of them properly, as I would normally have done, we were shown by this incredibly knowledgeable guide just a small number of ... maybe five or six really interesting artefacts. She explained the story and context behind each one in lots of detail – and it was fascinating. The experience didn't quite inspire me to want to become an expert on early Christian art, but it did make me reassess my whole attitude to organized tours.

A year later I went on a guided trip to Italy. Again, the guides were brilliant – mostly qualified archaeologists and historians. You know, to get that much information about somewhere, you'd have to do weeks, probably months, of reading beforehand. What surprised me too was how knowledgeable and interesting some of the other travellers were – not the sheep I'd ignorantly thought they'd be before ...

There are lots of other benefits too. Your transport, hotel, food: it's all taken care of; all the visits are pre-arranged, so you don't have to book anything. The convenience factor is *not* to be underestimated, like particularly if it's a more remote or not-so-safe place you're visiting. Imagine all the pressure and anxiety from planning and booking and missed connections that it cuts out. It's so liberating.

And, talking of liberating, what about free time? It's actually a myth that organized tours are too regimented – in fact, they've always factored in free time for people to go off and explore by themselves and these days they're even more sensitive to that than ever. A lot of operators offer you the option of not going on excursions if you'd prefer to make your own itinerary.

35
1 I do wish I had been able to spend more time there.
2 He did say that he'd help us.
3 We do prefer to take holidays close to home.
4 She does get very sunburnt.

37
1 Would you like to come to dinner one evening?
2 Do you need to borrow a pen?
3 Are you coming?
4 I didn't get the assistant manager job.
5 Are you going away this summer?
6 Do you like detective stories?
7 What are you doing here so early?

38
I've been on a few mystery tours, but the one I did in Prague was probably the best. And I'm not the only person to say so. If you look at reviews, you'll hardly find one negative one. I'm not going to give you too many details because that would spoil the surprise if one day you happened to do it too. What I will tell you is that it started at night and involved a segway, some canoes, a jazz band and a large breakfast. If that hasn't aroused your curiosity, I don't know what will.

39
Now when I was a little chap I had a passion for maps. I would look for hours at South America, or Africa, or Australia, and lose myself in all the glories of exploration. At that time there were many blank spaces on the earth, and when I saw one that looked particularly inviting on a map (but they all look that) I would put my finger on it and say, 'When I grow up I will go there.' The North Pole was one of these places, I remember. Well, I haven't been there yet, and shall not try now. The glamour is gone. Other places were scattered about the hemispheres. I have been in some of them, and ... well, we won't talk about that. But there was one yet – the biggest, the most blank, so to speak – that I had a hankering after.

True, by this time it was not a blank space any more. It had got filled since my boyhood with rivers and lakes and names. It had ceased to be a blank space of delightful mystery – a white patch for a boy to dream gloriously over. It had become a place of darkness. But there was in it one river especially, a mighty big river, that you could see on the map, resembling an immense snake uncoiled, with its head in the sea, its body at rest curving afar over a vast country, and its tail lost in the depths of the land. And as I looked at the map of it in a shop-window, it fascinated me as a snake would a bird – a silly little bird. Then I remembered there was a Company for trade on that river. Dash it all! I thought to myself, they can't trade without using some kind of craft on that lot of fresh water – steamboats! Why shouldn't I try to get charge of one?

I went on along Fleet Street, but could not shake off the idea. The snake had charmed me.

I got my appointment – of course; and I got it very quick. It appears the Company had received news that one of their captains had been killed in a scuffle with the natives. Soon after I left in a French steamer, and she called in every port they have out there. I watched the coast. Watching a coast as it slips by the ship is like thinking about an enigma. There it is before you – smiling or frowning, grand or mean, insipid, or savage, and always mute with an air of whispering, 'Come and find out.' This one was almost featureless, with an aspect of monotonous grimness. The edge of a colossal jungle, so dark-green as to be almost black, fringed with white surf, ran straight, like a ruled line, far, far away along a blue sea.

40
Very few people still hitchhike, these days. We all know that it can be dangerous. And actually, why would you take the risk when there are so many other cheap options available, like Megabus? But if you have the time – and that's important 'cos it's generally not a quick way to travel – if you have the time, you *can* have some amazing experiences. A year ago, a group of us from university had a competition to see who could get to Barcelona the quickest by hitchhiking. We were in pairs and we all set off from different points in London. Amazingly, within about ten minutes of our standing on the slip road to the motorway, we got a lift with a lorry driver who said he was going all the way to the Spanish border. We couldn't believe our luck. Once in France we drove for about six hours and then around midnight, the driver said he had to stop to get some sleep. He pulled over at a resting point, which by chance, happened to have an area for pitching tents. Thinking it would be better not to disturb him, we got out and put up our little tent.

The following morning, we woke up early, ready to get back in the lorry, but to our dismay, it had gone. We sat down and tried to rationalize the situation: he'd probably just had an emergency and couldn't help leaving in a hurry; we'd probably get another lift before too long – if anyone else stopped here – but the place was actually deserted. Feeling pretty miserable, we started to pack up our tent. But just at that moment, we heard a loud horn sounding. It was our driver. He pulled up, jumped out of the lorry and produced three cups of coffee and some fresh croissants.

41
Long vowel sound: amazement, annoyance, delight, dismay, frustration, relief, surprise

Short vowel sound: astonishment, embarrassment, horror, regret, shock

42
F = Friend, MA = Model answer
F: So, tell me what happened?
MA: Well, a couple of weeks ago I got the train to go and visit my aunt. She lives in Newville.
F: And what went wrong?
MA: I was really tired because I had been up late the night before and I started to doze.
F: Did you wake up in time for your stop?
MA: No, to my horror, I woke up just as the train was leaving Newville and the next station was fifty kilometres away.
F: Oh no! What did you do?
MA: Well, luckily, there was a really nice conductor on the train. And he explained to me the quickest way to get back to my station from the next stop. He also put a note on my ticket saying I didn't need to pay again.

Unit 6

43
In 1968, the Beatles turned up in Rishikesh to study transcendental meditation at Maharishi Mahesh Yogi's ashram. They wrote about forty songs here, many of which ended up on their famous *White Album*. I hadn't come to write music, but to get over chronic back pain – one of my vertebrae being severely out of line – or at least put off the day when I would have to face back surgery.

Perched above the Ganges River, Rishikesh is now a shopping mall for those looking for mental and physical healing, pulling in hundreds of thousands of foreign visitors each year. My chosen retreat was the Parmarth Niketan Ashram, which is less strict than other ashrams and allows guests to come and go as they please. I had also been attracted by the fact that it supports around 200 disadvantaged boys – some orphaned – putting them up in simple accommodation, and providing them with food and a basic education.

At 6.50 a.m. on the first day, I found myself sitting in a plain room with a wooden floor, white walls and a metal roof. We worked on a breathing technique that involved inhaling and exhaling through one nostril at a time. There were no other distractions – no New Age tunes playing, no yoga outfits, no blinding heat, no incense and no attitude; just students and a teacher. Meals were conducted in silence, something which I found odd at first but came to appreciate. During one of the meals, another guest sitting across the 20-centimetre high table broke this silence to comment on how horribly fast I ate. I felt a little taken aback, but thanked him and noted the point.

The yoga carried on in a serene way for two weeks, never causing me even to break sweat. In fact, more than once I wondered how it could be helping me. Yet by the end of my visit, the simple lessons – stretch, breathe, eat more slowly and more healthily, relax – had an effect. I can now touch my toes and even sit cross-legged for thirty minutes through a meal. My back? The persistent pain hasn't entirely gone away, but it has subsided. More importantly, I can now put up with it because I've given up worrying about it.

44
A: The other day I looked up what fitness classes there were available locally and I couldn't believe how many there were.
B: Did you come across any that you liked the look of?
A: Not really. I didn't know what half of them were: Boxercise, Boot camp, Aqua aerobics … and loads based on dance.
B: You mean like Zumba?
A: Yes. I knew Zumba was a craze that had taken off, but there were others: Jazzercise, Bodyjam. I mean, if you go in for dancing, why don't you just sign up for a dance class?
B: And do you? Go in for dancing, that is?
A: Yes, I do. I think that's what I'll do … take up samba or something.

46
I = Interviewer, E = Expert
I: What impact has globalization had on our idea of beauty?
E: Well, I guess the first thing to say is that not necessarily globalization, but general economic growth, has had a huge impact on the amount of time and money people spend on beautification. The global cosmetics and perfume industry is worth around $200 billion. Americans spend over a billion each year on their fingernails alone. And new markets keep being found. Male grooming, which twenty years ago was not a big

industry at all, now brings in over $30 billion. But I think the question you're getting at is: Has a globalized world made our ideal of beauty more homogenized?

I: Yes, I suppose what I'm asking is: Is there now a more global view of what beautiful is or means?

E: Well, that's an interesting question and I think the beauty industry is a good example of what has happened more generally in the world over the last 100 years or so. But I think we need to stress that there have been different stages of globalization – not just the most recent one that began in the 1980s. If you go back to the early 20th century and the days of western imperialism, you do find that cosmetics companies were peddling a Western and 'white' ideal of beauty. There was even the promise by some companies that regular washing with soap could help to turn a dark skin whiter.

I: Goodness!

E: Obviously, it was an effective marketing tactic: if people everywhere could aspire to the same notion of beauty, it would be far easier for the companies to mass-produce products. So using the ideals presented by Hollywood film stars and fashion magazines, they persuaded people not only that it was desirable to look a certain way, but that their collection of skin creams and lipsticks and fragrances would help them achieve that.

I: And did that marketing effort really work? Were people convinced by these ideas of beauty?

E: Well, yes and no. Local cultural values were never completely taken over by the global message of the marketers. People aren't stupid and they could see that they were being offered an American ideal. Henry Kissinger was right when he said that globalization in that era was just another name for Americanization. You know, I think generally people are able to differentiate between what they are being asked to aspire to and the reality of their daily lives.

I: And you talked about different eras of globalization. Can you just explain a bit more about that?

E: Sure, well, the more recent era of globalization – the one that began in the 1980s – is one in which companies definitely have to be more conscious of local traditions and values. You only have to look at how a company like McDonald's alters its menu to suit the tastes of each local market to see that. There is an increasing emphasis on diversity. So, as we all seem to get closer in a world of global communications, at the same time we want to celebrate individuality and local differences.

I: So now companies incorporate diversity into the products they make?

E: Definitely. Multinational companies can still accept the universal values of beauty that we all aspire to: a clear skin, healthy-looking hair, a youthful glow, and then they can adapt their products to include local and traditional ingredients: for example, black soap in Africa for skin cleansing, or the Huito fruit in South America – traditionally used for body painting – as an ingredient in hair dye.

47

Speaker 1
On the whole, I really like what the architect's done. But he's put in two lifts, which I think is excessive. A better alternative would be to have just one which can be a service lift and also be used for wheelchair access. That way, people will be obliged to use the stairs – it's only two flights – and that will actually be good for them. It'll help them stay fit. I realize that sometimes people who have heavy things to move or who aren't so mobile will sometimes want to use the lift, but we can easily work around that.

Speaker 2
I think the health problems associated with air conditioning systems are well documented. What you're getting is the same air – and so consequently the same germs and diseases – being recycled around the building. It would be much better just to have straightforward fresh air sucked in from outside, as Giovanni suggests. Admittedly, it wouldn't always be cool air, but it would be a lot healthier – and cheaper.

Speaker 3
I think the idea of a staff canteen is great, but we have to be very careful who we choose to run it. I think what we need to do is to make up our own list of what kind of food we think is acceptable – healthy options and so on – and then invite local companies to bid for the contract. I haven't really thought through who should be responsible for making the list, but I do think it's important to make one.

Speaker 4
I think the idea of forming a partnership with the local fitness and leisure centre is probably the best option. I love the idea of staff being able to do sports together – it'd be very good for morale. I know not everyone will want to join in in that way, but for a lot of people the social element will really be a big attraction.

49
C = Colleague, MA = Model answer

1
C: What do you think of the proposal?
MA: I think it's a great idea. It would really help staff to keep in shape and get exercise during their lunch hour or after work.

2
C: And do you think that staff will really make good use of it?
MA: I don't see why not. Admittedly, there will be some who aren't interested, but I think that they'll be the minority.

3
C: Don't you think that it's quite an expensive way to promote health among the staff?
MA: Well, I realize it's not going to be cheap, but I think that you have to look at all the benefits. Like reducing the number of days of absence and making people more productive.

4
C: And do you see other benefits too?
MA: Well, yes. I think it could help attract people to come and work for us. It's a good advertisement for the company.

Answer key

Unit 1

1a (pages 104 and 105)

1
1 his book about scientific inventions
2 some rules of life (that he read about 15 years ago in a book by Charles Sykes)

2
1 unjust 2 can't expect 3 more strict 4 a beginning
5 your 6 have to be done by everyone
7 seldom 8 technical expertise

3
1 Currently 2 about fifteen years ago 3 Before that
4 next year 5 Many years ago 6 at the time
7 Over the last twenty years 8 rarely 9 Sooner or later

4
1 am (*or* 'm) taking 2 attended 3 had never been
4 seem 5 have (*or* 've) been wondering 6 will (*or* 'll) have

5
1 said (than) done 2 valuable 3 guiding
4 point 5 from (my) mistakes 6 thumb

6
One of the problems with advice is that people tend to interpret it to suit their own purposes. An example of this is the wisdom of the 18th-century economist, Adam Smith. One of his main ideas was that if you allow people to seek wealth for themselves, they will naturally create jobs and wealth for others. He called this 'the invisible hand'. People trying to improve their own situation also help their neighbour to improve theirs, but without meaning to, as if with an invisible hand. Unfortunately, a lot of people took Smith to mean that it was all right to be greedy and selfish and not to help others directly, which is not at all what he meant.

1b (pages 106 and 107)

1
b

2
1 T 2 T 3 T 4 F 5 F 6 F

3
past perfect continuous: *Had they already been thinking*
present perfect continuous: *have been following*
past continuous: *were looking at*
present continuous: *are continually changing*
future continuous: *will be calling me*

4
1 a) is already b) is becoming, i.e. it's a trend
2 a) statement of fact b) suggests irritation about this situation
3 a) the list is finished b) the list isn't complete – they are still working on it
4 little difference in meaning although b) suggests they thought about it for some time
5 a) I decided after I got married b) I decided at or around the time of the marriage
6 a) statement of fact b) the speaker expects that they are hoping

5
1 Had you been waiting
2 Has someone been smoking
3 had been playing, fell
4 am working
5 have been living, are repairing *or* have been repairing
6 have heard

6
1 c 2 f 3 e 4 b 5 d 6 a

7
1 peace and quiet 2 as and when 3 short and sweet
4 aches and pains 5 Now and then 6 fun and games
7 First and foremost 8 By and large

9
1 d 2 b 3 f 4 e 5 a 6 c

1c (page 108)

1
1 T 2 T 3 F 4 F 5 T 6 F

2
1 b 2 a 3 a 4 a 5 b 6 a

3
1 b 2 a 3 b 4 a 5 b

4
1 larger 2 saver 3 walks 4 brings 5 fact 6 story
7 lifelike 8 time

1d (page 109)

1
Conversation 1
Place: conference
Teresa: conference organizer and lecturer in Social Sciences in Toronto
Ana: academic in Social Sciences at Deusto University in San Sebastian, Spain

Conversation 2
Place: bus stop at airport
Jeff: primary school teacher
Khalid: M.Sc. student of Quantum Physics. Has come from Amman in Jordan

2
Conversation 1
1 think of 2 should have 3 Whereabouts 4 fancy
Conversation 2
1 heading 2 by (the) way 3 going, studying 4 impressive

3
1 a 2 a 3 b 4 b 5 b

4a
1 What did you think of 2 Do you fancy
3 What kind of 4 What's it like 5 I should have mentioned
6 How are you finding 7 Shall we go and get a
8 have you been here

5
Students' own answers.

1e (page 110)

1
1 pay grade 6 2 line manager 3 18 months

2
1 weeks 2 that is *or* that is to say 3 months 4 years
5 to be confirmed 6 for example

3
1 approx. 2 re *or* ref 3 incl. 4 etc. 5 10 a.m. 6 hrs
7 NB 8 pc *or* % 9 2nd *or* sec (time) 10 p.w.

161

4

Jeff rang at eleven o'clock (this morning). He wants
you to go to London to discuss the contract details,
i.e. commission, quantities, etc. The time of the meeting is to
be confirmed. Note that he isn't in the office until Thursday.
(Note that *i.e.* and *etc.* are perfectly acceptable in writing.)

5

New policy
no limits on how much/little holiday staff can take
try policy out for limited period, i.e. 6 mths
not entirely sure if going to work, but pretty confident

Reasons for policy
much better to be adult and responsible – all have busy
working lives + busy lives outside work
given a little freedom, organize time better

Employee responsibilities
NB not an excuse to take as much time off work as possible
can't organize completely independently – negotiate with
colleagues to avoid disruptions
also still have work targets to reach

Details
start date tbc – 2nd half of this year
policy applies to every employee incl. part-time staff
reviewed after approx. 4 mths

Wordbuilding / Learning skills / Check! (page 111)

1
1 or   2 or   3 and   4 and   5 but   6 and   7 and   8 or
9 and   10 to

2
1 back to front   2 give and take   3 wear and tear
4 more or less, out and about   5 sink or swim
6 cut and dried, take it or leave it
7 slowly but surely, live and learn

3
1 You can sound more natural, impress your audience and
create more vivid images to support your arguments.
2 It can sound ridiculous.
3 a T   b F Putting a correct idiom in an otherwise incorrect
sentence could sound odd.   c T   d F Use idioms that have
widespread and established use.   e F Slang is very informal
language that is usually spoken rather than written.

4
1 no   2 yes

6
1 a sit   b work   c yourself   d blind
2 a dreamer   b joker   c outgoing
3 a nowadays, generally   b so far, recently
  c sooner or later   d prior to that

Unit 2

2a (pages 112 and 113)

1
1 in Tibet
2 a small fungus (called *yartsa gunbu*), because it is highly valued
3 herding yaks and/or sheep

2
1 searching   2 fungus   3 medicinal   4 caterpillar   5 stalk
6 energy   7 soared   8 yaks   9 overpicking

3
1 get by   2 get out of   3 get back   4 gets over
5 getting at   6 get round to

4
1 had dropped   2 are looking for   3 has been known
4 had been searching, found   5 have prescribed   6 started

7 has grown   8 are thriving   9 will have disappeared
10 will be searching
(Note that 4 *had searched* and 8 *thrive* are also possible.)

5
1 has shown (*or* shows)   2 helps   3 have criticized (*or* criticize)
4 is based   5 showed   6 had used   7 has not exploited
8 has been   9 will be developed   10 is

6
1 livelihood   2 task   3 trade   4 vocation   5 living

7
/ɪ/
med<u>i</u>cinal
spe<u>ci</u>men
spe<u>ci</u>fic
caterp<u>i</u>llar
art<u>i</u>st

/iː/
pr<u>e</u>vious
k<u>i</u>lo
v<u>i</u>sa

/aɪ/
pr<u>i</u>vate
unsc<u>i</u>entific
surv<u>i</u>ve
prescr<u>i</u>be
t<u>i</u>ny
rev<u>i</u>talize
f<u>i</u>nancial

8
1 I've been travelling in this region for many years and I'd seen
  this phenomenon before but never paid it much attention.
2 Well, often you'll visit a place with a particular story
  in mind. Then, while you're researching it, you find
  something else catches your interest.
3 I was very struck by how well off people in the village
  seemed compared to when I'd last visited.
4 So I decided to investigate and got this amazing story of
  the golden worm.

2b (pages 114 and 115)

1
1 They swim very fast; they are difficult to find (because of
  overfishing and the use of seine nets which has reduced
  the numbers by 80 per cent); they weigh in excess of
  300 kilos and so are difficult to land.
2 (deep-sea) line fishing

2
1 T   2 F   3 F   4 N   5 F   6 F

3
1 d   2 f   3 a   4 h   5 b   6 g   7 e   8 c

4
1 be on the safe side   2 wrap (your children) in cotton wool
3 second nature   4 cut corners   5 follow the correct
procedure/do things by the book

5
1 The trip had been organized by my friend, Troy.
2 Once the fish have been found, that's only the beginning
  of your task.
3 In 'purse seine' fishing, big circular nets are used to trap
  the tuna.
4 The Atlantic tuna population has been devastated by
  'purse seine' fishing in the last thirty years.
5 Troy jumped on the rod so that the line could be kept tight.
6 The fish started to get tired of being chased.

6
1 was (*or* got) called   2 being told   3 could/might get injured
4 being (*or* to be) driven   5 don't get paid
6 Have you been invited

Answer key

7
1 active better, but passive also possible
2 passive
3 passive better, but active also possible
4 active
5 passive better, but active also possible
6 active

2c (page 116)

1
c

2
1 a missing cat 2 a geography teacher 3 memorizing dots on a map 4 outdoor 5 adventures 6 reality of the city 7 by walking 8 think at a high level 9 how friendly the community is 10 creative and innovative

3
1 a 2 b 3 b 4 a

4
1 a 2 c 3 d 4 b

5
1 She got off on the wrong foot, but relations with her colleagues are much better now.
2 I hope I didn't put my foot in it when I told her how like her sister she was.
3 I've never been good at dancing – I have two left feet.
4 She really shot herself in the foot by not taking the promotion when she was offered it.
5 People often ask me why I didn't follow in my father's footsteps and become a doctor like him.
6 Hannah found her feet very quickly at university and made some good friends.
7 I'm now working for Google. I was very lucky to get my foot in the door because so many people want to work there.
8 She was going to jump from the ten metre board but she got cold feet.

2d (page 117)

1
1 conscientious 2 reliable 3 enthusiastic 4 motivated
5 focused 6 flexible 7 well-organized 8 resourceful

2
1 infrastructure projects 2 He spent one year working on a transport and metro hub, where he helped to design (or adapted) the programme for planning work schedules for staff.

3
1 conscientious – got a commendation for his previous work
2 well-organized – he says he's good at planning and organization
3 resourceful – he had to adapt a computer programme
4 enthusiastic and motivated – he's keen to work for an
5 international company and says he is enthusiastic about learning

4a
1 ex<u>pe</u>rience 2 commen<u>da</u>tion 3 <u>in</u>frastructure
4 au<u>tho</u>rities 5 suita<u>bi</u>lity 6 par<u>ti</u>cular 7 <u>re</u>levant
8 im<u>por</u>tant 9 enthusi<u>a</u>stic

5
Students' own answers.

2e (page 118)

1a
a attracts *or* attracted b available c response
d Currently e As, suitable f attached g taking, consider
h requirements

1b
1 c 2 f 3 d 4 e 5 a 6 h 7 g 8 b

2
The missing elements are:
1 when it was advertised
3 your present situation
4 why you are suited to the job
and 9 (possibly) give a personal touch

3
Example answers:
… in response to your advertisement on the Jobsonline website (1) this week … and relevant experience. …
(3) I am currently working in a temporary position for a local charity making calls to potential donors. (9) It is interesting and worthwhile work but desk-based and I am someone who likes to get out and meet people.
The job attracted me because … world of work again. (4) As someone who understands the education sector and has experience of fundraising, I think I am a suitable candidate.

Wordbuilding / Learning skills / Check! (page 119)

2
1 e 2 j 3 f 4 i 5 b 6 h 7 a 8 d 9 g 10 c

4
Possible answers:
1 a to inform b specific information c When will it be available to buy? How much will it cost?
2 a to inform, to persuade b gist c What is different about this book? Have attitudes to childhood changed?
3 a to inform, to give opinions b gist and specific information
c What is the film? Would they recommend it?

5
1 a eagle hunter b Moken c smokejumper
2 a wait a long time b see well c keep fit and healthy
3 back, later b *get*
4 a not, contact b my, in c I, hearing, you, d job, male
Name: Jimmy Chin

Unit 3

3a (pages 120 and 121)

1
Possible answers:

	Glastonbury	Ghent
Location	west of England	Belgium
Size of town	small (but growing)	large, like a city
Type of town	market town. now with mix of residents – older and more conservative vs younger and alternative, wacky	university town, historic town, port, industrial
Reasons for liking	NM	lively and friendly, open-minded people, masses to do – good music scene, interesting museums and galleries, beautiful architecture, nice parks

2
1 b 2 a 3 b 4 b 5 c 6 a

3
1 g 2 a 3 d 4 f 5 h 6 b 7 e 8 c

4
1 ghost 2 quaint 3 shanty 4 sprawling 5 scruffy
6 characterless 7 sleepy 8 resort 9 run-down

5
1 fairly 2 quite a sleepy 3 rather 4 a bit (*quite* is also correct)
5 quite like it 6 cheating slightly 7 quite 8 particularly
9 pretty 10 a bit

6
1 very 2 particularly *or* very 3 quite *or* fairly 4 quite
5 fairly *or* pretty *or* rather 6 quite *or* rather

7
1, 5 and 6 mean 'but probably not enough'.

8
A: How was your trip to Russia?
B: Great, thanks. We had quite a packed schedule, but it was very interesting. We started in Moscow and saw the sights around Red Square. Strangely, the thing I loved most was the metro. Each station is like a work of art in itself. The service is pretty efficient too.
A: And how did it compare to St Petersburg?
B: Very different. St Petersburg is a very grand and gracious city. Actually, it feels a bit closer in atmosphere to other cities in central Europe, whereas Moscow doesn't feel particularly European. But that's the thing about Russia. You don't realize what an enormous and diverse country it is until you travel there.

3b (pages 122 and 123)

1
1 Geography: Mustang is a former kingdom in north-central Nepal; Climate: the climate is incredibly inhospitable; (wind-savaged)
2 10,000 (conservatively estimated)
3 It was a centre of scholarship and art, and a key place on the salt trade route from Tibet to India.
4 most showed signs of domestic habitation; in others there were stunning treasures: in one cave, a 26-foot-long mural; in another, 8,000 calligraphed manuscripts; many seemed to be elaborate tombs full of amazing riches
5 burial chambers
6 For safety. Because the territory was frequently fought over, they placed safety over convenience and took refuge in the caves.

2
1 ~~absolutely~~ 2 ~~extremely~~ 3 ~~completely~~ 4 ~~absolutely~~
5 ~~absolutely~~ 6 ~~utterly~~ 7 ~~very~~ 8 ~~incredibly~~

3
1 incredibly *or* really *or* very 2 absolutely *or* completely *or* totally 3 absolutely *or* quite 4 incredibly *or* really *or* very 5 absolutely *or* really 6 incredibly *or* really *or* very 7 completely *or* totally 8 quite

4a
1 I'm utterly exhausted.
2 I'd really appreciate that.
3 It's so hot today.
4 It's OK. I quite understand.
5 You're absolutely right.
6 It's very difficult to say.

5
1 f 2 i 3 h 4 a 5 g 6 c 7 e 8 j 9 b 10 d

6
1 wildly optimistic 2 vaguely familiar 3 patently obvious
4 perfectly reasonable 5 deadly serious 6 painfully slow

7
a a garage/workshop, a walk-in wardrobe
b a gym, a sauna
c a conservatory, a roof garden
d a games room, a home cinema, a library
e en suite bathrooms, a state-of-the-art kitchen

3c (page 124)

1
1 It means copying good design from nature and applying it to things that are man-made.
2 the architect Gaudi took inspiration from nature in his design of the Sagrada Familia and the materials he used; the Swiss Re Tower is built in a shape taken from nature; the chimneys in the Eastgate Centre in Harare imitate the heating and cooling system in a termite mound

2
1 a 2 c 3 b 4 b 5 b 6 c

3
1 a 2 b 3 b 4 b 5 a

4
1 keeps (his) feet 2 Stand 3 grounds 4 new, in
5 get off 6 covered

3d (page 125)

1
For: 1) people won't have to waste time going down to the canteen to get their coffee; 2) it will encourage employee interaction
Against: staff might spend too much time there away from productive work

2
1 all, basically 2 recommend 3 have to 4 disagree with
5 shouldn't underestimate 6 mean
7 much, favour, given 8 by (the) way, touch

3a
1 d 2 y 3 r 4 t 5 w 6 w

3b
1 first‿of‿all
2 with‿a bit‿of luck
3 as‿a matter‿of‿fact
4 as far‿as‿I'm‿aware
5 between you‿w‿and me
6 let's be‿j‿honest
7 at the‿j‿end‿of the day
8 I've no‿w‿idea, I'm‿afraid

4
Students' own answers.

3e (page 126)

1
a 4 b 3

2
against
the benefits of high-rise building to the wider environment are great; it's not possible to keep expanding our cities outwards

3
1 b 2 e 3 d 4 f 5 a 6 c

Wordbuilding / Learning skills / Check! (page 127)

1
1 rent 2 studio 3 lets 4 furnished 5 share 6 move
7 budget 8 bills 9 charges 10 properties

Answer key

11 commission   12 tenant   13 landlord   14 deposit
15 advance   16 references

4
1 There are only <u>two</u> interesting <u>buildings</u> in the <u>a</u>rea around <u>New</u>port.
2 The <u>green</u> belt should <u>def</u>initely be pro<u>tec</u>ted from de<u>ve</u>lopers.

6
Across: 5 deprived   8 time   9 rich   10 compact   11 en suite
Down: 1 modern   2 a bit   3 seem   4 spacious   6 vibrant
7 debate

Unit 4

4a (pages 128 and 129)

1
Possible answers:
It's a play on words. *Boring* also means 'making deep holes'. In this case, it refers to making deep underground tunnels below cities to serve as a new transport system.

2
1 To go round it, over it or under it.
2 Building channels around sandcastles. (They fill up as soon as you build them.)
3 Accidents in the air could also impact those below.
4 It's expensive.
5 On sleds in underground tunnels.
6 By using single-lane tunnels and more efficient tunnelling machines.
7 By having everyone travelling in the same direction.
8 Vacuum.
9 900 km an hour.

3
1 ring   2 debris   3 pull   4 venture   5 hold   6 tried

4
1 likely   2 might (*could* also possible)   3 could (*might* also possible)   4 good chance   5 should   6 possibly

5
1 Such solutions will probably never work / probably won't work because …
2 Rather than removing the problem, the chances are you are just moving it somewhere else.
3 It's possible that collisions or accidents in the air (might/could) have an impact on those below.
4 Given his amazing record, he may well pull this off.
5 Musk's idea is that his techniques are likely to reduce the cost enormously.
6 In his mind is the idea that in future, the tunnels could use vacuum technology.

6
1 may well
2 will almost certainly come up with
3 probably will be
4 are likely to be driving (*or* are likely to drive)
5 should have
6 will probably be
7 is unlikely to change
8 the likelihood of that happening
9 is

7
1 doable, desirable   2 non-negotiable   3 unimaginable   4 irreplaceable   5 insurmountable   6 intolerable

8
1 returnable   2 unbreakable   3 drinkable   4 walkable
5 non-washable   6 contactable

4b (pages 130 and 131)

1
1 d   2 b   3 a   4 c

2
1 scientists   2 day   3 problem   4 money
5 afford   6 tests

3
1 a   2 b   3 b   4 b   5 a   6 b

4
1 d   2 a   3 f   4 e   5 c   6 b

5
1 I must have ridden   2 I should have taken   3 I didn't need to   4 I could have wheeled   5 I had to be   6 I had to find   7 I needn't have worried   8 Someone might have dropped

6a
1 have   2 have   3 have   4 to   5 have   6 to

7
1 about   2 across   3 up   4 up   5 down

4c (page 132)

1
1 internet and mobile communications
2 they are actively involved in spending their money (more 'hands on') whereas past philanthropists set up long-term foundations and scholarships for future generations; they want to see a quick return on investment as they would in business

2
1 T   2 T   3 F   4 T   5 F   6 F

3
1 self-made   2 counterparts   3 return   4 seed money
5 bring about   6 no strings   7 self-confessed   8 ethos

4
1 ethos   2 seed money   3 return   4 bring about
5 self-made   6 counterpart   7 self-confessed   8 no strings

5
1 all *or* best   2 thought *or* consideration
3 break *or* chance   4 go *or* try   5 ahead   6 time

4d (page 133)

1
1 (school) children   2 It's a bag that also functions as a desk.
3 Not all children have a desk at school or even a table at home.
4 It has compartments for notebooks, pens and a water holder.

2
1 so original, ask   2 would, want, that
3 how, people, be able

3
1 The bag also functions as a desk.
2 Not all children have a desk at school or even a table at home.
3 The price is a little higher in Europe to help lower the cost of a bag for a family in a developing country.

4
Possible answers:
1 So how does it work?
2 Isn't that rather expensive, you ask?
3 So why would I need one?
4 So, what's our ambition for this?

5
1 <u>Clear</u>ly   2 <u>Fi</u>nancially   3 <u>Essen</u>tially   4 <u>Prac</u>tically
5 Of <u>course</u>   6 <u>Hon</u>estly   7 <u>Ob</u>viously   8 To be <u>hon</u>est
9 <u>Ba</u>sically

6
Students' own answers.

4e (page 134)

1
1 Yes, but only in theory.
2 A scheduled discussion between colleagues every two to four weeks; the opportunity to visit other organizations.
3 Giving employees a structure; rewarding employees for good ideas; giving innovation and creativity a more formal role.

2
1 To tell the reader what the report is about.
2 Using bullet points and sequencing words – *first of all, secondly,* etc.
3 *In summary*

3
1 are   2 should   3 giving   4 have   5 should visit

Wordbuilding / Learning skills / Check! (page 135)

1
1 drop   2 stroke   3 bit   4 bit   5 gust   6 hint   7 plot
8 word   9 shred   10 bite

2
a a drop of water
b a hint of disappointment
c a shred of evidence

3
2 2

6
1 necessity   2 foldable   3 bionic   4 elevator pitch
5 social entrepreneur

7
1 thought   2 off   3 must   4 shrink
Name of company: TOMS

Unit 5

5a (pages 136 and 137)

1
1 Being with knowledgeable guides
3 Meeting fellow travellers
5 No planning – everything is arranged for you
7 Optional free time

2
1 b   2 b   3 c   4 c   5 b   6 a

3
1 sheep   2 million   3 wrong   4 nothing   5 out   6 of

4
1 by   2 and   3 to   4 in   5 from, to   6 to

5
1 What I want from travel is a bit of independence and freedom.
2 The thing that changed my mind was a guided tour I took.
3 I do like visiting museums.
4 It did make me reassess my whole attitude to organized tours.
5 What surprised me was how knowledgeable and interesting some of the other travellers were.
6 … particularly if it's a more remote or not-so-safe place you're visiting.

6
1 The thing I remember best about/from my childhood is how amazing family holidays were.
2 It was enough to have a rough idea of where we were going.
3 We did stop when we saw things that interested us.
4 It wasn't money that was the issue.
5 What I loved was the lack of any kind of routine.
6 I do like sleeping in the afternoon.
7 When I have children, what I'm going to do is (to) recreate a similar experience for them.

7
1 do   2 did   3 do   4 does

8
Across: 1 cosy   4 slow   7 romantic
Down: 2 officious   3 elegant   5 wary   6 grand

5b (pages 138 and 139)

1
1 to educate the rest of the world about Africa
2 the football World Cup in South Africa in 2010
3 They aim to reveal Africa as seen by Africans themselves rather than through the eyes of an outsider.
4 presenting a one-dimensional, clichéd view of Africa

2
a haphazardly   b seize   c conspicuous   d turbulent
e (her) portrait   f stereotyped   g decree

3
1 a Chinua Achebe Centre for African Writers and Artists   b writer
2 a (The fact that) many things are already familiar to them   b observing the details
3 a Africa   b series of travel books   c travel books
4 a be   b author(s)/writer(s)

4
1 one   2 (omit underlined words)   3 do (so)   4 others *or* other ones   5 This *or* That   6 one   7 to   8 so *or* it is

5a
1 B: <u>Yes</u>, I'd <u>love</u> to.
2 B: <u>No</u>, I've <u>got</u> one, <u>thanks</u>.
3 B: <u>No</u>, I'm <u>afraid not</u>.
4 B: <u>Oh</u>, I'm <u>sorry</u> to <u>hear</u> that.
5 B: I <u>hope so</u>.
6 B: Oh, <u>yes</u>. I <u>love</u> a good <u>thriller</u>.
7 B: <u>Catching</u> up on <u>emails</u>.

6
I've been on a few mystery tours, but the one I did in Prague was probably the best. And I'm not the only person to say so. If you look at reviews, you'll hardly find one negative one. I'm not going to give you too many details because that would spoil the surprise if one day you happened to do it too. What I will tell you is that it started at night and involved a segway, some canoes, a jazz band and a large breakfast. If that hasn't aroused your curiosity, I don't know what will.

5c (page 140)

1
1 He dreamed about exploring.
2 It had ceased to be a mystery. *or* It had become a place of darkness.
3 He got a job as a ship's captain aboard a steamboat.

2
1 blank spaces   2 rivers, lakes and names   3 an immense, uncoiled snake   4 It was used for trading.   5 He had been killed ('in a scuffle with the natives').   6 It was featureless, monotonous and grim.

3
1 positive   2 No, they haven't.   3 It is curled up/asleep.
4 b   5 a   6 cannot speak *or* not speaking

Answer key

4
1 laughing 2 mind 3 course 4 principle 5 way 6 that

5d (page 141)

1
1 To Barcelona. It was a competition amongst a group of university friends.
2 A lorry driver going all the way to the Spanish border picked them up within ten minutes.
3 In the morning, they couldn't see the lorry driver and they thought he'd had to leave in a hurry. The lorry driver returned with coffee and croissants.

2
1 these days 2 We all know that 3 A year ago
4 Amazingly, 5 believe 6 by chance, happened
7 The following morning 8 our dismay
9 Feeling pretty miserable 10 just at that moment

3
a by chance b Just at that moment, c Feeling pretty miserable d these days e Amazingly, f A year ago
g The following morning h To our dismay

4a
Long vowel sound: am**a**zement, ann**o**yance, del**igh**t, dism**a**y frustr**a**tion, rel**ie**f, surpr**i**se
Short vowel sound: ast**o**nishment, emb**a**rrassment, h**o**rror, regr**e**t, sh**o**ck

5
Students' own answers.

5e (page 142)

1
³ It is 1857 and the British Empire in India is facing severe unrest from the indigenous population. For the ruling British class in the northern town of Krishnapur, life is calm and polite until the sepoys at a nearby military fort rise in mutiny and the British are forced to retreat into the British Residency. Food and other supplies become short, disease sets in and the inhabitants' resources are tested to the limit.

This is the first part of J.G. Farrell's empire trilogy, ¹ an examination of the British Empire in its decline. *The Siege of Krishnapur* serves as a metaphor for this decline as each character is forced to examine their own view of the world.

Although the situation is desperate, ⁴ Farrell describes it with great elegance and humour, conveying the ridiculousness of the British position. Some would argue that in not describing the hardship and injustice suffered by the local Indian population, Farrell has done them a great injustice. ² But I do not think that was his aim. What he has done is to write both a gripping story and a thought-provoking study of colonial life.

2
d

3
1 provoking 2 going 3 uneventful 4 fetched
5 convincing 6 wrenching 7 uninspiring 8 poorly

Wordbuilding / Learning skills / Check! (page 143)

1
1 spot 2 managed 3 ruined 4 tough 5 coped 6 courage
7 expectations 8 make (it) out 9 set off 10 thrilling

4
1 officious 2 sustainable, expectations 3 magical, unknown
4 graphic 5 cartoonist 6 relief, worryingly
7 thought-provoking 8 transformative

Unit 6

6a (pages 144 and 145)

1
1 Rishikesh (India) 2 chronic back pain 3 yes – because he's given up worrying about his bad back

2
1 the Beatles arrived in Rishikesh to study transcendental meditation at Maharishi Mahesh Yogi's ashram
2 songs the Beatles wrote in Rishikesh
3 foreign visitors who go to Rishikesh each year
4 disadvantaged boys that the Parmarth Niketan Ashram supports
5 the man started his exercise regime on the first day
6 the table at which they ate their meals
7 the man's visit to the ashram
8 the man can sit cross-legged through a meal

3
1 a 2 b 3 b 4 a 5 a 6 a

4
1 intransitive 2 intransitive 3 chronic back pain
4 the day 5 mental and physical healing 6 hundreds of thousands of foreign visitors 7 them (the disadvantaged boys) 8 a breathing technique 9 intransitive 10 it (the pain) 11 worrying

5
1 put up 2 put up with 3 separable: pull in, put off, give up inseparable: get over, look for, work on

6
1 The pain is quite bad, but I've learned to put up with it.
2 I got the injury playing football and it took me a long time to get over it.
3 If you think going to yoga classes will help, then there's no point putting it off.
4 I used to ski a lot, but I gave it up.
5 Reducing the cost of the course for students really pulled them in.
6 Can you put me up for the night on Tuesday when I'm in town?
7 I'm not as supple as I used to be, but I put that down to my age.
8 I can't touch my toes yet, but I'm working on it.

7
1 come across 2 set aside 3 take up 4 put someone off 5 go in for 6 takes off 7 get out of 8 carry out
9 comes about 10 fall back on

8
1 keep 2 do 3 out 4 shape 5 on 6 am *or* keep
7 watch 8 for

9
A: The other day I looked up what fitness classes there were available locally and I couldn't believe how many there were.
B: Did you come across any that you liked the look of?
A: Not really. I didn't know what half of them were: Boxercise, Boot camp, Aqua aerobics … and loads based on dance.
B: You mean like Zumba?
A: Yes. I knew Zumba was a craze that had taken off, but there were others: Jazzercise, Bodyjam. I mean, if you go in for dancing, why don't you just sign up for a dance class?
B: And do you? Go in for dancing, that is?
A: Yes, I do. I think that's what I'll do … take up samba or something.

167

6b (pages 146 and 147)

1
1 Simply put, cross-training means practising other sports or forms of exercise to improve, indirectly, your abilities in your main or target sport. (para 1)
2 Finally, and most importantly, it prevents athletes from getting the kind of repetitive strain injuries that they often suffer if they only practise the same activities day in, day out. (para 2)
3 The lesson of cross-training is that the body reacts well to new experiences. (para 4)

2
1 c   2 c   3 a   4 b   5 a   6 c

3
1 help (more generally) to increase, tend(s) to be, learn to deal with
2 require(s) you to control, enable them to continue (playing)
3 let(s) you build, recommend everyone incorporate
4 mean(s) practising
5 succeed in performing
6 prevent(s) athletes from getting

4
1 to warm up   2 to do   3 doing   4 exercise, (to) see
5 playing   6 about getting   7 for getting   8 to be
9 playing *or* to play   10 playing, training

5
1 grazed   2 stubbed   3 bumped   4 chipped   5 bruised
6 lost   7 sprained   8 pulled

6
1 passed out   2 on the mend   3 run down   4 shaken up
5 off colour   6 in a bad way

7a
They all have the stress on the second syllable apart from *practise* and *welcome*.

7b
All the verbs with stress on the second syllable have common prefixes, e.g. *pre-, post-, de-, ex-*.

6c (page 148)

1
b

2
1 a is worth around $200 billion
  b spend over a billion each year on their fingernails alone
2 Male grooming (now)
3 regular washing with soap could help to turn a dark skin whiter
4 McDonald's alters its menu to suit the tastes of each local market
5 a black soap in Africa   b in South America as an ingredient in hair dye

3
Possible answers:
1 similar   2 selling   3 idea   4 changes   5 shine

4
1 long   2 straight   3 brave   4 it   5 lose   6 music

6d (page 149)

1
1 b   2 d   3 e   4 f

2
1 lift   2 air conditioning   3 staff canteen
4 staff to do sports together

3
1 sometimes people who have heavy things to move or who aren't so mobile will want to use a lift   2 fresh air from outside wouldn't always be cool   3 who should be responsible for making the list   4 not everyone will want to join in with doing sports with other staff

4
1 alternative, be   2 realize, easily (work) around
3 would (be) much   4 Admittedly, but   5 through
6 know (not) everyone

5a
1 I'm not <u>very</u> much in <u>favour</u> of the proposal.
2 It's not <u>exactly</u> what I had in <u>mind</u>.
3 It's not a <u>particularly</u> <u>cheap</u> option.
4 It hasn't proved to be <u>so</u> <u>successful</u>.
5 I'm not <u>entirely</u> <u>convinced</u>.

6
Students' own answers.

6e (page 150)

1
1 There is concern that children in the school are not eating healthily enough, and this is affecting both their general health and their academic performance.
2 Most children are not getting a balanced diet.
3 That school meals should be compulsory for all pupils and that they are given the choice of different meals, but not a choice of different elements within each meal.

2
1 In view of this   2 Overall   3 However
4 Accordingly   5 apparently   6 specifically

3a
1 pupils   2 lunches   3 good variety of foods
4 what packed lunches should include   5 choices
6 We (also) suggest

3b
Possible answers:
serving the meals
majority of the pupils
benefit children

Wordbuilding / Learning skills / Check! (page 151)

1
1 flashbacks   2 turnout   3 breakthrough   4 follow-up
5 catch-up   6 breakdown   7 lookout   8 faraway
9 break-in   10 showdown

2
a getaway   b cutback   c clampdown   d show-off
e turn-up   f break-up

4
1 a, c, d   2 a, b   3 b, c   4 c, d

5
1 jogging, swimming   2 Japan   3 India   4 very long
5 necks   6 only skin   7 calories   8 insurance

NATIONAL GEOGRAPHIC
LEARNING

Life Advanced Student's Book and Workbook, Split A, 2nd Edition
Paul Dummett, John Hughes, Helen Stephenson

Vice President, Editorial Director: John McHugh

Executive Editor: Sian Mavor

Publishing Consultant: Karen Spiller

Project Managers: Sarah Ratcliff, Laura Brant

Development Editors: Jess Rackham, Stephanie Parker

Editorial Manager: Claire Merchant

Head of Strategic Marketing ELT: Charlotte Ellis

Senior Content Project Manager: Nick Ventullo

Manufacturing Buyer: Elaine Bevan

Senior IP Analyst: Michelle McKenna

Senior IP Project Manager: Carissa Poweleit

Cover: Lisa Trager

Text design: emc design ltd., Vasiliki Christoforidou

Compositor: emc design ltd., Lumina Datamatics, Inc.

Audio: Tom Dick and Debbie Productions Ltd, Prolingua Productions

Video: Tom Dick and Debbie Productions Ltd

Contributing writers: Graham Burton (Grammar summary), Nick Kenny and Miles Hordern (IELTS practice test)

© 2019 National Geographic Learning, a Cengage Learning Company

ALL RIGHTS RESERVED. No part of this work covered by the copyright herein may be reproduced or distributed in any form or by any means, except as permitted by U.S. copyright law, without the prior written permission of the copyright owner.

"National Geographic", "National Geographic Society" and the Yellow Border Design are registered trademarks of the National Geographic Society ® Marcas Registradas

For product information and technology assistance, contact us at
Cengage Learning Customer & Sales Support, cengage.com/contact
For permission to use material from this text or product, submit all requests online at **cengage.com/permissions**
Further permissions questions can be emailed to
permissionrequest@cengage.com

ISBN: 978-1-337-28645-9

National Geographic Learning
Cheriton House, North Way,
Andover, Hampshire, SP10 5BE
United Kingdom

National Geographic Learning, a Cengage Learning Company, has a mission to bring the world to the classroom and the classroom to life. With our English language programs, students learn about their world by experiencing it. Through our partnerships with National Geographic and TED Talks, they develop the language and skills they need to be successful global citizens and leaders.

Locate your local office at **international.cengage.com/region**

Visit National Geographic Learning online at **NGL.Cengage.com/ELT**
Visit our corporate website at **www.cengage.com**

CREDITS
Student's Book Text: p15 'Shakespeare's Coined Words Now Common Currency', by Jennifer Vernon, National Geographic, April 22, 2004. http://news.nationalgeographic.com/; p22 'Moken: Sea Gypsies of Myanmar', by Jacques Ivanoff, National Geographic, April 2005. ngm.nationalgeographic.com/; p24 'Women Smokejumpers: Fighting Fires, Stereotypes', by Hillary Mayell, National Geographic, August 08, 2003. http://news.nationalgeographic.com/; p27 'Yosemite Climbing', by Mark Jenkins, National Geographic, May 2011. http://ngm.nationalgeographic.com/; p75 'The Enigma of Beauty', by Cathy Newman, National Geographic. http://science.nationalgeographic.com/.
Workbook Text: We are grateful to the following for permission to reproduce copyright material:
Extract from *Dumbing Down Our Kids: Why American Children feel good about themselves but can't read, write or add*, copyright © 1995 by Charles J. Sykes. Reprinted by permission of St. Martin's Press. All rights reserved; National Geographic for extracts adapted from 'Tibet's Golden 'Worm'' by Michael Finkel, August 2012, http://ngm.nationalgeographic.com; Interview with Daniel Raven-Ellison http://www.nationalgeographic.com; 'Sky caves of Nepal' by, Michael Finkel, October 2012, http://ngm.nationalgeographic.com; 'The City Solution' by Robert Kunzig, NG Magazine, December 2011, http://ngm.nationalgeographic.com; 'Here comes the sun' by Peter McBride, National Geographic Traveler, October 2012, http://travel.nationalgeographic.com/travel/countries/india-yoga-traveler.
Cover: © Subir Basak/Getty Images.
Student's Book Photos: 6 (tl) © Carl Court/Getty Images; 6 (tr) © Norbert Rosing/National Geographic Creative; 6 (bl) © American Institute of Architects; 6 (br) © Mauricio Abreu/Getty Images; 7 (tl) © Sebastian Wahlhuetter; 7 (tr) © Lynn Johnson/National Geographic Creative; 7 (mt) © David Edwards/National Geographic Creative; 7 (mb) © O. Louis Mazzatenta/National Geographic Creative; 7 (b) Jake Lyell/Alamy Stock Photo; 8 (tl) © Bobby Model/National Geographic Creative; 8 (tm) © Sasha Leahovcenco; 8 (tr) © Albert Dros; 8 (mtl) © Peter Dazeley/Getty Images; 8 (mtm) © TOUR EIFFEL – Illuminations PIERRE BIDEAU, Photo: © Fred Derwal/Getty Images; 8 (mtr) PCN Photography/Alamy Stock Photo; 8 (mbl) © Raul Touzon/National Geographic Creative; 8 (mbm) © W. Laui; 8 (mbr) © Jim Richardson/National Geographic Creative; 8 (bl) © John McEvoy; 8 (bm) © Shaaz Jung; 8 (br) © David Epperson/Getty Images; 9 © Bobby Model/National Geographic Creative; 10 (l) © XiXinXing/Shutterstock.com; 10 (r) © Chris Johns/National Geographic Creative; 12 © Bruno Schlumberger/Ottawa Citizen; 15 © Damir Spanic/Getty Images; 16 Christopher Vallis/Alamy Stock Photo; 18 © Norbert Rosing/National

Printed in China by RR Donnelley
Print Number: 01 Print Year: 2018

Geographic Creative; 20 Irene Abdou/Alamy Stock Photo; 21 © Sasha Leahovcenco; 22 Hemis/Alamy Stock Photo; 24 © Tim Matsui/ Liaison/Getty Images; 25 © Bates Littlehales/National Geographic Creative; 27 © Jimmy Chin/National Geographic Creative; 28 © Antonio Guillem/Shutterstock.com; 30 © Jimmy Chin/National Geographic Creative; 32 © Pete McBride/National Geographic Creative; 33 © Albert Dros; 34 (l) © Mlenny/Getty Images; 34 (r) Robin Weaver/Alamy Stock Photo; 36 (t) © Borge Ousland/National Geographic Creative; 36 (b) © Mike Clarke/AFP/Getty Images; 39 (t) VIEW Pictures Ltd/Alamy Stock Photo; 39 (b) © Hufton and Crow/Getty Images; 40 © Annie Griffiths/National Geographic Creative; 41 JLImages/Alamy Stock Photo; 42 © American Institute of Architects; 44 (left col) VIEW Pictures Ltd/Alamy Stock Photo; 44 (right col: l) © Albert Dros; 44 (right col: m) © Mlenny/Getty Images; 44 (right col: r) © Borge Ousland/National Geographic Creative; 45 © Peter Dazeley/Getty Images; 46 (t) Haiyin Wang/Alamy Stock Photo; 46 (b) © The Asahi Shimbun/Getty Images; 48 © Bettmann/Getty Images; 51 © Noel Vasquez/Getty Images; 52 ZUMA Press, Inc./Alamy Stock Photo; 54 Jake Lyell/Alamy Stock Photo;56 Igor Stevanovic/Alamy Stock Photo; 57 © TOUR EIFFEL – Illuminations PIERRE BIDEAU, Photo: © Fred Derwal/Getty Images; 58 © Pablo Corral Vega/National Geographic Creative; 60 Loop Images Ltd/Alamy Stock Photo; 63 Michael DeFreitas South America/ Alamy Stock Photo; 64 © Design Pics Inc/National Geographic Creative; 65 GlowImages/Alamy Stock Photo; 66 © Mauricio Abreu/ Getty Images; 68 © Mark Cosslett/National Geographic Creative; 69 PCN Photography/Alamy Stock Photo; 70 (t) Marcus Spedding/ Alamy Stock Photo; 70 (m) © Christopher Furlong/Getty Images; 70 (b) © Emanuele Ciccomartino/robertharding/Getty Images; 72 Fry Vanessa/Alamy Stock Photo; 74 (l) Catchlight Visual Services/Alamy Stock Photo; 74 (ml) Fancy/Alamy Stock Photo; 74 (mml) © O. Louis Mazzatenta/National Geographic Creative; 74 (mmr) Bill Bachmann/Alamy Stock Photo; 74 (mr) Photo Japan/Alamy Stock Photo; 74 (r) LJSphotography/Alamy Stock Photo; 75 © Frans Lemmens/Getty Images; 76 Werli Francois/Alamy Stock Photo; 78 © Sebastian Wahlhuetter; 80 © Lynn Johnson/National Geographic Creative.

Workbook Photos: 104 © Halfpoint/Shutterstock.com; 106 © Dan Westergren/National Geographic Creative; 108 Mike Booth/Alamy Stock Photo; 109 Tony Tallec/Alamy Stock Photo; 110 © Andrey_Popov/Shutterstock.com; 112 © Kevin Frayer/Stringer/Getty Images; 114 © Gary John Norman/Getty Images; 116 © Daniel Raven-Ellison; 117 © aslysun/Shutterstock.com; 119 (l) © Sasha Leahovcenco; 119 (m) Hemis/Alamy Stock Photo; 119 (r) © Tim Matsui/Liaison/Getty Images; 120 (t) Kumar Sriskandan/Alamy Stock Photo; 120 (b) david sanger photography/Alamy Stock Photo; 122 © Richard l'Anson/Getty Images; 124 (l) © funkyfrogstock/Shutterstock.com; 124 (m) © mambo6435/Shutterstock.com; 124 (r) © EcoPrint/Shutterstock.com; 125 imageBROKER/Alamy Stock Photo; 126 © oblong1/ Shutterstock.com; 128 © Gene Blevins/AFP/Getty Images; 130 © Bill Pugliano/Stringer/Getty Images; 132 Asia Images Group Pte Ltd/ Alamy Stock Photo; 133 © Fuse/Getty Images; 136 Justin Kase zsixz/Alamy Stock Photo; 140 Sergey Uryadnikov/Alamy Stock Photo; 141 © Peter Kim/Dreamstime.com; 142 © Luciano Mortula/Shutterstock.com; 143 © Fred Derwal/Getty Images; 144 © Peter McBride/ National Geographic Creative; 145 MediaWorldImages/Alamy Stock Photo; 146 © Ljupco Smokovski/Shutterstock.com; 148 GoGo Images Corporation/Alamy Stock Photo; 149 © ArtmannWitte/Shutterstock.com; 150 © Mike Flippo/Shutterstock.com.

Student's Book Illustrations: 18, 76, David Russell; 82 Laszlo Veres/Beehive Illustration.
Workbook Illustrations: 114, 138 David Russell.

ACKNOWLEDGEMENTS

The *Life* publishing team would like to thank the following teachers and students who provided invaluable and detailed feedback on the first edition:

Armik Adamians, Colombo Americano, Cali; Carlos Alberto Aguirre, Universidad Madero, Puebla; Anabel Aikin, La Escuela Oficial de Idiomas de Coslada, Madrid; Pamela Alvarez, Colegio Eccleston, Lanús; Manuel Antonio, CEL Unicamp, São Paulo; Bob Ashcroft, Shonan Koka University; Linda Azzopardi, Clubclass; Éricka Bauchwitz, Universidad Madero, Puebla; Paola Biancolini, Università Cattolica del Sacro Cuore, Milan; Laura Bottiglieri, Universidad Nacional de Salta; Richard Brookes, Brookes Talen, Aalsmeer; Maria Cante, Universidad Madero, Puebla; Carmín Castillo, Universidad Madero, Puebla; Ana Laura Chacón, Universidad Madero, Puebla; Somchao Chatnaridom, Suratthani Rajabhat University, Surat Thani; Adrian Cini, British Study Centres, London; Andrew Clarke, Centre of English Studies, Dublin; Mariano Cordoni, Centro Universitario de Idiomas, Buenos Aires; Monica Cuellar, Universidad La Gran Colombia; Jacqui Davis-Bowen, St Giles International; Nuria Mendoza Dominguez, Universidad Nebrija, Madrid; Robin Duncan, ITC London; Christine Eade, Libera Università Internazionale degli Studi Sociali Guido Carli, Rome; Leopoldo Pinzon Escobar, Universidad Catolica; Joanne Evans, Linguarama, Berlin; Juan David Figueroa, Colombo Americano, Cali; Emmanuel Flores, Universidad del Valle de Puebla; Sally Fryer, University of Sheffield, Sheffield; Antonio David Berbel García, Escuela Oficial de Idiomas de Almería; Lia Gargioni, Feltrinelli Secondary School, Milan; Roberta Giugni, Galileo Galilei Secondary School, Legnano; Monica Gomez, Universidad Pontificia Bolivariana; Doctor Erwin Gonzales, Centro de Idiomas Universidad Nacional San Agustin; Ivonne Gonzalez, Universidad de La Sabana; J Gouman, Pieter Zandt Scholengemeenschap, Kampen; Cherryll Harrison, UNINT, Rome; Lottie Harrison, International House Recoleta; Marjo Heij, CSG Prins Maurits, Middelharnis; María del Pilar Hernández, Universidad Madero, Puebla; Luz Stella Hernandez, Universidad de La Sabana; Rogelio Herrera, Colombo Americano, Cali; Amy Huang, Language Canada Taipei; Huang Huei-Jiun, Pu Tai Senior High School; Nelson Jaramillo, Colombo Americano, Cali; Jacek Kaczmarek, Xiehe YouDe High School, Taipei; Thurgadevi Kalay, Kaplan, Noreen Kane, Centre of English Studies, Dublin; Billy Kao, Jinwen University of Science and Technology; Shih-Fan Kao, Jinwen University of Science and Technology, Taipei; Youmay Kao, Mackay Junior College of Medicine, Nursing, and Management, Taipei; Fleur Kelder, Vechtstede College, Weesp; Dr Sarinya Khattiya, Chiang Mai University; Lucy Khoo, Kaplan, Karen Koh, Kaplan, Susan Langerfeld, Liceo Scientifico Statale Augusto Righi, Rome; Hilary Lawler, Centre of English Studies, Dublin; Eva Lendi, Kantonsschule Zürich Nord, Zürich; Evon Lo, Jinwen University of Science and Technology; Peter Loftus, Centre of English Studies, Dublin; José Luiz, Inglês com Tecnologia, Cruzeiro; Christopher MacGuire, UC Language Center; Eric Maher, Centre of English Studies, Dublin; Nick Malewski, ITC London; Claudia Maribell Loo, Universidad Madero, Puebla; Malcolm Marr, ITC London; Graciela Martin, ICANA (Belgrano); Erik Meek, CS Vincent van Gogh, Assen; Marlene Merkt, Kantonsschule Zürich Nord, Zürich; David Moran, Qatar University, Doha; Rosella Morini, Feltrinelli Secondary School, Milan; Judith Mundell, Quarenghi Adult Learning Centre, Milan; Cinthya Nestor, Universidad Madero, Puebla; Peter O'Connor, Musashino University, Tokyo; Cliona O'Neill, Trinity School, Rome; María José Colón Orellana, Escola Oficial d'Idiomes de Terrassa, Barcelona; Viviana Ortega, Universidad Mayor, Santiago; Luc Peeters, Kyoto Sangyo University, Kyoto; Sanja Brekalo Pelin, La Escuela Oficial de Idiomas de Coslada, Madrid; Itzel Carolina Pérez, Universidad Madero, Puebla; Sutthima Peung, Rajamangala University of Technology Rattanakosin; Marina Pezzuoli, Liceo Scientifico Amedeo Avogadro, Rome; Andrew Pharis, Aichi Gakuin University, Nagoya; Hugh Podmore, St Giles International; Carolina Porras, Universidad de La Sabana; Brigit Portilla, Colombo Americano, Cali; Soudaben Pradeep, Kaplan; Judith Puertas, Colombo Americano, Cali; Takako Ramsden, Kyoto Sangyo University, Kyoto; Sophie Rebel-Dijkstra, Aeres Hogeschool; Zita Reszler, Nottingham Language Academy, Nottingham; Sophia Rizzo, St Giles International; Gloria Stella Quintero Riveros, Universidad Catolica; Cecilia Rosas, Euroidiomas; Eleonora Salas, IICANA Centro, Córdoba; Victoria Samaniego, La Escuela Oficial de Idiomas de Pozuelo de Alarcón, Madrid; Jeanette Sandre, Universidad Madero, Puebla; Bruno Scafati, ARICANA; Anya Shaw, International House Belgrano; Anne Smith, UNINT, Rome & University of Rome Tor Vergata; Suzannah Spencer-George, British Study Centres, Bournemouth; Students of Cultura Inglesa, São Paulo; Makiko Takeda, Aichi Gakuin University, Nagoya; Jilly Taylor, British Study Centres, London; Juliana

Trisno, Kaplan, Ruey Miin Tsao, National Cheng Kung University, Tainan City; Michelle Uitterhoeve, Vechtstede College, Weesp; Anna Maria Usai, Liceo Spallanzani, Rome; Carolina Valdiri, Colombo Americano, Cali; Gina Vasquez, Colombo Americano, Cali; Andreas Vikran, NET School of English, Milan; Mimi Watts, Università Cattolica del Sacro Cuore, Milan; Helen Ward, Oxford; Yvonne Wee, Kaplan Higher Education Academy, Christopher Wood, Meijo University; Yanina Zagarrio, ARICANA.